Praise for *You Are N*

"*You Are Not Alone In This* is th   1e
needs. As I read it, I kept thinki..g ~. ......~ anu ram..y wno i could
send it to. It deals with complex issues without over simplifying, and
it's laid out like an instruction manual which makes it easy to follow
and digest. This book is going to help huge numbers of people."
**James Longman, foreign correspondent for ABC News and author
of** *The Inherited Mind*

"This is the book I wish my family had read when I was seriously
unwell. It's such a comprehensive, engaging and supportive guide
for anyone helping a loved one through mental illness. *You Are Not
Alone In This* is a must-have for all the millions of carers out there.
You are most certainly not alone with Sophie's incredible book."
**Jonny Benjamin MBE, award-winning mental health campaigner
and author of** *The Stranger on the Bridge*

"I genuinely believe everyone should read this if we want to get
stronger as individuals and as a society when tackling mental
health. Sophie writes with so much empathy yet offers practical
suggestions that all of us can start today."
Maya Raichoora, UK's leading mental fitness and visualization expert

"Everyone needs a book like this! As someone who's both
experienced the depth of mental health challenges myself and
in supporting those around me, this book is the toolbox everyone
needs to support those around them and most of all themselves."
**Dan Murray-Serter, mental health advocate and podcast host at
Secret Leaders.**

"Sophie has delivered such a valuable book, bringing light to the
struggle of those who care for a loved one who is suffering with
their mental health. Her book is a deep resource for both clinicians
and anyone who is caring for a loved one in crisis."
Robert Rees, Director of The Grove Practice London

"A book of this kind is long overdue. Combining lived experience with professional knowledge and practice, Sophie Scott has written a comprehensive, compassionate and accessible guide that is full of essential insight. *You Are Not Alone In This* is a real step forward."
Jonathon Clack, mental health practitioner and carer

"Sophie's book is a beacon of light that is destined to help so many people find support, resilience and hope. She's able to put into words the complexities of being human in a simple yet powerful way that reminds us we're never alone."
Michael James Wong, founder of Just Breathe and author of *Sen Baz Uru*

"None of us should have to suffer alone when it comes to supporting loved ones with mental illness. And thanks to this empathetic and inspirational companion, you no longer have to. I wish this was around when I was learning to cope on my own."
Pete Ward, co-founder and CEO of Humanity Inc

"This is a hugely important and timely addition to the mental health literature on offer. Sophie has written a comprehensive and heartfelt exploration of care for others and self-care. You Are Not Alone In This is a much-needed approach to the topic and a beautifully written book that both educates and inspires."
Malcolm Stern, author of *Slay Your Dragons With Compassion*, psychotherapist and co-host of Compassionate Mental Health

"*You Are Not Alone In This* is a nuanced and thoughtful manual on how to care for a loved one struggling with mental health problems. Sophie nicely balances the challenges of being there for someone and the need to care for yourself. A great, much-needed read!"
Dr Ryan Martin, author of *How to Deal with Angry People*

"This compassionate and practical guide is a must-read for anyone supporting a loved one with mental health challenges."
Talitha Fosh, psychotherapist and author of Hooked

YOU ARE NOT ALONE IN THIS

Supporting a loved one's mental health without losing your own

Sophie Scott
Foreword by Emma Willis

WATKINS
1893

You Are Not Alone In This
Sophie Scott

First published in the UK and USA in 2025 by
Watkins, an imprint of Watkins Media Limited
Unit 11, Shepperton House, 83–89 Shepperton Road
London N1 3DF

enquiries@watkinspublishing.com

Publisher: Fiona Robertson
Commissioning Editor: Brittany Willis
Copyeditor: Sue Lascelles
Head of Design: Karen Smith
Production: Uzma Taj

A CIP record for this book is available from the British Library

ISBN: 978-1-78678-890-0 (Paperback)
ISBN: 978-1-78678-891-7 (eBook)

10 9 8 7 6 5 4 3 2 1

Typeset by Lapiz
Printed and bound by CPI Group (UK) Ltd, Croydon, CR0 4YY

www.watkinspublishing.com

To my beloved parents, whose spirits
guide me every day.

To Daniel, my darling husband and steadfast
partner in life, and to our enchanting Billie.

And to my sister, Vikki, a Valkyrie – who
epitomizes human bravery and is the inspiration
behind every word of this book.

CONTENTS

FOREWORD

By Emma Willis

When Sophie Scott first approached me and my team about writing this foreword, I'll be honest, I felt a bit of imposter syndrome. I wasn't sure I was the right person for the job or that I was qualified enough to talk about something as important as mental health and supporting others. I'm a television host, after all. Yet, despite being fortunate enough to present some of Britan's best-loved shows over the past two decades, my life behind the scenes has been more complex.

In 2004 I met Matt Willis from the band Busted. After dating for just a few short months it became evident that he had issues with addiction. Yet 20 years later we are still together, married, with three wonderful children. He is very much the love of my life, and I feel immensely proud of how far we've come because, at times, things have been incredibly heavy.

Having never really talked extensively or openly about his issues, in 2023 he decided to film a documentary for the BBC called *Fighting Addiction*, in the hope he could help other like-minded people, and I was asked to contribute to it. It was the first time that I publicly shared some of my experiences. Afterwards, I was overwhelmed by messages from people who said hearing me talk about how Matt's addiction had impacted me had made them feel seen. This opened my eyes to the vast numbers of people who were affected by similar experiences. It was also a potent reminder that sharing our stories, no matter how personal or tough, can help others feel less alone.

Reading this book, I've been reflecting on my life and thinking about how much a book like this would have helped me 20 years ago. Back then, I was desperately trying to figure out how to support Matt through his addiction and, honestly, there were times when I felt completely lost. There was no manual, no guide to help me navigate the emotions, the anxiety, and the exhaustion. I was just taking it day by day.

I often think about what I would have done differently if I'd had the kind of insights that Sophie offers here. The truth is, when you're the one supporting someone else – whether it's a partner dealing with addiction, a friend struggling with mental health or a loved one with neurodiversity – your instinct is to throw everything you have into helping them. You put them first in every way imaginable. And while that comes from a place of love and care, it also comes with an incredible cost to your own wellbeing.

That's one of the reasons this book is so important. Sophie highlights something that I think so many of us forget; something that took me years to learn: you have to prioritize yourself, too. If you neglect yourself, eventually, you'll burn out.

Sophie understands that delicate balance between supporting someone and not losing yourself in the process. That's a lesson I wish I'd known sooner. It's easy to think of self-care as something indulgent, especially when you're in the thick of someone else's crisis. But Sophie reminds us that caring for yourself isn't indulgence; it's survival. You can't pour from an empty cup, as they say.

What I also love about this book is how practical and relatable it is. Sophie writes about such complex psychological theories and methods in a digestible way. Even after everything I've been through, after all the work Matt and I have done individually and as a couple, I found myself learning new things from the first chapter.

Going through something like a mental health issue or addiction with a loved one is a long journey. You never stop learning, and this book is a perfect example of that.

Above all, I was really touched by the case studies she shares, in particular, reading the words of those people who courageously chose to share their stories. I find it easier to open up when hearing about other people's lived experiences.

Sophie has written a book that I genuinely believe will change lives. It's full of wisdom, compassion and practical advice that will resonate with anyone who has ever been in the role of a carer or supporter. Whether you're just starting your journey or have been living through it for years, this book will offer you comfort, insight, and a reminder that your wellbeing is just as important as the person you're supporting.

I'm incredibly grateful to Sophie for writing this book, and I know it's going to make a difference to so many people. It certainly has for me.

Emma Willis

INTRODUCTION

My mum looked like an old-fashioned movie star. Fiercely loyal, wickedly funny and wholly instinctive, she could read a person a mile off. Her life revolved around her family, and that meant doing everything for us. I don't think I once laid the table – or cleared it for that matter – until I was an adult. Friends would come over and chuckle at the way she set out my toothbrush with toothpaste already neatly squeezed onto it.

Each day, she would manically scrub the house from top to bottom, as if trying to wash away her muddled feelings or channel her impulsivity. Today, she might be diagnosed with obsessive compulsive disorder (OCD) and attention deficit hyperactivity disorder (ADHD). But that's probably wishful thinking; she always refused to see there was a problem. When my sister suggested she speak to a counsellor, she was chastised. We were all exasperated by Mum's behaviour and it's only now, years later, that I finally get it. She was just finding a way to cope.

Mum was 52 years old when she tragically passed away from stage-four breast cancer. I was 14. All these years later, I still talk to her daily. And imagine what our relationship could be today.

My father was also a real character, and lived to be 80. But he was obsessional too and existed in a make-believe world. A gifted composer, he wrote a musical about Italian history that was his life's work. For 60 years he relentlessly pursued this one project, unable to think or talk of anything else.

I loved both my parents with every fibre of my being, but they weren't emotionally available. They barely functioned in the big, bad world.

After Mum died, my amazing and vivacious older sister (who also happens to be my best friend) descended into a pit of guilt, which lasted several years. Call it survivor's guilt or a saviour's complex, she blamed herself for not being able to rescue Mum and get her onto a less self-destructive path. She became overwhelmed with anxiety and intrusive thoughts, and experienced something known as pure O, which is a subtype of OCD that involves mental compulsions rather than visible ones. It took its toll.

Here I was, once again, faced with someone I adored who couldn't get past their obsessions. And I was still only a teenager. Still grieving. Our close bond meant that my sister leaned on me daily, looking for reassurance that she was a "good" person. Just how could someone who gave up a large part of her twenties to raise me, her teenage sister, think she was bad? It was crazy, and in truth, I became increasingly impatient and angry at the attention her (self-) affliction commanded. Hadn't we been through enough?

Eventually, unlike Mum and Dad, my sister recognized that something was wrong and sought help. Today she has a great life; working in publishing and happily married, she is also a leading psychotherapist. We've weathered many storms together and our love is about as deep as you can get. But the road wasn't always easy. Along the way, I've discovered how to set boundaries and occupy more space in the relationship (which mostly involves me just talking more about myself!). And she has learned to find the answers within herself. Our codependent relationship has morphed into a wholly healthy and balanced one, with both of us doing the necessary work to get there. And I can tell you, our connection has only expanded as our individual senses of self have developed.

On a side note, I should probably add that other close family members and friends have faced mental health challenges, too, which may explain why I've felt a deep connection to those navigating similar struggles. My friends joke that my dating history is chequered with every diagnosis going! It's possible that I have a saviour complex (more on that later).

Ironically, I have gone on to marry a neurotypical man, who is cognitively, emotionally and socially healthy (for now at least). In the end, I think that was a conscious choice – as part of my own healing, thanks to a ton of great therapy. Paradoxically, I'm now the anxious one in the relationship. In fact, I've experienced generalized anxiety disorder (GAD) on and off over the years, but I didn't always have the language for it. I had become so accustomed to looking after everyone else's needs that I neglected to reflect on my own problems.

My MO was to be resilient, high-performing, self-contained and externally calm. But my inner landscape often felt very different. I was highly fearful, full of self-doubt, melancholic and resentful. As someone with high-functioning anxiety, I can categorically say that I became so adept at coping and keeping my pain (and everyone else's) secret that I just kept piling more and more stressors onto my shoulders. Until one day, I snapped. And it wasn't until I stopped pretending to be Superwoman that anything changed.

The truth is that we all sit somewhere on the mental health spectrum – existing on the precipice, dancing somewhere close to the edge – and any number of factors might hurtle us into the abyss. No one is immune. That includes you. And me. I urge you to keep this in mind as you navigate this book. If you find yourself categorizing people, labelling "them" and "us", catch yourself and stop.

Why I Wrote This Book

I wrote this book because it didn't exist when I needed it. And I know that I'm not alone in this.

A lot of people come into therapy because someone close to them is struggling with their mental health and they're deeply affected. Whether it's worrying intensely over a partner battling depression and suicidal thoughts, a parent agonizing over their child's impulsive behaviour or witnessing a best friend succumb to addiction, these experiences can be overwhelming. Much of my therapeutic work centres on helping clients navigate these complex relationships, while ensuring they don't lose themselves in the process.

These individuals often feel like the forgotten ones. Today, there's so much emphasis on mental health, and rightly so, but here's the thing: the person in the supporting role often ends up struggling with mental health issues themselves. A 2015 UK report found that 55 per cent of people supporting others were experiencing depression and 78 per cent anxious thoughts.[1] Older adults and women have reported the highest levels of strain, often neglecting their own health conditions, which can worsen over time.[2] However, my own experience has taught me that the effects of loving and caring for someone who is struggling with their mental health can cause issues at any age.

In fact, it can seriously change the course of a young person's life, as younger caregivers frequently experience disruptions to their education, which can impact their future career and earnings.[3] Yet "caregiver burden", as it's known, remains a relatively under-researched area; far more support is required. One of the few recent studies showed that individuals experienced the highest levels of stress when their loved ones were treated for psychotic disorders, such as schizophrenia, in a hospital setting (rather than in a community setting).[4] This is hardly unsurprising, really.

It's possible you don't even consider yourself a carer. Unseen carers are everywhere. Regardless, I'm here to tell you that it's okay to admit you're struggling with the role you've been assigned. It's not an easy one. Often the wounded *wound*, so it may be that your loved one isn't always that nice to you. I wish to reinforce again and again that there's room for all your feelings. The good, the bad and the ugly. There's space for you here.

While I believe this book can help everyone, I am of course limited in how many different conditions I can give examples for, so please don't be deterred if the mental health or neurodivergent issue your loved one faces isn't specifically mentioned – a lot of the guidance in this book is still applicable. The same can be said of minors – as an adult psychotherapist, I wrote this book with adult-to-adult relationships in mind. When children are involved there are many additional ethical and legal complexities to consider, so take the advice you find applicable, but be sure to seek out other expertise that targets the psychosocial health of children or teens.

A Book of Two Halves

Mental health issues create a domino effect, spreading far and wide. Yet there's little guidance out there for the sentinels – for those who lovingly stand guard without any formal training of their own.

This book has two main parts: "Caring for Your Loved One" and "Caring for Yourself". In the first part, we will look at how to have difficult conversations about behaviours that concern you, and how to make an emergency plan. We will also cover presentations of the most common mental health disorders – and understand how these can directly impact relationships. Above all, we'll consider strategies to help your loved one get the right treatment plan and support in place.

However, I cannot stress enough the importance of the second part: "Caring for Yourself". Research shows that *loneliness increases caregiving stress, while having a sense of purpose in life reduces it.*[5] Read that last sentence again. That's why, in Part 2, we'll cover how to put your own support structure in place, as well as how to create space for your sense of purpose through forging healthier boundaries.

(I recommend starting a journal to accompany the exercises in both Parts 1 and 2.)

Please know this: you are not forgotten. It's entirely valid for you to ask: "*What about me?*" Just by picking up this book, you're engaging in a form of self-care, self-recognition and love. I truly hope it serves as both a retreat and a practical resource, guiding you with compassion through your journey. Above all, I hope the personal stories and anonymized case studies do more than just illustrate psychological theory; they're here to remind you: *You. Are. Not. Alone. In. This.*

Sophie Scott

PART 1
CARING FOR YOUR LOVED ONE

CHAPTER 1
NAVIGATING THE PATH TO HELP

"My physician husband is brilliant and charming, but his behaviour grew increasingly impulsive. His family wouldn't hear my concerns; to them, he was perfect. I worried constantly about him. After he went missing for two days, he was finally diagnosed with bipolar disorder. This, in turn, propelled him to manage his condition and change his lifestyle. Now he's able to look after his own health, as well as his patients."

Caroline, 39

It may surprise you to know that caregivers, most notably parents, often act as the "gatekeepers" to mental health services. This means you can play a vital role in whether your loved one seeks, receives and engages with professional help.[1] The best outcomes are usually achieved when active family support is combined with the right treatment plan. But what should you do if your loved one refuses to get help and dismisses your concerns?

This chapter aims to equip you with the necessary tools to support your loved one effectively. We'll weigh the pros and cons of obtaining a clinical diagnosis, look at how to initiate difficult conversations about seeking help and even discuss strategies for handling situations should a loved one use their challenges as a way to avoid taking personal responsibility.

To Diagnose or Not Diagnose?

Unlike a broken bone seen on an X-ray, mental health is visible only through the prism of someone's behaviour. Diagnoses aim to bridge this gap; to make the intangible tangible. So how essential is it to have a diagnosis in place? And is it ever ethically sound to label someone's behaviour?

Today, the American Psychological Association's *Diagnostic and Statistical Manual of Mental Disorders*, Fifth Edition (DSM-5, 2013), is the most widely recognized tool used by psychiatrists and mental health professionals. It categorizes 20 mental health disorders, with over 200 specific subset disorders listed.

Typically, a diagnosis follows an assessment by a health professional, which involves asking questions about someone's experiences (their feelings, behaviours and symptoms), the duration of these and their impact on daily life. While family physicians can often diagnose common conditions such as anxiety or depression, complex cases are referred to a psychiatrist. The psychiatrist meets the patient over a longer period of time, which is of the utmost importance; otherwise, a diagnosis might just capture a person based on how they appear on a particular day.

Some people argue that mental health diagnoses are simplistic labels applied by professionals to explain behaviours and experiences they can't relate to. They believe that categorizing someone as "personality disordered" or "schizophrenic" may stem from a lack of understanding, rather than genuine insight. Diagnoses can make the complexity of being human simpler – but in doing so, they can diminish a person to a set of symptoms.

Factors including a patient's age, cultural background, the physician's experience, how information is communicated and how participatory the whole process is also impact whether a diagnosis is deemed helpful, or not. Let's start to unpack the pros and cons a bit more.

Six main arguments for getting a clinical diagnosis:

1 **Mental health problems don't just go away if left untreated**: Conditions such as schizophrenia, bipolar disorder and personality disorders get worse if left unchecked.

2 **Facilitates treatment:** By understanding the precise nature of an issue, specialized treatment plans can be put in place. I mean, you'd probably want to know if you had a stomach ulcer versus a gallstone, so why should it be any different with mental health?

3 **Improves access to support:** Insurance companies, schools and services typically require a formal diagnosis to approve treatment.

4 **Provides validation:** It offers a framework for individuals to feel validated and understood in their experiences.

5 **Shared language:** Diagnoses provide a common language, enabling more effective communication and consistency when dealing with mental health care professionals.

6 **Enhances self-awareness:** A diagnosis can empower someone to understand themselves better, including identifying specific triggers and patterns.

Six main arguments against getting a clinical diagnosis:

1 **Over-pathologizing:** With over 200 disorders recognized, there is a risk that everything becomes treated as a medical condition. In the wrong hands, this can be problematic.

2 **Ambiguous distinctions:** The line between personality trait and mental health issue is not always clear-cut. For example, when do neurotic tendencies turn into obsessive compulsive disorder?

3 **Cultural differences:** Different cultures view mental health differently, and the diagnostic framework used in DSM-5 is grounded in a Western paradigm.

4 **Pharmaceutical influence:** Concerns exist about the pharmaceutical industry's influence on the DSM-5. In 2008, it was revealed that 28 per cent of the American Psychological Association's budget came from the pharmaceutical industry (around $14 million).[2]
5 **Trauma response:** We should be more curious about how a person's behaviour is perhaps a response to earlier trauma, rather than simply labelling them based on it.
6 **Can feel limiting:** As we'll touch on below, there's a real risk that a label can overshadow a person's sense of self or even be used as a weapon against them by other people, communities and institutions.

As you can see, the question of getting a diagnosis is highly nuanced and will ultimately come down to personal preference. However, I've seen time and again how getting the right diagnosis can be a crucial step toward getting the right treatment, which is in turn critical in determining the wellbeing of everyone involved – including you.

CHILDHOOD DETECTION

While this book focuses on adult-to-adult relationships, you might be interested to know that half of all lifetime cases of mental illness begin by age 14, but most go undetected.[3] Early intervention can improve prognosis, reduce symptom severity and, in some cases, alter the course of a disorder.[4] Yet pathologizing a child's behaviour is deeply complex. There's a delicate balance between acknowledging challenges and prematurely labelling natural variations of behaviour.

Adults who were diagnosed early report widely differing experiences. Some people have told me that an early autism diagnosis, for example, gave their parents and teachers a clearer understanding of their behaviour, enabling them to focus on strengthening their unique gifts and world viewpoint. However, my client Chloe, 33, felt being diagnosed with anxiety when young wasn't so much the problem as the way her parents dealt with it, which was to medicate her and put her in child psychoanalysis. Chloe felt her parents didn't seek to understand what lay beneath her anxiety.

Early diagnosis can be double-edged: it can provide a roadmap for support or, if mishandled, become a source of resentment and exclusion. It seems to come down to how understood the young person felt. For example, if their behaviour changed after the loss of a family member, a parent's divorce or bullying, was this recognized? Children, like adults, need to be invited to share their experiences and feelings. That's why you might find value in understanding more about when your loved one's symptoms first showed up, and how they felt received by those closest to them (including you). It's not about playing detective, but sensitively enquiring about how long they have felt this way for. Considering the whole life course of a person and not just the present moment can foster a deeper understanding of who they are – and more compassion.

Refusing to Get Help

When someone appears to be struggling or is affected by mental illness but refuses to get help, it can feel excruciating for those who want nothing but the best for them. The situation is not just emotionally draining but can take over everything, making your whole life revolve around trying to convince your loved one to seek support. I've lived through this myself, and I know how consuming it can become.

If you think your loved one needs help but is refusing to seek it, it can be incredibly hard to break this cycle, but getting into a longstanding debate usually proves ineffective. Instead, it's important to step back and understand the underlying reasons behind your loved one's reluctance. Often, it comes down to a fear of receiving a diagnosis. With that in mind, let's consider some of the very valid reasons why they might be refusing to see a doctor:

- Many people fear they will be discriminated against if diagnosed with a mental health condition; that they will be seen as "broken", "crazy" or "unstable", which will affect their employment opportunities and relationships.
- There's a lack of awareness about different mental health illnesses and what they look like. This means symptoms are often ignored or misunderstood. For example, symptoms of high-functioning anxiety might be dismissed as stress, preventing individuals from seeking necessary help.
- Society tends to prioritize physical health over mental health. This imbalance sends a clear message, meaning individuals may neglect their mental wellbeing because they don't trust that they will be listened to.
- Unfortunately, some people have had terrible experiences with the medical profession, such as feeling dismissed, misunderstood or even gaslit, which puts them off seeking further help.
- Mental health problems are still stigmatized in some cultures and religions. In certain religious communities, mental health issues might be interpreted as a lack of faith or even a moral failing.[5]
- People from marginalized backgrounds and ethnic minorities fear being misunderstood and wrongly diagnosed due to a lack of cultural competence in psychiatry. In the UK, for example, black people are four times more likely than white people to be detained under the Mental Health Act.[6]

- Prevailing gender norms may contribute to resistance to getting help. Men are conditioned from a young age to be stoic, suppress their emotions and shoulder burdens independently. Phrases like "be a man" perpetuate the notion that emotional vulnerability equates to weakness.
- Mental healthcare systems in many countries are under strain, with unclear pathways to access services and physical locations that are often inaccessible. Rural areas, in particular, often lack resources and long wait times can discourage people from pursuing treatment.
- Some people don't believe there's anything wrong with them and may feel scapegoated. This denial can be a coping mechanism to avoid facing the reality of their situation. Others can experience what's known as anosognosia, which is defined as an inability to recognize their own mental health condition. Someone with borderline personality disorder (BPD), for example, might view their fear of abandonment and tendency toward intense interpersonal relationships as part of their identity, rather than symptoms of a disorder.

Begin a Conversation

If your loved one is resistant to seeing a doctor or a mental health professional, gently encourage them to consider what's stopping them. It's not about trying to change their mind, but simply being curious. You might identify which argument(s) are driving their refusal and offer some other perspectives. (I would encourage you to read Chapter 2, on the foundations of good communication, before launching into this conversation.) Here are some ways to open up a conversation specifically about getting support, even if your loved one doesn't think anything is wrong:

- **Understand their perspective:** The key here is NOT to invalidate their feelings. Try to identify which arguments are driving their refusal and offer other perspectives simply to inform them of the full picture. (You might find some interesting counterarguments in the section above on the pros and cons of getting a diagnosis.)

- **Create space for dialogue:** Avoid using accusatory words and instead focus on specific behaviours. Arguing over what's "real" is counterproductive and potentially harmful. Therefore, use "I" statements and simply share your own experience and concerns for them (for example, "I've noticed that when we have disagreements, I feel worried about how it affects you").
- **Don't mention the word "diagnosis":** This word is extremely emotive and divisive. It can also come across as shaming or as a levelled criticism. As an esteemed psychiatrist explained to me: "It's a misconception that people seek out psychiatry for a diagnosis. They come with a challenge, a part of their life they feel is unravelling, and they're seeking a *resolution*."
- **Encourage self-reflection:** Consider asking open-ended questions that promote introspection (for example, "Do you have a sense of what prompts these intense feelings?"); there's a lot more on this in Chapter 2.
- **Highlight the benefits of support:** Discuss how support can improve quality of life, stress levels and enhance relationships (for example, "Talking to a professional could offer comfort and support, and provide some tools to help you navigate these intense feelings").
- **Demonstrate patience:** Understand that change takes time and your loved one may need to hear you express your love and care multiple times before they start to see things differently.

It's also important to realize that sometimes you're the wrong person to have this conversation with them. When dynamics are especially charged, it might be beneficial to involve a neutral family member with whom your loved one has a less involved relationship, or to ask them if there's anyone else they might be willing to speak to.

The Urge to Direct Our Lives

While the above strategies hopefully help, when all's said and done, you can't and shouldn't insist that anyone gets help if they don't want it. We all have free will. Convincing anyone to do something they don't want to do invites resistance, and, as Dr Deepak Chopra has said: "Stress is resistance to existence."[7] So, if you're unable to get through to your loved one without tensions escalating, stop trying. Acknowledge that's how it is for them. Instead, focus on expressing your love and care, not needing to be right, or to prove a point.

Ultimately, in the journey of helping those we care about, there comes a stark realization that not everyone seeks assistance, nor accepts it when offered. This is a painful truth, yet it's essential to recognize that every individual has the intrinsic right to chart their own path, regardless of how much we may wish to guide them toward help. Accepting this doesn't signify approval or indifference, but is an acknowledgement of personal autonomy. Our role may shift then from active helper to compassionate witness, honouring their right to self-determination while remaining present and caring, ready to support them should they ever choose to reach out.

Respecting self-determination is not only a profound act of grace, but it forms the basis of ethical caregiving and support. And, as a side note, acceptance may also become a critical part of your own self-care, as we'll see in Part 2.

However, respecting autonomy obviously has limits, especially if a person's choices pose a significant risk of harm to themselves or others. In such cases, ethical considerations shift toward finding ways to minimize harm while still respecting the individual's autonomy as much as possible.

This principle underpins the logic behind facilities like Insite in Vancouver, Canada, where individuals can use illicit drugs under medical supervision. The facility aims to reduce drug overdose deaths and infections from unsafe needle use, acknowledging that while the risk cannot be eliminated, it can be mitigated in a controlled environment that respects each person's choices.

From the bottom of my heart, I absolutely acknowledge that none of these outcomes is easy to navigate or accept. Ultimately, though, after doing everything possible to encourage a loved one to seek support, there may come a time when acceptance is the only option left. Throughout my interviews for this book, many shared that their loved ones only sought help after hitting rock bottom, not from a single intervention or conversation.

Nevertheless, the advice remains: do your best to facilitate support and be actively engaged in your loved one's treatment plan, which should ideally be holistic and personalized. If this proves impossible, striving to keep them as safe as possible under the circumstances becomes the goal.

The decision of when to step back is complex and should be guided by your personal boundaries. This is why it's essential you begin to understand what that means to you and when your efforts begin to impact your own mental health negatively. We'll go deeper into understanding and setting your boundaries in Chapter 8.

Contact with a Mental Health Specialist

If your loved one *does* want to go ahead and see a healthcare professional, the first thing is to ask them if they'd like you or anyone else to go with them to show support. But don't take it personally if they would prefer to go in alone – or with someone else. Obviously, if they're going to meet with a psychotherapist, it's important they go alone, although you could always offer to accompany them on their journey.

And don't worry if they go reluctantly; what matters is they're attempting to seek help. Mental health practitioners are used to meeting with people who are only attending sessions at the behest of concerned family members – typically young adults driven to appointments by their parents. It's their job (not yours) to unravel why someone doesn't perceive their mental health or behaviour as problematic. Even clients who have been seeing me for years still experience mixed feelings toward therapy, so it's only natural there's resistance if this is your loved one's first meeting with a mental health specialist.

Sometimes, a root issue is entangled in family dynamics or a specific relationship, and I urge you not to be afraid if this comes up during their consultation. Your loved one may say something like: "It's not mania; it's a response to my partner's suffocating behaviour", but it's the expert's job to navigate this path. Sometimes people suggest that their mental health practitioner speak to someone close to them to get a better perspective on them, and that might not be you. "My aunt understands me better than my mother, talk to her," they might say, so it's up to the mental health practitioner to do that. Never assume the right to know what your loved one shared in their appointment, and don't pester them to find out. They're entitled to privacy.

If you have serious concerns about what has or hasn't been shared, you can always contact the specialist separately. They are, of course, duty-bound by confidentiality, but they can listen to what you have to say. Of all the psychiatrists I've spoken to, none has an issue with relatives doing this. Sure, it can be challenging if a family member reaches out and says something along the lines of: "I've noticed Robin is declining, but please don't tell him I rang you." But professionals are used to making those decisions. An experienced mental health practitioner would never say: "Your mum told me you haven't taken your medication." Instead, they would simply contact their patient in the guise of following up with them.

That way, it's not technically a breach of confidentiality. The health professional will then make their own assessment as to whether it's you who's overestimating the problem or your loved one who's understating it. Similarly, if your loved one experiences manic phases when everything is fantastic, letting their psychiatrist know that everything's "a little too fantastic" can be precious information.

In my research and collaboration with psychiatrists for this book, one resounding principle emerged: the act of diagnosing should be a dialogue, not a decree. That said, the world of psychiatry still has a long way to go in this respect. Unlike in psychotherapy, the patient–doctor model pervades, depicting people as unwell and in need of repair (even the word "disorder" implies this). That's why it's imperative that you support your loved one in becoming an active participant in their care, rather than a passive recipient. Even if this involves refusing treatment – providing they can think for themselves.

A distinguished psychiatrist recently shared their approach with me. Upon meeting a patient, they ask: "Are you curious about my thoughts on our discussions? Would you like to hear my professional interpretation?" Invariably, the answer is "yes", as people have an innate desire to understand themselves better. A consultation with a psychiatrist should really be akin to a partnership: they bring the technical knowledge but, ultimately, it's about shared communication. Your loved one might benefit from knowing this context, so they go into a meeting feeling more empowered.

Modern-day psychiatry should not simply seek to diagnose and medicate people, but to understand their life experiences and the societal pressures they face. I love the words of the Scottish psychiatrist R.D. Laing, who famously said: "Insanity – a perfectly rational adjustment to an insane world." To me, this accepts that what we label as insane might just be a rational response to a dysfunctional and oppressive environment.

CONFIDENTIALITY AND ACCESS TO INFORMATION

More than half of caregivers report being told that their relative's mental health professional cannot talk with them.[8] Under health privacy laws, a healthcare provider may share relevant information with a family member or caregiver if the person in care:

- gives permission to the provider
- is present and doesn't object to sharing the information
- is not present and, in the provider's professional judgement, sharing is in the client's best interest

Providing information: Family members can share relevant information with the provider, but the provider is not required to acknowledge or explain how the information will be used.

Signed releases: Providers may ask for permission, inform the person they intend to discuss information, or infer from the circumstances that the person doesn't object.

If involvement is refused: If the person in care is of age and the provider believes they have sound judgement, the provider must not share information without their permission. If the provider decides the person lacks decision-making capacity, information may be shared if it's in the person's best interest, without requiring a court order.

Substance-use treatment: Federal confidentiality law concerning alcohol and drug treatment requires specific written permission from the person in care before disclosing substance-use treatment information. If stricter privacy policies interfere with mental health treatment, consider asking the clinic director for a more open policy.

Governing laws: Most of this information is relevant for the US and Europe. However, there are some differences in the legal frameworks and specific regulations. Therefore, it's important to familiarize yourself with the relevant laws and regulations regarding confidentiality and information, based on where your loved one lives. Policies are also subject to change.

Life After Diagnosis

If a diagnosis is made, it can usher in a new reality – not just for the individual it's assigned to, but for their entire support system. For some, a diagnosis can provide the much-needed illumination of how to navigate the path ahead. It can provide a framework for understanding previously perplexing behaviours, offering relief and a starting point for treatment. For others, a diagnosis can feel like an unwelcome label, the demoralizing reduction of a richly textured life into a set of symptoms. Mark, 38, puts it like this:

> My whole world came crashing down when I was diagnosed with schizophrenia. There was nothing positive about it. No role models; no healthy, helpful conversations on the subject matter. I felt like an alien. Certain I would be a burden to my family forevermore and that's when I knew I didn't want to live. In the end, ironically, the only thing that's got me here is talking about my issues.

Here are some common responses to receiving a diagnosis:

- withdrawing from others
- going into denial: "There's nothing wrong with me"
- trying to cope by using alcohol or drugs
- blaming others: "You're the one that's crazy!"
- spending money on things to temporarily feel better
- abandoning old interests or anything that serves as a reminder of the past
- weaponizing the diagnosis (see page 23)

With respect to your loved one, you may experience some initial validation – confirmation that your concerns and observations weren't without basis. But this validation might quickly be followed by fear and apprehension. It's not uncommon to start re-evaluating the person you know. Does the diagnosis reshape the narrative of past behaviours and future possibilities?

Who your loved one is to you will heavily impact the way you relate to their diagnosis. Over the years, I've spoken to mothers who worry sick about their child's bipolar disorder and blame themselves for "passing it down"; to sons and daughters of parents with alcohol-dependency, who are fed up with the constant gaslighting that their parents aren't addicted; to spouses of those struggling with OCD, who feel out of their depth until a diagnosis finally lands and a treatment plan is put in place. Some themes come up again and again, but everyone's stories are beautifully inimitable, every relationship a world unto itself.

REFLECTING ON YOUR OWN RESPONSE

When you're supporting a loved one with mental health issues, whatever you're feeling is perfectly natural – it can be shocking for someone to get a diagnosis, even if you were half-expecting it. Here's an exercise to help get to grips with some of the thoughts and feelings you may be experiencing.

1 In your journal, create three columns: everything you "know", everything you "feel" about your loved one's mental health and everything you "want to understand more about".

2 In the first, "what I know" column, include any clinical diagnoses they've received, information you may know about their psychiatric history, and what you know about their mental health condition(s), experiences and presenting symptoms.

3 In the second, "what I feel" column, note down your personal feelings about their mental health, diagnoses, behaviour and how this all impacts you.

Through doing this exercise, it may become clear how much or little you know, as well as areas you'd like to educate yourself about (put all that in the third column). This "what I feel" column may confront you with your own biases. Rather than shying away from these, or beating yourself up about them (don't do that; we all have them), get curious as to where they might have emanated from.

This is purely a self-reflective process; now is definitely not the time to share your thoughts with your loved one. It's important that you process your own response separately and try not to let it colour your interactions. Straight after receiving a diagnosis or treatment plan, your loved one is likely to be at their most vulnerable, and needs nothing but unwavering support. They need to be reassured that they're still the same person they were yesterday – and so are you.

Instead, this might be the time to reflect all their amazing qualities back to them and let them know you see them for who they *really* are – that they might "have X diagnosis, but they are not X". It's a bit like saying, "I sometimes struggle with anxiety", rather than "I'm an anxious person".

A diagnosis is not who a person is. And it should never overshadow them. To truly see someone is to look beyond the clinical terms and perceive the whole of their humanity – their unique perspective, dark humour, protective mechanisms, eccentricities, gifts and the essence of their soul. Diagnoses may have their place but should only be one component of a larger, more holistic understanding of an individual's wellbeing (more on this in Chapter 4).

Fiona, 32, explains the value of this approach:

> After my diagnosis of bipolar disorder, I found myself trapped in a new reality where every action, every mood swing, was attributed to my condition. It felt like my personality had been stripped away, replaced by a clinical label in the eyes of my family. They started interpreting everything through the lens of bipolar – every laugh a little too loud, every moment of introspection a sign of impending depression. It's as if my diagnosis became the sole narrative of my life …
>
> Sometimes, it feels like they've forgotten that I'm still the same person. I wish they could understand that while the diagnosis is a part of my life, it doesn't monopolize every moment. I'm more than a bunch of symptoms.

By Their Side

Helping your loved one to metabolize a diagnosis might require patience, as well as encouragement to explore what their condition means for them. A diagnosis is not a full stop; it's a comma in someone's story. They may need reminding of this. Above all, it could be seen as an invitation to a deeper understanding of one's self, a call to adapt and to grow in new ways. Individual therapy and peer support can prove invaluable in this regard (see Chapter 4). A question for your loved one and you to reflect on might be: in what ways can this new information be respectfully integrated and assimilated? With the right support, time and again I have seen people find ways to extract the "gold" from their struggles. Hold this in your heart and mind.

For family and friends, this period is often one of adjustment and adaptation. Roles may shift, and the balance within relationships can change. It may involve creating a shared language around mental health, one that respects the individual's experience while, in time, also acknowledges its impact on the relationship.

It's true that a diagnosis can subtly shift the power dynamics. It can become an unspoken participant in every interaction, every decision, every argument. Yet, in reality, nothing has actually changed. A diagnosis doesn't make a condition any more – or any less – real.

When children are part of the family dynamic, the impact of a diagnosis can ripple through the household in unexpected ways. Siblings might struggle with feelings of neglect or confusion. They require support to understand what's happening, often needing assurance that they, too, are seen and valued. Family or relationship therapy can help to open up dialogues that honour each member's experience.

Handling Doubt

What if you or your loved one experiences doubts about a diagnosis, or questions the treatment plan put in place? I always tell my therapy clients, "You're the expert on yourself. You know yourself far better than I could ever know you, so if this doesn't feel right, stop me." However, I'm aware that most medical doctors wouldn't be caught dead saying this! This is why self-education is so important, which means researching everything from medical terminology to understanding some basic neuroscience, different symptomology and even the common side effects of drugs. Knowledge gives us the power to have more informed conversations with healthcare providers. But always make sure you and/or your loved one read from reliable sources, such as peer-reviewed medical journals, reputable health organizations (for example, the Mayo Clinic, WebMD and NIMH), and books written by experts in the field. Avoid relying solely on anecdotal information or non-expert advice found in forums or unverified websites. By playing "Doctor Google" responsibly, you can empower yourself with knowledge while ensuring that your loved one receives the best possible care.

The more armed we are when we go into medical appointments the better. That means helping your loved one to keep detailed records of their symptoms (or doing this on their behalf), changes in mood, behaviour and additional health concerns, for example. Part of your role is empowering your loved one to be an active participant in their care.

If your loved one is unable to advocate for themselves, consider who is best placed to be their spokesperson when it comes to liaising with medical professionals – it might not be you, and that's fine.

PROMPT: Who can you delegate tasks to that will also support your loved one? Ensure they document everything thoroughly.

When a treatment plan is created, ask the provider how long it should take to determine whether it is working; this helps to create some metrics around both the diagnosis and treatment. If it doesn't seem to be helping within that period – or helping enough – it's crucial to tell the provider.

If your loved one expresses concerns about their care, including the behaviour of a medical professional, listen attentively and let them know you're taking their experience seriously. First off, encourage them to put their experience in writing, citing dates, names and specific interactions. If necessary, offer to support them in making a written complaint and then focus your energies on helping them to find a new healthcare provider (which I do appreciate isn't always straightforward).

Having said that, I've worked with several individuals over the years who've made complaint after complaint, and who were either thrown out of, or voluntarily left, every service offered to them. Unfortunately, this can often be the case with people who are prone to splitting, which is a psychological phenomenon when people view themselves or others as either all good or all bad (with nothing in-between). This can lead to them metaphorically "leaving different parts" of themselves in different services, so no integration or cohesion of treatment can be achieved. If you recognize this to be your loved one, there is little you can do other than listen attentively and document any patterns you see for their healthcare providers. You might wish to express your concerns and ask for guidance on how to best support your loved one. For example, you might say, "I've noticed that [name] frequently feels mistreated by different providers. Could this be related to their mental health condition, and how can we address it?" When it comes to discussing this with your loved one, it's best to focus on the impact of their behaviour on *themselves*, but read Chapter 2 first.

If your loved one doesn't think there's anything wrong with them or the diagnosis is incorrect, they're unlikely to want to take the medication prescribed to them – I mean, would you? Anosognosia is a neurological condition where a person is unable to recognize they have a health or psychiatric condition – it's not about being stubborn. If you suspect anosognosia, tell your loved one's healthcare provider. A strategy tailored to this condition might include slowly introducing the idea of treatment and involving your loved one in more decision-making. You might also wish to suggest a trial period for medication to see if your loved one notices any improvements.

Remember, it's fully within a person's right to seek a second opinion. Or even a third one. This isn't unusual. In fact, getting multiple perspectives is standard practice in medical care because it helps to confirm a diagnosis or treatment plan is correct, and ensures all options have been considered. However, it's worth checking with your healthcare provider or insurance company if they cover this; if not, it may be something that needs to be covered separately. So, if you or your loved one are unsure, it might be worth exploring your options, and, if possible, paying for additional perspectives. You can utilize online resources to evaluate providers based on patient reviews, obtain a second opinion online without a referral through places like the Mayo Clinic, or access more affordable telehealth services. In a 2017 study, the Mayo Clinic reported that as many as 88 per cent of patients go home with a new or refined diagnosis – changing their care plan and potentially their lives.[9]

Ultimately, we know that caregivers experience reduced stress and improved mental health when their loved ones receive effective treatment. This relief comes from knowing they're getting the help they need, which in turn alleviates the constant worry and emotional strain that caregivers often experience. So, if you can, make every effort to support them to get this.

Weaponizing a Diagnosis

While getting a diagnosis often marks a valuable turning point, it can give rise to its own set of challenges. It can create a narrative of victimhood, for example, where the individual feels that something is "happening" to them, casting a shadow over their agency and autonomy. During my sessions with Sarah, it became evident that her husband Tom's diagnosis of clinical depression had become a shield of sorts that he employed to deflect responsibilities and expectations. This "weaponization" of his diagnosis was evident in his refusal to engage with life's routines, staying in his pyjamas all day and relying on Sarah to manage both their lives. Each time Sarah encouraged him to take action, Tom retreated behind his diagnosis, stating that his condition made it impossible for him to participate in normal activities.

This pattern of behaviour created a dynamic where Tom's depression wasn't just a medical condition to be treated, but an ever-present entity in their marriage, excusing him from even the smallest effort. For Sarah, this raised a question: was Tom's diagnosis being used as a convenient rationale for his not taking personal responsibility, or was it truly the depression speaking?

The challenge was how to broach this with Tom. It was a sensitive issue, and discussing it risked invalidating his experience. However, it was also important for the health of their marriage that Sarah was able to express her concerns in a way that showed she was coming from a place of love and support.

In a session together, we planned for her to share her feelings with Tom, focusing on the impact of his behaviour on her and their relationship, rather than on the impact of the diagnosis. Sarah could acknowledge the realness of his depression, affirming her commitment to supporting him while also conveying how his behaviour made her feel.

I emphasized to her the importance of timing and tone: this conversation needed to occur when Tom was at his most receptive and in a manner that underscored their partnership, rather than creating an adversarial dynamic. The aim was to help Tom see that while his depression was a valid and significant struggle, it didn't have to define the entirety of his being or their life together.

Through this process, Sarah and Tom both began to see that while a diagnosis can explain behaviour, it shouldn't excuse anyone from striving toward personal growth and mutual support within a relationship. The idea wasn't to deny the depression but to ensure it didn't wield an unchecked power over their collective wellbeing.

Weaponizing a diagnosis can materialize in several ways, but typically it means that an individual brandishes their mental health problems to avoid taking personal responsibility. This can even take the form of someone seeking a more extreme diagnosis than perhaps is fitting. The desire for a clinical label may sometimes stem from a deeper longing for validation. I'm encountering this more and more often in my therapy practice. Some clients have been deeply frustrated by my inability or unwillingness to label them. But here's the nuanced truth: feelings of sadness, for example, need not always be pathologized or justified. There lies a distinction between melancholia, which accounts for the complexity and limitations of being human, and depression, a diagnosable ailment that actively hinders our ability to live fully.

Besides, getting a diagnosis is just the start of a process. It's not a magic bullet. It isn't about taking a pill and being "fixed". The same is true for a physical illness or injury, too. If you go to a physiotherapist, you'll likely be given an exercise or treatment plan that you then have to implement. And addressing mental health issues is no different.

This also played out in Sarah's case. Her husband Tom's passivity meant he could remain angry at the world, instead of looking at what he could do to help himself.

Through therapy, Sarah began to discover that she herself was mirroring his behaviour. She would continually make allowances for Tom, only to scold him for his depression later in arguments. Through throwing his mental illness back in his face, she was doing exactly what she found so challenging about his behaviour: basically, reducing him to being just a depressed person!

Together, we worked on her finding ways to communicate her feelings without demoralizing him. This softened Tom's tendency to hide behind his diagnosis. During calm moments she might say something like: "I appreciate you may have clinical depression, but you're also an amazing husband who's always been a dab hand in the kitchen, so please can you make dinner tonight?" Through this simple action, she was inadvertently reminding him of who he was – and still is – aside from his depression. And she found a way to step into her own sense of agency, too.

Later in this book, we'll explore strategies for creating more authentic, balanced relationships, and ways to help your loved one foster a positive identity in the face of mental health challenges, including in the aftermath of a diagnosis. As we will see, communication is key at every stage of the journey.

CHAPTER 2
COMMUNICATION AND BUILDING DIALOGUE

"I just need you to understand, to give me that look that says you get it, that you know today is a tough one for me. That's it. No magic cures, no elaborate plans – just understanding. You with me?"

Emily, 26

Over the years, my sister and I have had just one recurrent fight. Regardless of whether it started over vacuuming duties, a misconstrued remark or a surreptitiously borrowed skirt, it always boiled down to this: "When I'm struggling, support me better." It's taken years to get to a place where we both agree that the other can't be expected to be a mind reader. Or a saint. Sometimes you're too in your own head to notice what the other person needs. Sometimes you're itching to give advice even when you know it's not welcomed. Sometimes you're compelled to share a piece of your mind even when you know it won't end well. You're a perfectly imperfect human, after all.

Communication is a skill so intrinsic to life, I don't know why it isn't a core curriculum in every school. And when mental health enters the equation, the intricate dance between words and their meaning can take on new layers of complexity. The stakes skyrocket. Every turn can seem precarious, every gesture loaded.

As a therapist, I've stumbled over my words more times than I can count, sometimes inadvertently piercing the veil of a client's emotional armour. But these moments, uncomfortable as they are, form the raw material of transformation – the grist for the therapeutic mill. The essence of communication isn't about flawless delivery; it's about the courage to remain engaged, to recalibrate and continue when we veer off course.

In this chapter, we'll establish the tenets of how to have better communication with your loved one. That means thinking about the practicalities around choosing the right time, space and place for important dialogue; what to do when your loved one doesn't feel safe enough to open up; how to deal with conversations that don't go to plan; and how best to utilize nonverbal communication.

May we all find the words, the pauses and the gestures that reach across the divide, extending a hand where it's needed most. But above all, please remember this simple truth: *you're doing the best you can*. If, in a given moment, your loved one isn't receptive or is simply too unwell, understand there are limits to your influence. No single conversation will change things, but the cumulative effect of your patience, behaviour and love has the potential to lead to healing for all. And as we journey through this chapter, avoid chaining yourself to past regrets. There is no guaranteed formula for a breakthrough, but every genuine effort you make lays a brick on the path toward understanding and recovery.

First off, let's explore your current thoughts and feelings about your communication with your loved one.

COMMUNICATION CONCERNS

Ask yourself the following questions and jot down your answers in your journal:

1 On a scale of 1 to 10, how concerned do I feel about my loved one? (NB: If your loved one is facing an urgent mental health crisis – such as expressing intent to harm themselves or others, experiencing severe disorientation, or showing signs of a drastic personality change – it's crucial to seek professional medical help immediately. For further guidance on how to handle these scenarios, go to Chapter 5 on emergency planning.)

2 What is it that I might like to express to my loved one?

3 What would good and bad communication look like?

4 How might our shared history be impacting our communication?

5 How do I feel about having a conversation with my loved one about issues concerning their mental health?

6 What would hold me back from speaking with them – and are these concerns justified?

Time, Place, Space

The right conversation at the wrong time can have unfavourable consequences, as can the right conversation in the wrong environment (note to self: a department store changing room is not a good space, no matter how much you both enjoy shopping). So how do you know when to pick your moment, and where to do it?

If you take one thing away from this chapter let it be this: avoid having big conversations when big emotions are present. Constructive conversations don't come about when either party is feeling overwhelmed – this simply clouds judgement and impedes communication. This also stands true when someone is relapsing, experiencing psychosis or appears to be disassociated. These are not times to discuss major issues, medication adjustments or future plans. Such topics are best tackled when both of you can engage calmly and meaningfully. But even a simple challenge at the wrong time can cause damage, like when someone is in the throes of heightened anxiety – something my husband will attest to, if he endeavours to make an otherwise totally logical point when I'm feeling particularly stressed or anxious.

Once a crisis has been navigated or a particularly stressful episode has concluded, this could be the optimal time to open dialogue. Emotional clarity often follows a storm, allowing for more productive and sensitive conversations, where both parties can come together for a joint purpose. Allowing 24 to 48 hours to pass before a post-conflict debrief is generally advisable, and best practice is to agree on a mutually convenient but specific time in advance.

Important conversations are best done when walking. When you're side by side, rather than face to face, the dynamic is less confrontational. There's a common purpose that makes the conversation feel more like a shared journey, which facilitates open, honest conversation. Not to mention, being outdoors provides oxygenation and physical movement, both of which have been shown to reduce stress hormones and increase the release of endorphins. Being surrounded by nature can offer a sense of expansiveness, too, which you might mirror psychologically, giving the other person more emotional "space".

Being in a public setting while maintaining the intimacy of a private conversation offers another interesting advantage: the presence of others. Even if they're at a distance, this can serve as a subtle but important safety net. Especially if the conversation is at risk of escalating or becoming volatile.

If taking a walk isn't feasible, opt for a cool, calm room to serve as neutral ground, and consider playing some unobtrusive music at a low volume. Research has shown that listening to classical music, particularly pieces with a slow tempo, can reduce stress levels, lower blood pressure, and even boost dopamine production.[1] The calming effect of music is thought to slow down the brain's neural pathways, creating a more relaxed and focused state conducive to mindful communication. Similarly, too much heat can cause cortisol levels to spike, so you might want to make sure the radiators aren't blasting, and the room is aired.[2]

Picking a neutral environment like a quiet café may offer the emotional distance needed for a tough discussion. Be aware of how the setting may impact the conversation and be ready to adapt your strategy accordingly.

One of the key factors that makes therapy a transformative experience is the existence of a well-defined set of ground rules. These boundaries provide a safe structure within which both the therapist and client can explore emotional terrain that is often fraught. While I appreciate that real-world relationships can be more complex than those confined to the therapy room, consider how the following principles may still be relevant for you:

1 **Time-capped conversations:** Consider time-capping discussions related to mental health matters. Keep these conversations consistent so they are short but regular in occurrence. This is not about avoidance but about maintaining emotional sustainability, which allows you both to approach each conversation with the energy and focus they deserve.

2 **Confidentiality:** Assure your loved one that what they share with you stays between you both. Yet let them know that if you are concerned for their safety, or the safety of anyone else, you will inform their doctor or emergency services, but only with their knowing first.

3 **Non-judgemental space:** Create an environment where your loved one feels they can express themselves without fear of judgement or criticism. You may do this by simply telling them: "I'm not judging you."

4 **Understanding their needs:** Have a mutual understanding of what you hope to achieve in your discussions. Rarely

in life do we ask the other person what they need, yet it would transform most of our conversations: we'd know whether the other person simply wanted to offload, or whether they were looking for solutions.

5 **Emotional buffer zones:** In therapy, there is often a "cooling-off" period toward the end of a session where you can discuss less intense topics. This can also be useful in everyday interactions, too, offering a period for emotional decompression. This is a great time to signal that your visit/ chat is coming to an end and you have "10 minutes left".

Far from making someone feel rejected, establishing some guidelines can feel reassuring, while protecting your own energy.

Asking the Right Questions

No matter the depth of love, there is always space between people. Our realities are subjective, and we can never know what's going on in another person's head. I spent my early life behaving more like a coach to my loved ones and even clients, barking motivational orders at them, instructing them on the actions they needed to take to improve their lives and so on. It never ended well. Tell someone they need to change and they'll rarely listen. Whereas curiosity builds bridges.

People are much more likely to open up when you express a genuine interest in them. And that's when they're asked the right questions, which are open-ended.

A good open-ended question can't be answered with a simple "yes" or "no". It invites the respondent to think, reflect and explore their thoughts and feelings. Open-ended questions typically start with words like "what", "how" or "why", prompting a more in-depth reply. These questions stimulate critical thinking and emotional processing, offering the respondent the opportunity to contribute more than just factual information (which is what closed questions do). They provide space for a richer dialogue.

Some examples of open-ended questions that tend to come up in the therapy room include:

- "How did that experience make you feel?"
- "What was going through your mind when that happened?"
- "Can you tell me more about your relationship with your parents?"
- "What are some of the challenges you've faced in this area?"
- "Can you describe a typical 24 hours in your life?"

Addressing sensitive topics around mental health requires a special touch. Here are some examples of how to turn the closed questions you might want to ask your loved one into more productive open-ended ones:

Topic	Closed question	Open-ended question
Feelings and emotions	"Are you feeling okay?"	"Can you share what you're going through right now?"
Medication	"Did you take your medication today?"	"Can you help me understand your thoughts on your medication regimen?"
Professional help	"Did you see the doctor?"	"What was your experience like at the doctor's office?"
Treatment plan	"Do you like your treatment plan?"	"How do you feel about your current treatment plan and its effectiveness?"

The above examples will allow your loved one the space to express themselves more freely, which can lead to a better understanding of their needs and concerns.

PROMPT: Before you ask someone 20 questions, justify their usefulness to yourself first – this is something all good therapists should do, too!

The Art of Storytelling

If you can't get through to someone, tell them a story. Stories resonate deeply because they're woven into the fabric of our existence; we're naturally attuned to them from childhood.

And where advice never works, storytelling often does. Stories lower defences. Instead of feeling confronted or judged, the listener can immerse themselves in a narrative. This detachment allows them to reflect on the underlying message without feeling targeted. By using stories, you'll engage the heart and mind, offering gentle guidance without confrontation and making your interactions a lot richer.

Here are some practical tools for communicating through stories that resonate with your loved one's situation:

- Share short personal anecdotes, but frame them as something you heard about from someone else; for example, "I once heard about someone who faced a similar challenge..." This is an old trick for a reason: it works!
- Use stories from friends and associates (without breaching confidentiality) or even public figures. This can create a sense of relatability and broaden the perspective.
- Referencing well-known stories from literature or film can help illustrate a point, while engaging the listener in a familiar context. For example, discussing a character's journey can parallel the challenges faced by your loved one.
- Research classic tales and parables that could be relevant to what you're trying to convey. Old favourites like "The Tortoise and the Hare" can be useful, as they come with built-in morals that can guide thinking.

- Never follow up with an explanation or interpretation. Let the story breathe, and allow the other person to draw their own meanings and insights in their own sweet time.

Don't Play the Expert

Remember that it's not your responsibility to "mend" your loved one, as Saul, 46, makes clear when voicing what he wants his husband to know:

> You don't have to fix me; you really don't. Trying to do so just heaps more weight and pressure onto the relationship, and honestly, it makes me feel like I'm some kind of broken object that needs mending. I start thinking I have to "get better" to be worthy of your love. I get it; your intentions are pure gold. But it's taken us years to realize that fixing isn't what's needed here.

While Freud might have believed that the therapist was the expert attempting to "cure" his patient, modern psychotherapy has moved on a great deal. The reality is that people only learn through experience (or through other people's stories!). As such, a therapist isn't there to diagnose or imprint ideas on their client, but to offer a supportive relationship and environment, conducive to someone's own change. And I think this is an important lesson for us all. My belief is that given the right environment – one that provides genuineness, acceptance and empathic understanding – we can all realize our potential. Just like a plant needs a suitable climate to grow, so do people.

You might have heard of Carl Rogers, who pioneered the person-centred approach in therapy.[3] He's a real inspiration to me and I'd like to share his main teachings with you, as they may be helpful when it comes to communicating with your loved one. Alongside these, you'll find specific exercises to help you develop that quality or skill. These exercises are, of course, not just for use with your loved one, but can help improve all relationships.

1. Unconditional Positive Regard

Unconditional positive regard is the cornerstone of creating a safe and nurturing emotional space. It means that you show love, respect and support for a person's inherent worth, no matter what they say or do. I know this isn't always easy. Especially if you're struggling with feelings such as rage, despair or ambivalence. Unconditional positive regard doesn't mean you condone or support any behaviour, but rather you accept someone for who they are at their core, separate from their actions. As a result, the other person's defensive mechanisms may reduce – and a safe space for open dialogue is more likely to be established. You see, through modelling unconditional positive regard for your loved one, you give them the opportunity to develop unconditional positive *self-regard*. Tone, facial expression and body language can all convey unconditional positive regard, sometimes even more strongly than words.

BLOOMING

In this exercise, you'll encourage your loved one to bloom like a flower. Here's how:

1 Spend a few moments each day thinking about your loved one's positive qualities. Make it a point to share one of these thoughts with them daily to foster an environment of unconditional positive regard.
2 In time, you might make this a two-way exercise, so you both name each other's positive qualities.

Some ideas of what to say:

- "I love you, no matter what."
- "Take all the time you need, I'm here."
- "You're more than just this moment or this situation."
- "I see you. I want to hear you."

2. Empathetic Understanding

This involves attempting to understand someone from their point of view, not just sympathizing from your own perspective. Putting yourself in someone else's shoes can be incredibly validating, and lessen feelings of isolation and alienation, which can be pronounced in those experiencing mental health issues.

SILENTLY SHARE YOUR FEELINGS

When it comes to developing empathic understanding, sometimes it's easier to write things down than to say them aloud.

1 Suggest that each of you writes down a recent personal challenge or worry.
2 Swap notes and read them in silence, taking the time to consider how you would genuinely feel if you were in your loved one's shoes.
3 Share your empathic understanding without attempting to solve the problem; for example, "If I were facing this, I think I would feel pretty overwhelmed because…"

Some ideas of what to say:

- "I sense you're going through a difficult time. How are you feeling about it all?"
- "What you're feeling is important, and I want to understand it fully. Can you help me do that?"
- "What you're saying makes sense to me. I can see why you'd feel that way."

3. Congruence

It might sound straightforward, but being genuine and transparent establishes trust. When there's mutual trust, all conversations, including those about mental health treatments or lifestyle changes, can occur more smoothly. Congruence means your external expressions match your internal feelings. Usually, we can sense incongruence in another, so it's important to say only the things that sit right with you. If you don't feel something, then can you find other ways to offer support, other than through verbal agreement or reassurance?

BE TRUE TO YOURSELF

If you don't know how you really feel, it can be difficult to act congruently. To address this:

1 Regularly take time to assess your feelings. If you notice any emotional blocks or hesitance in discussing specific topics, reflect on why that is.
2 Daily meditation and regular journaling can also help build self-awareness.

Some ideas of what to say:

- "I'm really concerned about you and think we should talk."
- "It hurts me to see you in pain."
- "I'm scared you're not wanting to face things and that makes me worried about the future."

4. Active Listening

Active listening involves more than hearing words; it's about understanding the emotions and intentions behind them, and allowing the other person to express themselves without fear of criticism or misunderstanding. The language someone uses is very important. Really listen to your loved one's subjective experience of living with mental illness without needing to respond or fix anything. Here's the thing: when someone feels genuinely heard, their body undergoes positive physiological changes. Research indicates that levels of inflammation decrease, heart rate variability improves, and the prefrontal cortex, responsible for problem-solving, becomes more active. Simultaneously, the brain's threat response centre, responsible for the fight, flight or freeze reactions, is deactivated.[4]

THE MIRROR EXERCISE

To develop active listening, try the following exercise.

1 Ask your loved one an open-ended question and hear them out fully.
2 Then reflect what you've heard and ask whether you've understood them accurately. Make sure not to add your own thoughts, judgements or assumptions.

3 Your loved one should then provide feedback on the accuracy and completeness of your understanding. Were you able to capture the essence of what they were saying?

Some ideas of what to say:

- "I want to make sure I'm understanding you correctly. Are you saying…?"
- "Let me see if I've understood… Does this sound right?"
- "I trust your judgement."

5. Non-Directivity

Let your loved one take the lead in discussions to show respect for their autonomy and give them a sense of control. Remember, an individual knows themselves best. Even if someone is very unwell, they need to feel as though they have agency and the potential for self-expression. It also makes people far less defensive when they feel they can ultimately follow their own path.

TAKE A STEP BACK

Here's an exercise that allows your loved one to take the lead. Don't do this if they're in a state of mania.

1 Spend some uninterrupted time with your loved one where you let them take the lead.
2 Simply accompany them and go at their pace. Notice the impact on them when you're not trying to change anything.

Some ideas of what to say:

- "What do you think you should do?"
- "How do you feel about that?"
- "Is there something specific you'd like for me to do to support you better?"

The Power of the Nonverbal

When Mara, 20, first walked into the therapy room, her presence was as faint as a shadow. I was at the start of my career and felt ill-equipped to work with this ghost-like figure, who had been diagnosed with PTSD, an eating disorder and depersonalization. For months, Mara would barely lift her eyes to acknowledge me, her whispered words disappearing into the drab grey room.

Most of the time we sat in silence. If I was lucky, she'd half-respond to one of my enquiries. Yet it never felt rude. Or boring. Instead, I did my best to engage with her on another level; smiling at her mostly through my eyes, sometimes putting my hand up to my chest, to feel my beating heart and steady myself with a slow breath or two. I'd gently remind her, "I'm here, Mara. Whenever you're ready."

Slowly, her life story unfolded. Beneath her long sleeves, the angry lines of self-harm told of a tumultuous past dominated by an abusive, drug-addicted father and a mother whose own anxiety rendered her absent.

Our weekly sessions became an example of consistency in her chaotic world. Over time, an unexpected form of communication emerged: illustrations. Mara took refuge in the world of Japanese comics, which offered a parallel universe that felt far safer than the one she inhabited. She started bringing her sketchbook to our sessions. Her talent was undeniable, and through these Chibi drawings, I glimpsed her resilient spirit in the form of a lead character named "Haiko", who had weathered a lot but was still a kick-ass fighter, slaying evil monsters and terrorizing corrupt institutions. For a long time, Mara would only speak about Haiko – but I sensed she was really telling me about herself.

What couldn't be spoken of – at least for now – was shared through art. It took several months before I told her, "Haiko came from you. She's a part of you, Mara. The fact that you have created such an awe-inspiring character fills me with a lot of hope for you. You're every bit as kick-ass as her."

I wanted to share this story, because even if your loved one is not yet ready to have an important conversation with you, communication *is* in fact happening; it's just nonverbal. Nonverbal cues, such as facial expressions, eye contact, tone of voice, gestures, body posture and even the pace and rhythm of speech, can all reveal hidden emotions and underlying attitudes that may not be easily articulated through words. Being attuned to your loved one's nonverbal signals can provide clues to their state of mind and needs in that moment. For example, constant shifting in their seat, playing with their hands or foot tapping may indicate anxiety, which calls for a calming presence or even a distraction that helps them to relax. Consistently crossed arms suggests defensiveness, requiring a need for patience and a less confrontational approach. Changes in proximity indicate whether someone desires more or less space.

Being mindful of cues – both in yourself and in others – can significantly enhance the quality of your interactions. Remember, nonverbal signals are not just ways to convey messages; they're also ways to connect on a more intuitive level. You may find that certain gestures, like a tender touch or an understanding look, can say more than any words when comforting someone who is in emotional distress. What's more, being attuned to nonverbal cues can alert you to incongruences between what is being said and what is being conveyed through body language or tone, which can be particularly useful when dealing with someone who may not be fully transparent, or aware of their own feelings.

Becoming comfortable in silence can be the access point to nonverbal communication, as it was for Mara and me. Sometimes just "being" with the other person is enough – something many of us are out of practice at. Yet connecting, quietly, through simple presence of mind can be transformative. Especially when words fail us. This is when doing a shared activity can be linctus for the soul. Making someone a nourishing meal or taking time to watch something they enjoy are both forms of expressing love. And may be particularly useful when a person is depressed, or simply "not ready to go there".

Discovering Another Language

When someone has a mental health issue like schizophrenia or severe neurodiversity, the realm of relating can shift dramatically. Someone with schizophrenia may experience delusions, hallucinations and disorganized speech, otherwise known as "word salad". These symptoms often distort the individual's perception and expression, making conventional communication strategies less effective, or even counterproductive. In such cases, alternative modes of connection become crucial. A type of soul-to-soul connection is required. A way of relating that transcends words and dives into the essence of our shared humanity. Activities like painting, music therapy or simply sitting together in nature can foster this level of connection. These activities don't rely on verbal exchange but activate other, subtle pathways to shared experience and understanding.

Similarly, for those who are neurodiverse, conventional "norms" of eye contact, body language and even vocal intonation may not apply in the same way. Instead, communication with your loved one becomes about joining them in their world, and investing time in finding their language. Engage in activities that appeal to their interests. Familiarize yourself with their distinct expressions. Use visual aids, pictures and even role-play to understand their intentions and feelings. Sensory experiences, such as dancing, jumping or finger painting, can also serve as potent connectors. The focus is simply on meeting an individual where they are, and validating their unique way of interacting with the world. If they can't come to you, go to them.

Remember, connecting at this level isn't about interpreting symptoms, but about acknowledging the profound essence that exists beyond categorizations. Simply hold the intention to recognize the being within each of us.

Which brings me to humour. An unlikely topic in a book about mental health, you might think! Except that some of the most brilliant comedians of our time have struggled with their mental health – from Robin Williams to Sarah Silverman and Jim Carrey, to name just a few. Whether they were born with funny bones or adapted to making people laugh to survive a dark, depraved world is up for debate. But laughter is one of the great uniters (and relaxants) of our world. I know my own family have found the funny in the darkest and most absurd of times.

Above all, what leaning into nonverbal communication can do is chaperone you from the mind to the heart, opening the channel for a different kind of communication to emerge. To do this, it can help to visualize a warm light emanating from your heart and filling your entire body.

When Conversations Veer Off Course

A client, Beatrice, 33, recounted a recent experience to me:

My long, silk dress caught underneath my stiletto as I stormed off to find the exit to the wedding. It was gone midnight and I had just seen that our nine-month-old was back at the villa, sleeping under a blanket her sitter had put on her. Which everyone knows is a big no-no. Our friends had laughed at my behaviour and rolled their eyes as they handed me another glass of champagne. My husband gave me that look; he wasn't impressed. I waited for a taxi for several minutes, incensed he hadn't run straight after me.

We rode home in silence; all the while I was shaking and sobbing. *How can he be so callous? Doesn't he care about our baby? Clearly, he doesn't care about me.* These thoughts were rushing through my head.

We didn't speak for two days – until I told him his behaviour had "changed something for me and I didn't know how to come back from it".

During our subsequent therapy sessions, Beatrice and I unpacked what had happened. By way of background, she had been diagnosed with anxiety a few years earlier and had taken Citalopram for a year, but was no longer on it. Generally, she was a high-functioning person – to date, her success had been both a cause and effect of her perfectionism. But Beatrice had also experienced a considerable amount of loss for someone of her age, and death never felt far away.

"It sounds to me like you feared you would lose your baby that night, and sheer panic took over. The fact that your husband couldn't see that made you question the fabric of your marriage," I told her. "But is it possible that he had no idea why you behaved the way you did? And that your response, which was primitive, was baffling to him – even deeply concerning? My guess is that it might have triggered his own trauma. His memories of his first wife just suddenly pulling the plug on their marriage. If you agree, perhaps it might be worth talking about this with him. To explain your position and enquire into his."

When Beatrice returned the following week, she told me that she had talked to her husband and felt much closer to him. Together, they had been able to decode what had happened. Now they had identified their triggers, they vowed to be much more aware of each other's going forward.

Here's the thing: trauma disrupts the natural ebb and flow of communication. Those affected by it often struggle to find the appropriate words for the tempest raging within. This internal turbulence can lead to external conflicts, presenting challenges for even the most well-intentioned of us. The fact is, trauma can rise up without a moment's notice (think of it like an open wound that's suddenly touched) – whether expressed in a sudden flare of anger, an inexplicable display of distrust, a panic attack or a retreat into disengaged silence.

For those who stand beside loved ones ensnared by trauma's shadows, understanding becomes key. The raw emotions that emerge, often perceived as overreactions, are essentially remnants of intense experiences lingering in the nervous system.

Instances that seem benign or innocent can inexplicably trigger these survival responses. This unpredictability is not a reflection of volatility but a testament to the deep-seated scars left behind. With this knowledge, we can learn to reframe and reinterpret our loved one's reactions, seeing them not as erratic behaviours but as echoes of past pains.

But trauma is not a one-sided coin. Just as you navigate your loved one's triggers, it is paramount to recognize your own. Close relationships always step on old wounds, evoking reactions in both parties. There will be times when both of you experience emotional overwhelm – often at the same time. This emotional "flooding" can make it challenging to think clearly, listen well and respond appropriately. When emotions are heightened, the brain's ability to process information diminishes, and this can screw up communication.

Signs of emotional flooding include raised voices, accelerated heart rate, feeling extremely defensive, aggressive or feeling the urge to run away. In other words, it's when our fight, flight or freeze goes from zero to a hundred. When this happens, it's a prompt to pause dialogue.

By identifying and understanding our triggers, both big and small, issues can be approached with caution and care. As human beings we attach meanings to words based on our past experiences. This is why being mindful of our words and what might provoke us or our loved one is key. We can never assume to know what this looks like, so if something is said that puts the other person into a state of fight, flight or freeze, it's a good idea to pay attention to what that is, and check in by saying something like: "I noticed that perhaps saying X triggered something unhelpful? I'm so sorry."

PREPARE A SHARED VOCABULARY

You can create your own prompts to pause dialogue.

1 Sit down with your loved one during a calm moment and discuss which words or phrases to say when a pause is required. Phrases like "I'm overwhelmed" work well, but go ahead and find the words that work for you both.

2 If pre-agreeing such words isn't feasible, you can still model this behaviour yourself. During an intense conversation, you might say, "I'm feeling overwhelmed right now; can we take a break and revisit this later?"

3 By taking the lead, you're not only advocating for your own emotional wellbeing but also setting an example for your loved one. You're showing that it's okay to recognize and articulate emotional limits. Over time, your loved one may start to adopt a similar strategy, making your communication more effective and less emotionally charged.

4 During a cooling-off period, I'd recommend getting some fresh air and space. Ideally, wait to pick things up the following day.

Becoming Aware of Projections

As a therapist, I've been trained to work with unconscious communication using various frameworks. Transference is when a client transfers a significant relationship – usually the one with their primary caregiver – onto the therapist. Over the years, I'm sure I've been cast in several roles, ranging from a client's neglectful father to their doting mother. If you consistently feel that your loved one is relating to you in a way that doesn't necessarily reflect your actual relationship, it may worth spending time considering who you might "be" for them. Simply knowing this might be liberating enough for you to stop taking their responses quite so personally.

We all transfer powerful experiences and strong feelings onto one another *most* of the time. (You don't need to have a mental health diagnosis to do this.) Here's what Andy, 38, a client of mine, ended up saying to his wife after we identified a potential transference was playing out:

Something has come up during my own therapy, and I wondered if I could share it with you? Is now a good time? [He waited for her consent.] Sometimes I get the sense that you see me a bit like your father, who I know you've found quite harsh and cold. I totally understand why you might do this – he's been an important and challenging figure for a long time – and I'm the "other" significant man in your life. But I want to assure you that I'm not him. I'm very much me. And I love you, just as you are. I feel hurt when I'm cast in this role, and it can leave me feeling unappreciated. If it makes you feel any better, I sometimes notice I do this, too, and treat [X] like they're my [X], who affected me in [X] way. I just wanted to share this with you in case it's helpful, as I think it might be useful for us to reflect on the dynamics that sometimes play out between us. But what do you think?

It's important to note that Andy's wife was experiencing moderate long-term depression and low self-esteem, but that she was generally functioning well and was in psychotherapy herself. Otherwise it wouldn't have been prudent for Andy to share his reflections with her.

Another useful framework to be aware of is projective identification. In therapy, that's when a client projects a rejected part of themselves onto the therapist. It can also happen in relationships outside the therapy room. Have you ever sat with someone and felt surprisingly overcome with emotion, while they seemed totally emotionless, even though the upsetting incident was happening to them? Perhaps you sensed the feelings somehow didn't really "belong" to you, even though you were the one experiencing them. This happens a lot when feelings are disowned and someone hasn't faced their shadow material.

In short, we all have a shadow self – the primitive part of ourselves we deny. It's where our unprocessed feelings and pain is stored; without mindful awareness it gets unconsciously projected onto others. Recognizing if this is playing out in the moment can make strong emotions seem more manageable. When we're less stuck in the weeds, we can take a more considered, aerial view of what's happening in our interactions and know how to navigate them safely. Even if we choose to keep this information to ourselves.

Threats and How to Handle Them

"I can be very manipulative," Sylvia, 26, declared within minutes of our first session.

Sylvia was warning me of the games she played – yet surely manipulative people manipulate, rather than let on? I asked Sylvia to consider whether she was pushing me away before the work had even begun.

Sylvia came over to England with her mum when she was two years old. Life was hard. Her mother worked several jobs to keep them afloat. Sylvia always felt alone and longed for a "normal family".

During one session, when Sylvia boasted that she had stopped taking her medication for bipolar disorder, I drafted a letter to her doctor. Ethically, it was important to share this with Sylvia and seek consent first. I explained I was doing this for her own wellbeing, but she saw red and declared: "Normally I punch someone in the face when I feel like this." My heart skipped a beat. I took a breath and repeated back what she had just said, adding that it sounded threatening before ending the session and saying we would resume next week. I knew I needed to show strength and implement clear boundaries.

I was shocked when she turned up uncharacteristically early to our next session. I reiterated that I would not accept threatening behaviour, but that I ultimately wanted to support her and could we think together about what played out. I used the SET model of communication – by focusing on speaking with support, empathy and truth.

At the end of the session Sylvia admitted that previous counsellors had all found her "too much". The fact I expressed my desire to continue working with her and proved to be reliable and robust enabled us to build a positive therapeutic alliance for a time. However, I knew that setting firm boundaries was equally crucial, especially after her veiled threat toward me.

People like Sylvia, who endure a tumultuous emotional landscape, benefit from the steady, empathic presence of someone who can model emotional stability. In this capacity, you can become a guiding anchor in someone's emotional storms. Your consistent responses can act as a grounding force. Achieving this kind of steadiness isn't easy, but it can influence the climate of an interaction – and lay the groundwork for more balanced emotional exchanges in the long run.

It also helps to build a robust sense of safety measures internally – so that you are better prepared if a conflict does arise. Ultimately, learning ways to self-regulate is beneficial for everyone, including you. Here are some practical things to do in your own time:

- **Slow down**: Learn to slow down your breath to centre yourself. This pause gives you a brief window to tune in to your feelings before reacting.
- **Body check**: Pay attention to physical sensations. Does your stomach tighten or do you feel tension in your shoulders? Become attuned to your body's signals.
- **Get grounded**: It's easier for people who are grounded to step back and offer space to the other person and themselves. The best way to ground yourself is to spend time regularly in nature, especially walking barefoot.
- **Reflect**: After the situation has de-escalated, take some time to think back. Was your gut feeling accurate? Understanding when it was can help you trust it more in the future.
- **Journal**: Keep a record of times when your gut instinct was spot on and when it wasn't. Look for patterns that can offer insights into how to listen to your internal signals.

These simple practices may enable you to pre-empt a conflict more easily, when you can offer gentle yet clear feedback. This can be as simple as saying, "I notice you seem a bit more tense than usual. Is something bothering you?" The objective here is not judgement but observation – providing a calm, external viewpoint that the other person might lack. By doing so, you're helping your loved one become more aware of their own fluctuating emotional states.

According to the FBI's Crisis Negotiation Unit, maintaining a calm demeanour and avoiding an authoritative tone helps create an atmosphere of trust and cooperation.[5] Speaking in a low and calm way (I like to think of it as my night-time radio voice) works best.

If you find yourself feeling threatened, repeat back what the other person has said to you word for word, adding no extra detail. Reflecting back offers you both some time to reshape your thinking and, if necessary, rephrase hurtful or harmful words toward each other. This active listening helps your loved one feel heard and can de-escalate the situation.

Should you have immediate concerns for your safety, remove yourself from the situation rather than try to manage it on your own. The guiding principle should always be the safety and wellbeing of all involved. If you anticipate a threatening situation, ensure a neutral third party is present, such as a therapist, counsellor or trusted mutual friend. This can provide an additional layer of safety and mediation.

Working with my client Sylvia was, indeed, a rollercoaster of ups and downs. She continued attending therapy with me for a year. Slowly, she began to trust that I was committed to our therapeutic relationship. Yet, in the end, she did sabotage our work together, and I had to make the difficult decision to terminate therapy. The lesson here is that despite our best intentions, outcomes aren't always within our control. Setting firm boundaries, even painful ones like ending a therapeutic relationship, can be essential for both parties involved (there's more on this topic in Chapter 8). It's an important reminder that while we may deeply desire to assist, there are limits to what we can endure or overlook – emotionally or otherwise.

Can There Be Two Different Thoughts in the Room?

Some individuals find it very difficult to consider another person's point of view. This can be associated with having a personality disorder, but it may be more commonplace than that. A lot of people have a fragile ego that makes it challenging for them to handle criticism, confrontation or even simple differences of opinion. This might manifest in an array of behaviours – from being overly defensive to avoiding relationships altogether.

It's worth noting that the strength of our ego is not fixed. Learning to acknowledge that different viewpoints exist is an ego-strengthening exercise that builds empathy, self-reflection and emotional regulation. But this should not be done in haste (and ideally left to a professional). The shock of being confronted can set back even the most established of egos. So, a hurried or misplaced challenge can crush a fragile movement toward growth.

Over time, you might start to introduce phrases such as, "Is it possible there can be two opinions in the room?" This can help open doors to healthier discussions. You might also try saying things like, "We don't have to agree to understand each other", or "Hearing you out doesn't mean I'm necessarily agreeing, but it means I respect your right to feel the way you do."

But what if one person's point of view is objectively and factually correct? Let's say your loved one drinks excessively every day – we know that's far from advisable. Yet arguing the point over and over again will only get you so far. You see, it's not enough to be right. If your partner is drinking to the point of blacking out, for example, your conversation is going to be layered with more than just the facts about their health. You'll likely be contending with your own fears about where they could end up, the undue risks they'll face, worries about their behaviour, your indignation at not feeling heard, concerns about whether they'll be able to continue working or that you'll be left to do all the childcare … and so on. For them, there will also be countless things going on. Perhaps they drink to deal with chronic pain, or they derive purpose from socializing, or they are dealing with complex feelings. Maybe drinking is the one thing they feel they have for themselves and now you're looking to take that away.

Trying to get your partner to admit they're an alcoholic is likely to be an uphill battle.

The possibility of change is greater if you try to understand one another's perspective. What feels so good about going to the pub? How does drinking impact their mood? What is your partner trying to get away from? What do they need you to know about how they feel? They may not be ready to answer these questions, but you can share how their behaviour impacts you. Avoid blame statements and saying "you"; instead, own your own experience: "I feel …", "I worry …" Share your own mixed feelings when it comes to family life and about your own relationship to addiction (whether that be shopping, social media, other substances, exercise, food and so on), drawing on any significant experiences that have shaped you. Talking about your own strong feelings is not only acceptable, it's important.

The other piece involves disentangling from our own assumptions about the other person's behaviour through thinking things like, "Clearly they don't care about me, because if they did they would change." The way another person behaves doesn't necessarily reflect their intentions.

Once you've shared the impact on you, it's a good idea to clarify the other person's intent. You might say something like, "I'm noticing that now I've told you how I feel and you continue to drink, I'm assuming it's because you don't care about me. That leaves me feeling neglected and like you want out of this family. Is this the case?"

This is a conversation you're likely to need to have a few times. It's usual for someone to feel defensive when you're sharing this type of information. That's why the more open you can be – about your fears and the things you're doubting – the more likely it is that the other person will eventually hear you and share their intentions.

Dealing with Accusations

Gaslighting involves making someone doubt their own reality. If you find yourself being gaslit by a loved one to whom you've expressed concern, it's essential to take a step back and re-establish your own emotional and psychological footing (see Chapter 8 for more on this). Gaslighting is inherently manipulative, and can distort your own sense of sanity and self-worth. If this happens, you might find it helpful to distance yourself temporarily from the situation. Use this time to consult your feelings, perhaps write down your observations and concerns, and talk to trusted individuals who can help affirm your experiences. This space allows you to return to the issue at hand with a clearer mind and reinforced boundaries, crucial for any healthy interaction.

Separately, when someone is very unwell, they might find it hard to recognize themselves and you. This could lead to confusion or accusations against you or other family members, which can be very upsetting. Yet it's important to remain calm and centred, understanding that their accusations stem from their illness rather than any actual wrongdoing. Gently remind them of your identity and your relationship, using grounding statements like, "I understand you're feeling upset, but remember, I'm [your name], your [relationship], and I'm here to help you."

It's important to not make assumptions about how someone else feels. They may be having an experience that you can't relate to. Sometimes the best thing to do is to openly admit this: "No matter how hard I try, I can't come close to knowing what you're experiencing, but I'm here to support you through this."

Seeking clarification by asking your loved one to share more about their perspective can also help de-escalate the situation, showing them that you're there to listen and support, not to argue or defend yourself.

People who experience mental health difficulties can be extremely sensitive. So, keep reassuring them that they are wanted and say, "I love you", even if they don't say it back.

Tailoring Your Communication

Finally, I must reiterate that sometimes, despite your best intentions, your efforts might cause more harm than good. This realization can be both painful and liberating. It's essential to understand that you may not always be the best person to provide the necessary support, and that's okay. You may have to accept that your role in your loved one's life is not to be their primary source of mental health support, and that they would benefit more from the help of a professional, such as a therapist or counsellor, or possibly even another loved one. Your presence, however, remains invaluable. For example, your loved one might cherish your interactions with them when you don't ask about their mental health and instead focus on creating joyful, light-hearted moments. This can provide them with a sense of normalcy and a relationship that isn't defined by their struggles.

It may be useful to have open and honest conversations about what kind of support they truly need from you. Ask them directly, "How can I best support you?" and be prepared to listen to their response. They might express a desire for you to play a different role – perhaps as a fun presence rather than a caregiver. Respecting someone's wishes and boundaries can pay dividends when it comes to your communication with them. In the next chapter, we will address different ways to tailor your communication depending on the issue at hand. From my perspective, this might be the best argument in favour of diagnoses.

CHAPTER 3
UNDERSTANDING MENTAL HEALTH CONDITIONS

"Showing up for myself helps me show up for my mother, and so our time together is a navigating of ourselves and each other and a surrendering to how we are just as we are."

Sally, 53

Imagine a book that covered every health condition – from the common cold to liver disease, from a broken bone to adrenocortical carcinoma. You probably wouldn't trust it, and you'd be right not to. It couldn't possibly speak to the complexity, specificity and comorbidity of each illness. Well, the same is true for this book. Regrettably, we simply cannot cover the depth, nuances and range of every mental health issue. If you want a manual that goes into detail about every single condition, I'd recommend looking at the DSM-5.

The aim here isn't to give an overview of every diagnosis or even to talk about treatment. Instead, we'll take a brief look at some of the most common diagnoses – the ones that seem to show up a lot in my practice, in any case:

- anxiety disorders
- obsessive compulsive and related disorders
- clinical depression
- bipolar disorder

- schizophrenia
- eating disorders such as anorexia and bulimia
- borderline personality disorder
- narcissistic personality disorder
- antisocial personality disorder
- substance-related and addictive disorders

In particular, we'll explore the influence these conditions can exert on personal relationships. While I can't stress enough that it's not your job to become anyone's psychiatrist or therapist, we are experiencing a crisis of care, so understanding what might be going on could prove essential.

Even though the guidance in this chapter is tailored to specific diagnoses, remember that nothing matters so much as approaching exchanges with empathy and an open mind, which is why we covered the foundations of good communication in the previous chapter. Offering your heart, not just your ears, fosters a space where both you and your loved one can evolve. While pain can change a person, love also has the same potential.

> **PROMPT:** Reflect on how your own experiences resonate with some of the conditions we explore in this chapter. We all have parts of us that can be compulsive, anxious, depressed or impulsive. This can help build empathy for those who face more persistent or severe challenges.

Anxiety Disorders

While anxiety manifests differently in everyone, it prompts a primal and physiological defence response. Physical symptoms can include tightness in the chest, accelerated heart rate, sweaty palms, headaches, digestive issues, shallow breathing, tense muscles, unexplained pain, restlessness, insomnia, dizziness, jumpiness and a pervasive feeling of being on edge. These physical symptoms are probably why it accounts for around 30 per cent of all mental health problems seen by doctors in the UK.[1]

These symptoms are hallmarks of the fight-or-flight response – a state where the sympathetic nervous system is in overdrive due to a perceived threat. It's like an alarm has gone off in the body and continues to ring even after the "emergency" is over. When this response becomes chronic, individuals fail to return to a baseline of calm, missing out on the restorative "rest and digest" state. I believe this is why when someone is experiencing acute anxiety they may struggle to metabolize food, feedback or find focus.

Anxiety is pernicious and pervasive; it doesn't motivate us, but locks us into fear. It depletes our energy and output. I'm sure my own anxiety is linked to losing my mother when I was still a child. Often, those with anxiety have experienced a significant life change early on, which compounded the sense they weren't safe in the world. Stressors such as job uncertainty, the end of a relationship, work demands or life transitions can act as catalysts, heightening anxiety levels. So, keep an eye on your loved one if they're going through any major changes, as this can exacerbate old wounds. In fact, there's a saying, "if it's hysterical, it's historical", which means if someone's response seems unusually charged or perhaps disproportionate, its roots likely belong in the past.

Anxiety can escalate later in life (from middle age), too, when fears around mortality can take hold. Therapists believe that leaning into these concerns and applying cognitive reframing to them can turn existential anxiety into an opportunity for growth – and motivate us to consider how we choose to spend our time.

There is also a crossover between anxiety and depression. In my practice, I've observed anxiety's role as a potential defence against depression, which often presents more subtly and gradually. It's important to be aware that the two often exist alongside each other and that to understand how anxiety affects your loved one, you also must understand their depression – or the fear of the helplessness depression brings.

Anxiety itself can manifest in different ways, ranging from social anxiety and separation anxiety to selective mutism (when someone has an inability to speak in certain social contexts), panic attacks, health anxiety and phobias. It can also be connected to substance use or withdrawal and certain medical conditions. All of these present their own challenges, and while there isn't room to cover them here, it's important to know that at the heart of all these behaviours lies anxiety and a sense of disconnection from self. However, I will say one thing: never force anyone to confront their fear. This may cause setbacks and mistrust. No matter how upsetting it feels to watch someone you love impacted by anxiety, their journey must be self-led, and they must initiate their own change; this isn't something you can do for them.

There are usually two main ways people defend against anxiety: through avoidance or control. Both strategies can affect interpersonal relationships. Susannah, 32, explained to me how she struggled to support her best friend:

> She's become so anxious about everything, even the smallest things like catching the bus to meet up for an arrangement, or whether she should have sent a certain email brings about huge turmoil in her. I try to listen and find the right words to support her, but I often seem to unknowingly upset or trigger her. It's like she's putting her anxiety onto me … I leave our conversations feeling incredibly anxious myself and then I don't want to speak to her again for a while.

Susannah's concern and confusion captures the complex dynamic often present when supporting a loved one with generalized anxiety disorder (GAD). The issue here is that as the world feels scary to her best friend, she unknowingly looks to Susannah to make it better. But Susannah, equally, can make her feel more anxious through her responses. The fact is the world is full of uncertainty and the best Susannah can do is model how she herself lives with this. Unwittingly, her best friend was attempting to control her, as she was with most things in her environment. This wasn't out of ill will, but she did need to understand that most things in life are a shade of grey.

When a loved one is entangled in a web of anxiety, this can trap you too in a cycle of reassurance and accommodation. It's essential to recognize how actions that you might think helpful can sometimes perpetuate this cycle. For example, consistently altering plans to avoid triggering your loved one's anxiety could actually reinforce their fear.[2]

It's also important to understand the concept of "anxiety-speak" – a language pattern dominated by what-ifs and worst-case scenarios that is characteristic of GAD. This may require learning a new lexicon of supportive dialogue. For example, you might say: "Let's look at the likelihood of [X] happening. How often has that worry turned out to be true? We can think about strategies to handle it if it does, while keeping in mind that other outcomes are more likely based on past experiences." This response acknowledges the person's feelings while helping them consider the factual likelihood of their fear and to prepare constructively.

Why bother doing this? It's to do with "emotional economy" in relationships. Just as an economy can experience inflation, so too can the emotional responses in relationships with someone who experiences anxiety. What may have once been a reassuring comment can, over time, lose its value as the person experiencing anxiety seeks ever greater reassurance. Being cognizant of this can help you strategize more sustainable forms of support, like encouraging professional help or developing a shared language for when space is required to maintain both your emotional stabilities.

Strategies to help a loved one with anxiety:

- **Be grounded:** Your own emotional stability can be an anchor. Avoid feeding into the anxious atmosphere. Focus on your breathing – and encourage them to do the same.
- **Mindful presence:** Practise naming things you can see, hear, feel, touch and smell in the present moment. This can be very stabilizing when fight, flight or freeze kicks in, and serves as a reminder that the environment is safe.
- **Verbal reassurance:** Saying something like "we'll get through this together" can be incredibly comforting.
- **Physical presence:** A reassuring touch or a gentle massage may offer relief. Anxiety often shows up in the body, and that's where it needs to be met. The end goal is for your loved one to form a greater connection with their own body and learn ways to self-soothe.
- **Practise four–seven–eight breathing:** That is, breathe in to a count of four through the nose, hold for seven and exhale to a count of eight (see page 189). This is particularly useful if someone is in the throes of a panic attack.
- **Rhythmically squeeze their hand:** If your loved one is experiencing a panic attack, you can hold their hand and gently squeeze it in a rhythmic pattern. Encourage them to squeeze back. This can refocus their energy.
- **Offer calming scents:** Certain smells such as lavender have been shown to reduce stress and promote relaxation by affecting the brain's limbic system.
- **Get into nature:** Being surrounded by the great outdoors is arguably the greatest antidote to anxiety. It reminds us how beautiful and resilient nature is – as well as how big the world is, outside of our worries.
- **Notice if you're feeling controlled:** Anxious people are more likely to attempt to control their environment and may resort to obsessive behaviours. Sometimes this comes across as self-righteous. It's important not to get sucked into this, but try to understand where it's coming from.

- **Encourage agency:** Over time, gently encourage them to take an active role in decision-making. Ask them to consider when they can put aside a worry and come back to it.
- **Educate yourself:** Whether it's about a related medical condition, or the effects of medication or substance withdrawal, research information that could be used as part of a comprehensive treatment plan.

Things to avoid:

- **Minimization:** Saying "don't worry about it" can make the person feel like their fears are being undermined.
- **Sudden changes:** Try not to introduce unpredictable elements or surprises, as these can exacerbate anxiety. Gradual exposure is always recommended.
- **Escalation:** Controlling behaviour stemming from anxiety can express itself as anger toward the other person. Learn when it's useful to remove yourself from a situation in order to de-escalate tension.
- **Speaking in absolutes:** Using phrases like "you always" or "you never" can make a person feel criticized or overwhelmed, which can heighten anxiety.

Obsessive Compulsive and Related Disorders

The term OCD is flung around a lot these days and is often the hallmark of highly organized or meticulous individuals. However, obsessive compulsive disorder is a debilitating illness that can severely constrain a person's life, dictating their daily choices through a series of obsessions and compulsions. Alongside OCD, several other compulsive disorders fall into this category: hoarding, hair-pulling, skin-picking and pure O.

At their core, these behaviours are about control – control over ourselves and our environment to stave off or prevent a feared event. One client I worked with believed his intrusive thoughts could manifest as the death of his loved ones. In a desperate attempt to switch off his thoughts, he resorted to counting everything superstitiously and then sought refuge in alcohol. OCD is the way someone attempts to control or suppress unwanted images, impulses or thoughts.

The compulsions characteristic of OCD – whether they be mental rituals like continuous checking or physical acts like excessive washing – are deeply personal. These behaviours are a defence against the unbearable weight of internal fears and a guard against unmanageable feelings.

Indeed, OCD frequently coexists with anxiety and depression, and some recent research also shows a notable correlation with those on the autism spectrum, since the repetitive and habitual behaviours that define OCD can offer a semblance of comfort.[3] Similarly, those with schizophrenia may engage in compulsive behaviours to manage overwhelming thoughts and perceptions.

Individuals with OCD often possess above-average intelligence, and many are very successful, often employing black-and-white thinking and rigour in their pursuit of perfection. Intellectual interests may feel safer than emotional ones. Other people, with their messy feelings, may be avoided altogether.

However, while your loved one may appear to others as a very well-put-together person, this may not be how they feel on the inside. Perhaps they feel they need to keep themselves on a tight leash, or they would run themselves ragged. This is often seen in those who experienced "parentification" as children, taking on adult responsibilities prematurely. As adults, they may attempt to exert control within relationships, mirroring their need to manage the unpredictability of their environment. These individuals may withhold information or affection, becoming angry when they feel threatened – they often have a monopoly on the truth.

It can be taxing to live with someone who has OCD, as they may foster a very different public persona. Because of their perfectionist nature, these people might struggle with interpersonal relationships and be unduly critical of others' flaws. Perhaps they're overly polite, wanting to keep up appearances, or are overly conscientious and punctilious, whereas at home they might be irritable and almost tyrannical. Supporting loved ones involves recognizing the disorder's complexities, guiding them gently toward effective therapies, and helping them to reconnect with the emotional aspects of their experiences that they may have intellectualized or distanced themselves from. This does not mean making excuses for unacceptable behaviour. Rage, or repressed rage, can be worked through in a therapeutic setting. However, this might take time, since these individuals often find it hard to "let go" in therapy.

For those supporting a loved one with OCD, it's crucial to foster a present-focused environment for everyone's benefit, encouraging mindfulness and grounding techniques to mitigate the compulsion to project into an uncertain future. Understanding that compulsive behaviours are a person's way of creating a sense of security in a world that feels chaotic can inform a compassionate approach. However, the fundamental goal is always to NOT feed compulsions.

There's a small subsection of such individuals for whom therapy is unlikely to work, whose lives are so riddled with obsessive rituals that they have no time for real life. If your loved one is on that end of the spectrum, you might need to focus on rejoicing in those magical, fleeting moments when beauty does flow in; when, for example, you can appreciate the summer breeze on your faces or an awe-inspiring sunset together. For if they can't let go beyond that, it's you who will need to.

Strategies to help a loved one with OCD:

- **Educate yourself about OCD:** Understanding the nature of OCD and related disorders is critical, as it's really about warding off anxiety.
- **Encourage professional help:** Support your loved one in seeking therapy, particularly cognitive behavioural therapy (CBT) and exposure and response prevention (ERP), which are highly effective for treating OCD.
- **Respect their boundaries:** Be mindful of the need for routines or rituals. Avoid forcing anyone to confront their fears prematurely.
- **Acknowledge efforts:** Recognize and praise your loved one's attempts to resist compulsions. Positive reinforcement is a motivator.
- **Model stress-management techniques:** Demonstrate healthy ways of coping with stress, such as mindfulness, meditation or exercise, which can help reduce the intensity of OCD symptoms.

Things to avoid:

- **Participating in compulsions:** Avoid participating in or enabling their compulsive behaviours, as this can reinforce the cycle of OCD.
- **Constant reassurance:** Avoid providing constant reassurance, which can feed someone's anxiety and compulsions. Instead, encourage them to tolerate any uncertainty.
- **Dismissing their fears:** Never dismiss or trivialize their fears, no matter how irrational these may seem. Understand that their fears are very real to them.
- **Pressuring them to stop:** Don't pressure them to stop their compulsions abruptly or without professional guidance. This can increase their anxiety and make the situation worse.

- **Assuming control:** Do not take over their responsibilities or decisions in an attempt to help, as this disorder is all about exerting control.
- **Making jokes about OCD:** Refrain from making jokes or offhand comments.

Clinical Depression

Clinical depression isn't just a bad mood; it's a condition that affects a person's thoughts, feelings and overall health. It can range from pervasive feelings of despondency to severe self-neglect and risk to life. Its causes are broad-ranging, from difficult experiences in childhood to stressful life events.

Beneath depression's apparent numbness are lots of repressed feelings. These may relate to unresolved trauma or unmet emotional needs. But those with depression become adept at swallowing them (often turning to alcohol and food to do this). Why? Because usually, at some core level, they don't believe they're worthy. Their behaviour might then reinforce that belief, so it becomes a kind of self-fulfilling prophecy. Hence, they habitually underperform or self-sabotage.

The journey through depression is deeply personal, yet there are some shared elements. A sense of isolation is common, stemming not just from the condition, but from the perception that our struggles are a unique burden that others couldn't possibly understand. However, the reality is that depression affects millions globally. It's this shared aspect that can become a bridge to recovery – understanding that others have walked this path, too, and found ways to reclaim their lives.

One of the hallmarks of severe depression is a paralysing sense of hopelessness – a belief that things won't get better. There can be a certain stuck-in-the-mud quality to depressed people, as though they're mired in despair. You might feel this way, too, in their company. Alternatively, you might be left feeling all the feelings, like sadness, that they themselves are pushing away.

The challenge is to offer care without reinforcing the helplessness that depression engenders. It's about being present and listening without judgement, acknowledging the person's feelings while gently encouraging manageable steps toward activity and re-engagement.

Hopefulness comes from the belief that we can fundamentally put things right. Rather than trying to convince your loved one that they can surmount life's difficulties and prevail, the greatest gift you can give them is to model resilience, wisdom and healthy behaviours yourself, as Diane, 55, describes:

> Harold's depression was like a thick fog that settled over our lives. After he lost his job, his vibrancy and the intimacy we shared seemed to vanish into thin air. Night after night, I lay beside a man who was physically present but emotionally a million miles away... I felt helpless, watching the man I love dissolve into the background of his own life.
>
> Then, hope came from where we least expected it. It wasn't a breakthrough with therapy or a wonder pill that brought him back – it was our daughter's insistence on evening walks. Initially, he was reluctant, but her persistence won. Slowly, the natural world began to work its gentle magic. With every step, every breath of fresh air, I witnessed the subtle lift in his spirits. These walks became our salvation. And though he still has his struggles, we now walk them together, hand in hand.

I love what Diane says because it speaks to a gentle kind of communion. And of trusting the cycles of time, which nature also teaches us. As hard as it is to sit with depression, giving it space is important – as is giving yourself the space you need.

Finding ways to refuel your oxygen supply and the joy you require to keep going is critical. Don't dampen your own light but trust that, perhaps, little by little, it may illuminate your loved one's path forward.

If your loved one is catatonically depressed – motionless, mute and unresponsive for extended periods – this is a severe mental health condition requiring professional medical intervention. Try to remember that their lack of responsiveness is not a reflection of the quality of your relationship, or a deliberate withdrawal. They're undergoing a profound internal struggle that has manifested in a physical and psychological stasis.

Even if it seems one-sided, simply being physically present can offer profound comfort. Speaking to a person without expectation of a response ensures they're not isolated within their silence. This includes verbal reassurances of love and support, as well as maintaining normalcy in communication. Recovery from catatonic depression can be slow, and expecting quick changes can lead to disappointment, so it's essential to prioritize your self-care and establish the necessary support required for everyone involved.

The greatest risk with depression is suicide, but assessing that risk is complex and requires a multifaceted approach (see Chapter 5). If your loved one is on medication and you believe there is a risk to their life, please seek urgent medical care. Also, try to remove any medicines or instruments that could cause harm. However, remember that the buck does not stop with you, or anyone, other than the individual.

Through working with severely depressed clients over the years, I've witnessed how even the poorest eye contact, barely audible speech and a crippling distrust of others can be slowly transformed through effective mirroring and being heart-centred. But it takes time. I've also found that drawing on positive psychology – that is, helping people to think about their strengths, resilience and positive qualities even when they're at their lowest ebb – can be powerful.

Strategies to help a loved one with depression:

- **Offer simple activities**: Suggest activities that require minimal effort but provide a change of atmosphere, such as sitting in the garden.
- **Be patient**: Allow them to open up in their own time.
- **Play music and find ways to feed the soul:** People with depression can hugely benefit from the arts and finding nonverbal ways to express themselves.
- **See what lies beneath:** When people are depressed, they may avoid their feelings. If your loved one is keeping themselves "busy" with something like work or cleaning, you may want to reflect this back to them gently.
- **Notice if you're feeling drained:** Sometimes supporting someone with depression can feel like a bottomless pit, so acknowledge when you need some space, too.

Things to avoid:

- **Focusing on what's lacking:** Their self-esteem is likely to be low, and they may struggle to recognize their capabilities. Sometimes these people sabotage their achievements, but it's not for you to point this out. Instead, praise their achievements, however small.
- **Using clichés:** Phrases like "just be happy" aren't only unhelpful but can be harmful.
- **Forcing activity:** Understand that for someone with depression, even small tasks can be daunting.

Bipolar Disorder

Bipolar disorders encompass a category of mood disorders previously referred to as manic-depressive illness. These disorders are characterized by cyclical shifts in mood, energy and activity levels, from emotional highs to extreme lows. The cyclical nature means that the manic joy and productivity are often followed by episodes of deep, dark depression, where a person might experience overpowering sadness, lethargy and a loss of interest in life. At its most severe, this illness can manifest in psychosis, where the individual loses touch with reality.

Yang, 71, explains what it can be like to live with a bipolar loved one:

> Living with the knowledge that your child has bipolar disorder is like being perennially braced for a storm. Over the years, I've learned that managing this uncertainty is not about control but cultivating resilience. You become adept at crisis management, at gathering a community of support, at advocating fiercely. But most importantly, you learn to appreciate the standard days, and navigate the tumultuous ones with boundless love.

If you're navigating the ebb and flow of a loved one's bipolar, it's likely you've experienced the full gamut of heightened emotion – from confusion to fear, exasperation, overprotectiveness and everything in between. Acknowledging these emotions is key, not just for understanding the chaotic tides of bipolar disorder, but for anchoring your own wellbeing amidst the turbulence. It's important to understand that these feelings are a valid and natural response to a challenging situation.

In a society that often glorifies productivity, fun and extroversion, the symptoms of bipolar disorder can often be misconstrued. Perhaps you yourself mistook the early signs of mania for a positive development, not realizing it could be the precursor to a dangerous high or a subsequent devastating low. Please know that's perfectly normal. Maybe it took some time before you realized that your loved one's mood swings were down to more than an "artistic nature".

It's not unusual to find a streak of brilliance running through the lives of those with bipolar disorder. In moments of mania, the mind can race with ideas, drawing connections and inspirations that might elude the typical bounds of thinking. This vibrancy can give a magical allure to their persona, drawing others into their captivating orbit.

However, the cost of these flights into brilliance can be steep. The very same energy that propels someone to the stars can accelerate toward a crash. It's in these moments, when the party is over and the admirers have retreated, that the vulnerability of the person behind the "genius" is laid bare. And it's now that they need understanding and support the most – not for their talents or charisma, but for their humanity.

I worked with Ava, whose husband, Jamie, was diagnosed with bipolar disorder. Over time, she became skilled at recognizing the early signs of Jamie's manic episodes, such as a sudden flurry of grandiose plans. Together, we identified these as signals to initiate their communication plan. A key part involved setting clear, non-negotiable limits, including maintaining fidelity. Open and honest discussions about the consequences of crossing these boundaries were held during calm periods, ensuring mutual understanding and consent.

With her newfound knowledge of bipolar disorder, Ava was able to disentangle the person she loved from the symptomatic behaviours of the illness, addressing each episode with wisdom rather than taking it as a personal affront. This nuanced approach allowed Ava to trust and support Jamie's commitment to treatment and find a relevant community for herself, learning to navigate her own emotional journey alongside her husband's.

Dealing with bipolar disorder calls for a well-rounded approach. It's important to consider not just the personal and work-life impacts, but the broader societal costs. For example, there are laws that limit driving during acute episodes. There is more detail on recognizing the signs of mania on page 135.

Strategies to help a loved one with bipolar disorder:

- **Reality check**: During manic phases, gently question grandiose thinking or unrealistic plans. Ask questions like, "Do you think this is something you might want to think through a bit more?"
- **See the person behind their behaviour**: However wild or precarious their actions might be, remember to see and communicate with the human being behind them.
- **Remind them of consequences**: Without being confrontational, remind them of past experiences; for example, "I know you feel unstoppable, but remember the last time?"
- **Establish boundaries**: Make it clear what behaviour is unacceptable, especially during calm periods; this is also the time to agree to watch collectively for warning signs.
- **Be a steady emotional support**: Encourage positive steps without pushing too hard. Let them know you value them just as much when they're down.

Things to avoid:

- **Enabling mania**: Society rewards extroversion, humour and highs, which can all be signs of mania. Don't get swept along for the ride. Participating in risky behaviours or endorsing delusional plans can be dangerous.
- **Minimizing depression**: Saying things like "but you were so happy yesterday" misunderstands the condition and implies they're only acceptable one way.

Schizophrenia

Schizophrenia remains one of the most complex psychiatric conditions, characterized by a constellation of symptoms that can dramatically affect perception, cognition and emotional processing. Friends and family are often the first to detect early warning signs, as they can recognize when something is amiss. For example, you may notice your loved one speaking to themselves or reacting to unseen stimuli, hallucinating or expressing beliefs that seem out of touch with reality. Or you might notice paranoia, social withdrawal or disorganized actions. Such behaviours may escalate to the point where they interfere with daily functioning if not dealt with.

Those who love someone with schizophrenia may find themselves on a journey that is at times both surreal and heart-wrenching. To stand beside someone whose reality has diverged from your own is a profound act of love. It is a path marked by challenges that can test the strength of any relationship. Sally, 53, told me that she couldn't claim to understand her mother's sense of reality, and explained:

> I've learned that for a meaningful connection to be possible, I must be "real" and resist arriving with contrived jollities.

Today, we know that delusions should not be challenged since their preservation is essential to the individual's concept of themselves. Doing so can lead to immense stress and volatility, a sort of shattering of the self and increased defensiveness, and can threaten the bridge of trust you've built. However, eliciting information and helping the person to identify any associated feelings and behaviours can be helpful, if handled with skill. But challenging thoughts, and that includes offering other interpretations, is rarely prudent.[4]

Of course, that doesn't mean it's easy to go along with something you believe to be untrue. Navigating this terrain requires an understanding that these "delusions" aren't just ideas for the other person, but anchors in a precarious world. Preserving your own truth without invalidating theirs is a difficult dance. I certainly don't have the answers, but there feels something important in hearing the emotional truth *behind* the illusions. The same may be true for how we respond to signs of regression (when a person goes back to behaving in a child-like manner). In some instances, a psychotic episode might appear more like regression, but the advice, again, is to keep your loved one in the regression rather than to shatter it.

Having said this, of course, if a delusion steers anyone – including yourself – toward danger, it's imperative to step in and find safer alternatives. This isn't so much about attempting to shift the other person's belief, as focusing on the potential consequences of actions stemming from those beliefs. It may be particularly distressing if your loved one casts you in the role of a threat. As ever, attempt to find a way to listen to their concerns and acknowledge their feelings without validating the false belief.

I supported one woman whose sister, dealing with schizophrenia, unexpectedly brandished a knife. This was a watershed moment, one that crystalized the need for clear boundaries for safety. Together, we established a crisis plan (see Chapter 5), which involved securing potentially dangerous items and setting clear rules about personal space and acceptable behaviour. Such plans aren't just precautionary; they're a means to provide a structure within which your loved one can navigate their reality more safely.

Here's the thing: people with schizophrenia face profound discrimination, not only socially but within the very systems meant to aid them. Helping your loved one to know that they're cared about can be deeply healing. It's a reassurance that they're not an "other" to be feared, but a cherished individual whose experiences and challenges are recognized and met with love.

Schizophrenia is a condition that usually requires comprehensive care, addressing multiple facets of an individual's life – from stable housing and meaningful employment, to the management of other health conditions and finding one's place within the community. This holistic care is best coordinated by community mental health teams, which typically include social workers, mental health nurses, occupational therapists, psychotherapists and psychiatrists. Regular assessments are a critical component of this approach, facilitating ongoing adjustments to your loved one's care plan.

Cultivating your own quality time with them is key. These important building blocks of a shared life also create a backdrop of memories that can be a tremendous source of comfort during turbulent phases. Engaging in physical activities together, like walking or dance, can be especially beneficial. Movement has a way of grounding us, connecting us to the here and now, and it can offer a gentle reprieve from the turbulence and incessant chatter of hearing voices.

Strategies to help a loved one with schizophrenia:

- **Keep them safe:** Don't try to challenge delusions or hallucinations, but instead listen and provide emotional comfort. You might say: "I see this is really scaring you", rather than agreeing with the content of the paranoia. Keep your voice gentle and your body language open and non-threatening. Avoid sudden actions that could be misinterpreted as hostile. And seek urgent professional intervention if you feel unsafe.
- **Artful congruence:** Not challenging a belief doesn't mean you're colluding in it. Is it possible to convey that you take their point of view seriously while not necessarily explicitly agreeing?
- **Clear communication:** Use simple, clear language to avoid any misunderstandings. Hearing voices can interfere with attempts to communicate, so be mindful of this.
- **Encourage self-expression:** People with schizophrenia are often gifted creatively. Art or music therapy with a qualified practitioner may help them to explore their experiences, but this cannot happen during psychosis.

If this is unavailable due to funding cuts, you can still encourage them to draw or paint when you visit (but never interpret what they produce).

- **Let them know they're not alone:** Research has found that 96 per cent of people with a diagnosis of schizophrenia experience the effects of stigma on a daily basis.[5]
- **When lucid, initiate open conversations:** In periods of lucidity, initiating gentle conversations about their experiences can be enlightening and healing for both of you. Asking about voices, for example – "When did they begin? Have they changed over time?" – can help your loved one feel understood.

Things to avoid:

- **Confronting delusions:** Challenging their altered sense of reality can be not only ineffective but potentially dangerous.
- **Overloading information:** Keep all your conversations manageable and background stimulation to a minimum to avoid sensory overload.
- **Challenging alternative beliefs:** It's okay to take an interest in how these are impacting their life, but avoid taking a stance that beliefs are "wrong". Rather, focus on helping your loved one through supporting them to find places and people that make them feel safe.

Anorexia Nervosa

Characterized by an overpowering drive for thinness and a distorted body image, anorexia nervosa is often an endeavour for control or purity – one that overrides that most primal of human needs, nourishment. Those afflicted with anorexia might project a veneer of self-discipline, yet underneath they grapple with a poor self-image, emotional turmoil and an existential void that no degree of weight loss can fill.

Driven by the compulsion for perfection, those affected by anorexia often struggle to accept their own humanity. Typically, they believe a different set of standards applies to them; that somehow they must be super-human (and not eat). Even the smallest admonishment might make them feel ashamed, since they have impossibly high standards. I had a client who developed anorexia shortly after being rejected by an Ivy League university, when she struggled to cope with her own failure. As is often the case with those with anorexia, she felt prized and loved by her parents because of her achievements. Starvation dulled her painful sense of not being enough and gave her a type of spiritual high.

Unlike other psychiatric conditions, assessment and diagnosis will consider the physical consequences and associated risks. Malnutrition can be life-threatening and, unfortunately, those with anorexia often reject treatment, fearing the loss of their control mechanism. This resistance is not obstinacy; it's a fortress built around their vulnerabilities.

While anorexia can provoke a lot of anger in loved ones who find themselves witnessing the profound distress this disorder can cause, it's important to tread lightly, offering support without encroaching on the boundaries that the individual fiercely guards. Encouragement should be directed toward helping your loved one discover their own intrinsic motivations for recovery, for example, the desire to have children and therefore a healthy menstrual cycle through adequate nutrition, or to be well enough to do the job they love. Their weight is not something that you, as their loved one, should address head on. It can come across as neglectful of their deeper, emotional drivers. It's also deeply threatening for an anorexic person to be cajoled into putting on weight; so it's best to leave this to the professionals.

If you're reading this as a parent of someone with anorexia, you may be experiencing guilt and helplessness. Please remember that anorexia is a complex illness with many contributing factors. Your role now is not about looking back with blame, but looking forward with love, understanding and support. Discover how to practise self-care and self-regulation through practices such as mindfulness. Maintain a calm atmosphere around mealtimes and gently encourage balance and moderation. Treatment is most successful when the whole family is involved in the process, creating a supportive environment in the present and future, rather than dwelling on perceived past mistakes. It's also about recognizing your own emotions, since individuals with anorexia often won't take in nourishment and they might throw affection or kind words back at you instead.

Strategies to help a loved one with anorexia:

- **Be a role model:** Demonstrate healthy eating habits without making a big deal out of it. Your actions will speak louder than words.
- **Share the responsibility and offer choice:** Sharing the mental load of meal planning and eating can be helpful. It lets your loved one feel more in control and know you're not working against them. Also let them have control over what they eat whenever possible.
- **Acknowledge the effort:** Compliment your loved one when they make a step, however small, in the right direction. "I appreciate your being here with me for this meal" can go a long way.
- **Reinforce their inherent qualities:** Praise their worth and their characteristics that have nothing to do with appearance – and are unchanging.

Things to avoid:

- **Making food the centre of attention:** If possible, engage in light conversations that don't focus on the act of eating, or the food on the table.

- **Commenting on appearance:** Even well-intended compliments can trigger anxieties or preoccupations related to body image. This also means not talking about your own weight or appearance.
- **Emotional blackmail:** Remarks like "you're hurting me by not eating" add guilt to an already challenging situation.
- **Polarizing statements:** Saying things like "healthy versus unhealthy" or "good versus bad" can reinforce disordered thinking around food.
- **Monitoring physical health:** Measuring BMI and levels of nutrition are medical jobs for a doctor or psychiatrist. Not for you. If you need to break your loved one's confidentiality to contact their doctor, let them know and do what's necessary.

Bulimia Nervosa

Olivia, 34, described going up to the bathroom as a teenager and shoving her fingers down her throat while her parents sat drinking. She told me:

> Sure, I wanted to be thin; but I had a far bigger driver – to have my own secret world. They went off to their drunk happy place and left me and my brother to it. Well, I wanted to have a place of my own that no one could reach. It was also a way of me saying, "Fuck you, I won't eat your fancy food." Did I want them to notice what I was doing? Yes, I think a part of me was always secretly hoping for that day to come.

Bulimia is far less discussed than anorexia – perhaps because it's not usually associated with dangerous weight loss. While individuals living with anorexia nervosa often exhibit traits of being quiet, controlled and perfectionistic, this contrasts with those living with bulimia nervosa, who tend to display social and sexual confidence and impulsivity.

Research indicates that while avoidant personality traits are common among individuals with anorexia nervosa, borderline personality disorder (BPD) is more frequently observed in those with bulimia nervosa.[6] If you suspect your loved one's bulimia is part of a wider issue, such as BPD, it may be worth reading that section in this chapter.

Bulimia is often a (maladaptive) way to cope with impulse control issues resulting from trauma.[7] At the heart of the disorder usually lie feelings of inadequacy, shame and low self-worth, and the binge–purge cycle may serve as a coping mechanism for dealing with these negative emotions. The association between bulimia and other impulsive behaviours such as promiscuity can similarly stem from low self-esteem and a desperate need for validation. It's important (but not always easy) not to judge, and to recognize your loved one's behaviour as the symptom of something deeper. Despite their apparent confidence, they're likely to feel bad enough about themselves as it stands. What's more, the behaviours associated with bulimia are often shrouded in secrecy. In close relationships, the strain may manifest as volatility or an avoidance of intimacy as they navigate their own feelings of disgust. Binge eating can momentarily satisfy an insatiable hunger, not just for food but for love and connection. Later, the purging becomes a way to expel these overwhelming feelings.

Family therapy can help address the patterns that bulimia can impose on familial dynamics. As a therapist, I often find that bulimia is a lot to do with being unable to digest and hold on to "the good", and so it needs vomiting up. You might sense that your loved one appears to take in a lot of TLC and nourishment, but then they later seem to have forgotten about it, or "vomit" it back out at you. The sense of being constantly on edge around a loved one can be exhausting, but it's important not to take their behaviour personally. Instead, focus on offering consistent love and support, and try not to mirror their own volatility and self-destruction.

Sometimes we can't explain why people do the things they do, and it's arguably not your job to.

Strategies to help a loved one with bulimia:

- **Create a judgement-free zone:** Those with bulimia often feel deep shame and secrecy about their behaviours, so instead of appearing to judge, say, for example, "I'm here to listen if you want to talk about what's going on."
- **Support emotional regulation:** Help your loved one develop healthier strategies to manage their emotions. Encourage activities like journaling, mindfulness or art therapy.
- **Promote impulse control strategies:** Encourage techniques to help manage impulsive behaviours, such as delaying tactics (for example, waiting 10 minutes before acting on an urge), or engaging in a distracting activity.
- **Acknowledge their strengths:** Recognize and praise their abilities and achievements unrelated to their physical appearance or eating habits. This can help build self-esteem.
- **Be mindful of triggers:** Help them identify and avoid situations or conversations that may trigger impulsive-eating behaviours. This can include stressful social settings or discussions about weight and dieting.

Things to avoid:

- **Pressuring them to reveal secrets:** Avoid pushing them to disclose their purge behaviours. This can increase feelings of shame and secrecy.
- **Focusing on food and weight:** Steer clear of conversations about food, weight or body image. These topics can be particularly triggering for those with bulimia.
- **Ignoring impulsive behaviours:** Be aware of impulsive behaviours besides eating, such as spending or risky

actions. If impulsive behaviour is prevalent, you might want to read the sections on BPD (see below) or bipolar disorder (page 70).

- **Overlooking emotional dysregulation:** Understand that emotional dysregulation is a core issue. Avoid reacting emotionally to their behaviour; instead, respond calmly and supportively.

Borderline Personality Disorder

Firstly, is there such a thing as a "standardized" personality – and, if so, would you want one? Me neither. However, personality disorders are characterized by persistent, entrenched patterns of behaviour; those with them tend to lack the necessary self-awareness to get help, often leading their loved ones to seek therapy instead.

Among the various personality disorders, three are particularly prevalent and challenging for loved ones: borderline personality disorder (BPD), which we will discuss now; narcissistic personality disorder (NPD); and antisocial personality disorder (ASPD). BPD is characterized by intense emotional instability, impulsive behaviour and turbulent relationships, so if your loved one has BPD, you're likely to have a highly complex relationship with them. On the one hand, these individuals crave love but, on the other, they believe getting close to someone is dangerous; that either they will become harmed in the process or that they will bring harm to others.

To illustrate how BPD can begin, allow me to share an example. For a few months, I met with a wealthy Brazilian client. She sought therapy after the end of a fling, which had completely destabilized her. By the time we met she was using drugs and bedding every man she met. She kept falling out with people, but her wealth allowed her to keep throwing parties without needing to hold down a stable job. Because her paid staff (her adopted family) had stayed loyal to her all these years, she was protected from the potential consequences of her behaviour.

Her real family had been deeply neglectful: her mother was a model with addiction issues, she never knew her father and her maternal uncle was a drug baron who sexually abused her. My client had deep trauma and found it difficult to trust people and maintain relationships. I was aware that building an ongoing therapeutic relationship was likely to be challenging.

In the end, she ghosted me after I had to call in sick two weeks in a row. Despite my assurances that I still wanted to work with her, the perceived rebuff felt too overwhelming. And because she was in a heightened state of stress, her paranoia that "everyone leaves me" was strengthened. Those with borderline personality disorder often have families who've been suspicious of the outside world – and being raised in a wealthy drug cartel would have instilled this in her. Although our ending was painful, I had to accept my own limitations. If we had carried on working together longer, it's possible I would have done something else to disappoint her, so she could find a way to leave. She existed in a web of complex, unrewarding relationships; everything was experienced as push–pull. A disorganized attachment style is highly correlated with BPD (see page 245), and the disorder typically creates chaos for the individual and those around them.

Those with BPD often sabotage healthy relationships. Care (which is usually foreign to them) can be perceived as abuse, as this echoes their early experience. Therefore, if you're in a relationship with someone with BPD, you may feel confused a lot of the time – as though you're damned if you do and damned if you don't. Get too close and they'll run; be aloof and they'll run. It takes time and a lot of effort to find a pace and distance your loved one may feel comfortable with.

There is no simple solution, but try to balance giving enough reassurance and tenderness with holding your boundaries.

The SET system of communication can be super helpful – communicating with support, empathy and truth.[8] However, what's unique about this framework when speaking with those with BPD is the use of the word "you" – for example, "It must be really hard for *you* to feel that way" – as this helps your loved one to feel validated in their experience. The emphasis is on *their* feelings and experience, not on yours. It's also helpful as a device when you don't necessarily agree or identify with someone's experience.

Unpredictable people need predictability, so it's best to be consistent in your responses. Which isn't always easy – especially if they say unkind things (in an attempt to test you), or you doubt if what they're telling you is even true. Try to disconnect from their words and listen with your heart. These people have grown good at keeping secrets and altering the narrative as a survival strategy. It's rarely coming from a place of malice.

Having said all this, those with BPD need to learn there are consequences to their behaviour. For example, if they start accusing you of something fictitious such as cheating, lying or talking about them, kindly reassure them that's not the case. But if their accusations become more heated, let them know you will not tolerate threats and remove yourself from the conversation immediately. This not only de-escalates the situation, but models the impact of their behaviour on others, which can be a step toward change.

The natural thing might be to end all contact (I did with a previous boyfriend I loved), but evidently you are committed to this individual, or you wouldn't be reading this book. Your loved one is one of the lucky ones. Most people with BPD struggle to have meaningful relationships and often get in with the "wrong crowd". They might seek out sexually inappropriate or abusive partners. And their interpretation of events might leave them feeling (re)victimized, leading to a perception that the world is always against them.

It can help to see the person struggling behind their behaviour. Foster a positive feeling toward them, as though you're their loving parent. But hold boundaries, as they will continually try to push them. Above all, those with BPD are seeking consistent love, which is exactly what they might push away. While reading this book doesn't mean the journey will be any easier, hopefully you will be more informed.

Strategies to help a loved one with BPD:

- **Remember it's an illness, not just a way to get attention**: Seeing your loved one as a wounded child may help you to find greater empathy when their behaviour is challenging.
- **Know you're treading a fine line**: Demonstrate love and tenderness regularly, but too much and the individual will likely run away. Be aware of this and attempt to find a middle ground in the things you say and do for them.
- **Set boundaries**: Make it clear what behaviours are unacceptable to you.
- **Be consistent**: Consistency in your responses is vital for establishing trust.
- **Use the word "you"**: This validates their experience *and* creates a healthy separation for you.
- **Take threats seriously**: Don't allow threats to be treated as emotional blackmail. If you or your loved one are at risk of being harmed, contact emergency services immediately.
- **Be truthful**: Model authenticity in a predictable manner when impulsive behaviour strikes. Be honest about how what they do affects you, and the need for professional support.

Things to avoid:

- **Feeding the drama**: These disorders often involve manipulative or dramatic behaviour. Maintaining a calm demeanour helps you not to get pulled into the chaos.

- **Giving absolutes:** Using words like "always" or "never" can trigger defensive responses and create conflict.
- **Veering off course:** People with personality disorders may drop bombshells in an attempt to shock you – especially as you're about to say goodbye. If necessary, say you can discuss that more when you next meet.

Narcissistic Personality Disorder

Most of us display some narcissistic qualities – self-involvement, vanity and a tendency to be selfish. You just have to look at social media! However, narcissistic personality disorder (NPD) is not this. It's a complex mental health condition characterized by an inflated sense of self-importance, a deep need for excessive attention and admiration, troubled relationships and a lack of empathy for others. But behind this mask of extreme confidence lies a deeply fragile person, unable to accept feedback or take personal responsibility. Their grandiosity is actually a defence mechanism, usually to mask a deep sense of shame. In fact, narcissists are disconnected from their vulnerable "true self", so they construct a false self that dominates their lives and their relationships.

A relationship with someone who has NPD can leave you feeling like a spectator in the grand theatre of their self-constructed world. They seek an audience – a constant stream of praise to fuel the narrative of their superiority – and you may be called upon to supply admiration unconditionally and without pause. It can be taxing, especially when it feels like a one-way street, with little if any acknowledgement of your own needs and feelings.

Chances are your loved one seizes the limelight in every situation, as Savannah, 39, described about a friend:

I always knew she had a flair for the dramatic, a sort of magnetic pull that left little room for anyone else in the spotlight. But I never imagined she'd cross into the shadows of my personal life. When she tried to seduce my boyfriend, it wasn't just a breach of trust – it was the shattering of our friendship's foundation. That was the moment I saw the depth of her narcissism: not just an innocent craving for attention, but a voracious hunger that would stop at nothing to be fed.

Those who have an untended-to narcissistic wound almost always go on to wound others. The narcissistic defensive structure, once established, tends to be self-perpetuating, and the cycle of trauma continues as the individual, now armed with a narcissistic framework, interacts with the world around them. The child who had no attention from their narcissistic mother then doesn't give their own children the attention they deserve, and so on …

When a loved one has NPD, your own emotions seem to dissipate into the background as they exhibit an inability – or unwillingness – to engage with them. This lack of empathy can manifest in dismissive, insensitive or cruel behaviour, leaving others feeling misunderstood, unappreciated or neglected.

You may also notice a competitive streak in your loved one. They might harbour resentment toward the accomplishments of others, convinced that any success but their own is an affront. It's a challenging trait that can cast a shadow over your own achievements, leaving you wondering if your successes are actually silent threats in their eyes.

I worked with one young woman whose whole life had been scripted by her mother's needs. My client always had to stay two steps behind; close enough to reassure her mother and placate her if she was upset – but never ahead of her. This meant she held herself back in social gatherings and in her career. Unsurprisingly, she became a photographer like her mother. During the course of therapy, she started to redefine her work and use herself as the subject. Stepping into focus in this way was both challenging and healing for her. But she realized how important it was for her to start changing her role. Not because it would change her mother. But because it would change her. And she deserved that chance.

When my client became more successful in her own right, she was painfully belittled by her mother. But she realized she didn't want a life guided by her mother's deep-seated insecurities. Her mother ultimately didn't change, yet the choices my client made for herself did – and that included starting a relationship with a lovely man, while her mother remained single.

Having a romantic relationship with someone who has NPD is complex, but it often follows a recognizable pattern. Initially, there might be a "honeymoon" phase, where the narcissistic partner engages in love-bombing, making their new partner feel incredibly special. However, cracks begin to show. The same grandiosity and need for admiration that initially seemed to affirm the relationship can become oppressive. Partners may find themselves increasingly side-lined as the narcissist seeks validation from a broader audience. Eventually, many partners experience a sense of being discarded, devalued or even replaced by a new interest.

You see, in the narcissist's pursuit of self-esteem, they might leverage relationships as mere stepping stones. It's a utilitarian approach that typically reflects the way they were treated in childhood – as an appendage or status symbol. Regardless, it can leave you feeling valued only for your usefulness rather than your intrinsic worth , even if done "kindly".

If this sounds familiar, it's crucial to reflect on your reasons for choosing to stay with a person like this. If there's a pattern of seeking out relationships with narcissistic individuals, it might be worth exploring what that's about. Is there a need for validation from someone who appears confident and self-assured? Or perhaps it's a replication of a familiar dynamic from your family of origin? Therapy can be a valuable space for examining these choices and the personal histories that inform them. Developing a strong sense of self that is independent of the narcissist's influence is crucial for boundary-setting. If you're in a relationship with a narcissist who is destroying your self-worth, get out now before it's too late.

Strategies to help a loved one with NPD:

- **Empathy with boundaries**: Understand that beneath the surface bravado of NPD lies a fragile self-esteem. Empathy can be your guide, but it must be balanced with firm boundaries that are consistent.
- **Steady affection**: While it's important to show your love, be mindful of overpraising or feeding their ego excessively, which may reinforce narcissistic behaviours.
- **Use leverage**: Make continued participation in the relationship conditional on the narcissist's commitment to behavioural change and therapy.
- **Transparent communication**: Be honest and clear. Narcissists may not respond well to perceived criticism, so communicate your feelings assertively yet with compassion.
- **Professional support**: Encourage them to seek therapy, emphasizing the benefits for their personal growth.

Things to avoid:

- **Excessive admiration**: It's important not to perpetuate the narcissist's need for excessive admiration, as this can feed into the cycle of narcissistic behaviour.
- **Ignoring misconduct**: Do not excuse abusive or harmful behaviours. Address these issues directly and seek help for yourself.
- **Losing yourself**: Maintain your work, relationships and hobbies. Your loved one may try to erode your sense of self because they don't have one. Don't let them do this.
- **Playing the enabler**: Watch that you don't go out of your way to please the narcissist to keep things "nice" and end up gaslighting others in the process.

Antisocial Personality Disorder

Better known as sociopathy, antisocial personality disorder (ASPD) is a complex and often misunderstood condition. Characterized by a pervasive disregard for social rules, those with ASPD are impulsive and largely indifferent to the rights and feelings of others. It's significantly more common in men than in women, and is prevalent in the prison population.[9] However, what people don't realize (thanks to popular culture) is it's a condition that exists on a spectrum, and not everyone with it is a serial killer or inherently evil. In fact, I believe there are many undiagnosed people walking around with ASPD, leading relatively ordinary lives.

You see, while the terms sociopathy and psychopathy are often used interchangeably, there are differences. Psychopathy is considered a more severe form of ASPD, characterized by specific brain abnormalities (the two brain structures that regulate emotion and social behaviour don't communicate as they should).[10] While psychopaths experience basic emotions, they lack the capacity for social emotions, which include guilt, empathy and remorse. Sociopaths, on the other hand, can learn social emotions and, with the right professional and personal support, they can develop some capacity for empathy and social engagement.

There is an uncanny fearlessness in those with antisocial personality disorder. For most, engaging in antisocial behaviour becomes a way of coping with emotional problems, and provides a sense of relief. Without intervention, personality disorders like ASPD can worsen over time. What starts as a coping mechanism can evolve into a lifestyle necessity, creating a compulsion that drives behaviour.

If your loved one has antisocial personality disorder – or you suspect they do – you're likely to be in a challenging situation, and I'm so sorry. You may live in fear of their unpredictable behaviour and deal daily with the reality of deceitfulness, impulsivity, aggressiveness and a reckless disregard for safety and the law. It's vital to get support for yourself and recognize the impact this will be having on your mental health. When it comes to those with extreme sociopathy or psychopathy, the advice is clear and unequivocal: recognize the abuse, escape and get yourself support.

However, since most individuals with ASPD don't fall into this extreme category, this section will focus on how to support your loved one if they feel lost but *do* want to live differently. Sometimes it takes reaching a breaking point or having a major revelation to get there. To help get to that point, emphasize that it's someone's behaviour and actions – not their feelings and impulses – that matter. That way, they can start to see the importance of change.

As a loved one, setting boundaries is key, but even more so is reinforcing them (see Chapter 8). Consistent boundaries can help create a more predictable environment for you both. This structure can help reduce impulsive and reckless behaviours by providing clear consequences. But only say things you're willing to follow through on.

It's essential to reflect on your responses and emotions. Sometimes, the appeal of the other person's boldness can blur the lines between acceptable and harmful behaviour.

> **PROMPT:** Consider if you're excited, titillated even, by their fearless behaviour – does your loved one behave in ways you wish were available to you?

It's important to understand that most individuals with ASPD never seek help or therapy. This reluctance stems from the very nature of the disorder; people with ASPD often don't see their behaviour as problematic or feel genuine remorse for their actions. No amount of external pressure or persuasion can help if they lack the internal motivation to change, and you will have to accept that you cannot force change upon someone. Instead, redirect your energy toward managing your own responses and setting healthy boundaries.

Strategies to help a loved one with ASPD:

- **Positive reinforcement:** Immediately and specifically praise positive behaviours to encourage repetition.
- **Set clear boundaries:** Establish and consistently enforce clear boundaries to protect yourself and provide structure. Even if that means walking away from the relationship.
- **Model appropriate behaviour:** Demonstrate respectful and empathetic behaviour in your interactions to provide a positive example.
- **Focus on behaviour:** Encourage your loved one to reflect on their actions and their impact on others.
- **Educate yourself:** Learn about ASPD to better manage your interactions, so you take their behaviour less personally.
- **Seek support for yourself:** Join support groups or seek counselling to set up the emotional support you need.

Things to avoid:

- **Trying to change them:** Change must come from their own desire.
- **Engaging in arguments:** Avoid confrontational arguments, as these can escalate quickly and are often unproductive.
- **Ignoring boundaries:** Do not allow boundaries to be crossed; consistency is key to maintaining respect and safety.
- **Taking behaviour personally:** Understand that their actions are a manifestation of their disorder and not a reflection of your worth.
- **Enabling negative behaviour:** Do not excuse or enable harmful behaviours; hold them accountable in a firm but fair manner.
- **Minimizing the problem:** Do not downplay the severity of the disorder or the impact it has on your life.

Substance-Related and Addictive Disorders

Most of us are addicted to something, be it a substance, food, caffeine, social media, shopping, relationships or stress itself (goddamit!). Yet when we hear the word "addiction", the image of a junkie comes to mind. Except junkies are people too, with families and histories and lives. Society's view often fails to consider the person *behind* the disorder.

What causes addiction is hard to pinpoint. However, I've found that addiction is frequently connected to the desire to live in an altered state, usually because real life feels too bleak or painful. (It's worth noting that drug or alcohol addiction often occurs alongside other mental health issues.) Addiction – whatever it attaches itself to – can be seen as a distorted way of seeking wholeness. This viewpoint emphasizes the inner disconnection and spiritual void that the individual is attempting to fill.

Supporting a loved one through addiction is like walking a tightrope. There's a fine line between aiding their recovery and enabling their habit. Understanding the nature of addiction and recognizing that it is a mental health issue can help loved ones to not see the addiction as a moral failure. After all, addiction is the symptom. At its root is pain.

Finding ways to support someone emotionally without enabling their behaviour is extremely testing, as is not taking on the full weight of responsibility, which is easier said than done. I've spoken to many people over the years who see it as their responsibility to rescue the person they love. I remember Benji, 30, whose mother was addicted to drugs and later alcohol. Benji spent his childhood trying to save his mother, who sadly passed away when he was 20. He would research the latest treatments, cook nutritious food for her, make sure she was safe and tend to her. For years, he kept what he was going through a secret. He explained to me:

There was a codependency that formed. I would have done anything for Mum. A lot of my childhood memories involve drug dealers turning up at the house. When I was five, she tried to commit suicide and my older brother whisked me away. But I knew what had happened ... My brother, who is 11 years older than me, has been more screwed up by it all. He resents how I always tried to help her because he can't get his head around how a mother could behave like that. But I saw her mental illness; I was able to separate that from who she was as a person. Plus, I always felt showered in love.

This is a deeply moving story of a parentified child who was his mother's keeper. But Benji also beautifully described to me the lighter moments, which enabled him to hold on to who his mum was. As a result, he came out of his childhood relatively unscarred. What was important for him to know now is that he was not responsible for his mother.

This section would not be complete without also acknowledging that being in a relationship with someone in recovery can present unique challenges, as their focus on sobriety may seem self-centred. Early recovery takes priority over everything else, though this can change as self-awareness grows. For those starting a new relationship with someone in recovery, AA advises avoiding new romantic relationships in the first year to prevent distraction from healing. For those in existing relationships, read on!

Strategies to help a loved one with addiction:

- **Express concern, not disappointment**: Make it clear that you're worried about their wellbeing, rather than disappointed in them.
- **Communicate your boundaries**: If your loved one is in recovery, boundaries allow you to support their journey without losing yourself.

- **Give space and be patient**: Allow them the space they need and respect their focus on their recovery.
- **Write things down**: It helps both parties remember what was discussed and agreed upon.
- **Offer support in other ways**: While they may ask for money, show up for them in other ways – such as driving them to medical appointments or job interviews, etc.

Things to avoid:

- **Lecturing**: This can push the other person further away and reinforce feelings of guilt and shame that often fuel addiction.
- **Ultimatums**: If the situation is dire and presents risk to the individual's or someone else's life, then an ultimatum may be imperative for safety reasons, but not to induce change. The stress from an ultimatum could lead to a higher chance of relapse.
- **Making excuses**: Covering for them or making excuses can prolong the addiction cycle.

What to Do Next?

So often, what we're really talking about when it comes to mental health disorders is trauma or PTSD. The mind deals with trauma (such as a loss, a car crash, rape or assault, for example) differently to how it deals with ordinary day-to-day events. Instead of processing and making sense of what's happened, the experience of the trauma gets "stuck" and is *re-experienced again and again*, rather than recalled in the usual way. Often refuge is sought – whether in alcohol, delusions, obsessive thoughts or rituals. Taking a holistic approach can help you and your loved one to navigate the past and find a path that suits your needs in the present.

CHAPTER 4
TAKING A HOLISTIC APPROACH

"I never had a fixed routine and just went with the flow. But I was forced to implement structure in my life after experiencing a nervous breakdown, which led to a suicide attempt. These days, I'm asleep by 11pm, wake up at 7am, have a healthy diet, don't drink and exercise regularly. Sometimes I miss the person I was, but I'm a lot more stable these days. And that comes first. It's true a part of me had to 'die' in order to find the new Bianca."

Bianca, 34

We live in a world where we're squashed into boxes. Squeezed into stats. Yet we're wondrously complex beings with unique histories, needs, preferences and biology. A holistic approach to health respects the principle of bio-individuality – that no two people are exactly alike, so no two people will respond to treatment in the exact same way. This is the case for both you and your loved one.

Take four individuals all diagnosed with clinical depression. The prevailing one-size-fits-all model of treatment would mean these four individuals are given the same (or similar) pharmaceutical interventions that target their brain chemistry. Yet, on closer inspection, one has a hormonal imbalance, another complex trauma, another a vitamin B12 deficiency and yet another is facing abject poverty. Common sense would tell us the treatment plans for each person should be tailored to their specific needs. Rocket science that ain't – especially when research continually backs up the fact that a person-centred approach significantly enhances the chances of recovery. Why? Because this type of approach holds recovery to be the key objective of any mental health treatment plan! It recognizes that recovery is an ongoing journey determined by a person's connectedness, *hope* about the future, *identity*, *meaning* in life and *empowerment* (CHIME) – and not just by their neurochemistry.[1] You see, mental health issues are often signs, not diseases in themselves, indicating that the holistic network of wellbeing is out of balance.

Since this isn't a view shared by many physicians, it's a philosophy that needs to be safeguarded by you. You may already share this belief, or have arrived here by another route. Regardless, please know this: psychiatry is not the only way. In fact, for someone managing a mental health issue, a holistic approach can help reduce the recurrence of severe symptoms, build resilience, increase long-term stability and improve quality of life. In this chapter, we will explore the core principles that underpin this integrative approach to mental health, and why it matters. We will also talk about a framework of holistic health, which has eight pillars. By the end of this chapter, you'll be equipped to help your loved one create a holistic care plan – with the goal that they can lead a more balanced life.

Empowerment is the Goal

The Western medical model tends to prioritize the treatment of symptoms over the exploration of root cause, and often relegates patients to a passive role, positioning healthcare providers as the "experts". However, empowerment of the individual is a central tenet of holistic health, challenging the notion that health is something that is simply prescribed or administered by external authorities. All the research shows that when someone is empowered, they're much more likely to engage in their treatment plan consistently and proactively.[2] For example, that might look like:

- self-education and seeking out reputable information on integrative mental health approaches
- tracking progress through mobile devices, wearables and/ or logging symptoms, sleep and mood, etc.
- bringing questions and ideas to discussions with healthcare providers
- setting SMART goals (see page 128) that support their personal values and preferences
- trying self-care practices aligned with these goals
- playing a central role in decision-making about treatment plans

Mental health challenges can often lead to feelings of despondence, dependence and a loss of control. Offer support and encouragement, but let your loved one take the lead. If they're incapacitated and unable to do this, go to page 124 on "How Does This Model Apply to Severe Mental Illness?" And remember, people with a severe mental illness are still people.

Fundamentally, holistic healthcare requires a collaborative partnership between an individual, their support network and healthcare providers – one where the lived experience and innate wisdom of the patient is prized. Ultimately, it's about shifting the locus of control from external authorities back to your loved one, while also recognizing the impact community, family and systemic factors have in shaping health outcomes.

The Eight Pillars of Holistic Health

As I mentioned earlier, your loved one's wellbeing (and indeed, your own) is the sum of eight pillars:

1 physical
2 emotional
3 intellectual
4 occupational
5 social
6 spiritual
7 financial
8 environmental

This model demonstrates the multifaceted nature of human health – that our wellbeing is the sum of many interconnected parts. Each of the pillars plays a role in supporting our overall wellbeing and can significantly affect mental health outcomes. The objective is to achieve a personal balance with the aspects that truly resonate.

The holistic circle of health

Wellbeing can be viewed as a fluid, circular journey where physical needs (like sleep) can directly influence emotional wellbeing, financial stability can bolster intellectual growth (like learning) and so on. For most of us, there is rarely a singular cause of distress in our lives, but rather a complex interplay of factors. That's why supporting your loved one – and yourself – across relevant pillars can have a powerful cumulative effect. It's not about striving for perfection (what even is that anyway?), but making manageable changes that have a sustained impact. Even small lifestyle adjustments can create a positive effect. It starts with an acceptance that good health requires active awareness and commitment.

The Physical Pillar

The mind and the body are entirely connected: whatever happens in the body affects the brain, and vice versa. So, this pillar is about everything to do with our physical health. That's a HUGE area, so let me try to simplify it. My equation for the physical pillar is:

**REGULAR MOVEMENT + BALANCED DIET +
QUALITY SLEEP + HEALING THROUGH THE BODY
= THE PHYSICAL PILLAR**

Let's dig into these a little more now ...

Regular Movement

Not only does exercise build physical resilience, but it develops *mental* resilience. In fact, a recent study proved that exercise was as effective as psychological or pharmaceutical treatments for reducing depressive symptoms.[3] That's because exercise releases endorphins, which are natural mood lifters, and reduces the stress hormone cortisol. Phil, 37, describes the benefits to his mental health:

My depression has notably improved since I started playing football. I'm not saying it's a simple fix, but it's improved my motivation, sense of achievement and gives me social interaction on a weekly basis. It's also strangely improving my self-image. As a result, I've started eating better, finding pleasure in cooking, and preparing more nutritious meals for myself, so that after footie I can enjoy a cheeky kebab with my teammates.

Additionally, exercise stimulates the birth of new neurons, particularly in the hippocampus – the area of the brain associated with memory, learning and mood regulation. And it enhances sleep quality, which in turn can make it easier to maintain a healthy diet and exercise routine. In short, exercise, nutrition and rest create a virtuous cycle!

If your loved one is unwilling or unable to exercise, don't underestimate the impact of gentle movement – nothing beats a walk in the fresh air. Research also shows that aquatic exercise can help alleviate symptoms of depression and anxiety: almost half a million British adults with mental health problems have stated swimming has helped to reduce the number of visits to a medical professional regarding their mental health.[4] The sensory experience of being in water can also be a calming and grounding force for those with sensory processing difficulties, such as autism. For individuals who are obese and struggle to move, the buoyancy of water supports the body, reducing the impact on joints and allowing for a greater range of motion, which can be liberating and empowering for those who ordinarily face physical limitations.

Anyone experiencing anxiety or heightened stress would benefit from doing low-impact activities such as yoga, tai chi and Pilates regularly.[5] Conversely, if your loved one is depressed and sleeping endlessly, they could benefit from vigorous physical activities that stimulate endorphin production. That's when running, shaking out the body, dancing, weight training and creating resistance (like through pushing against the wall) are helpful. I've also worked with clients who have experienced abuse or physical violation, and who have found learning self-defence to be empowering.

Balanced Diet

At the core of the physical pillar is maintaining a balanced diet (yes, that old chestnut). This means consuming a variety of nutrient-dense foods from all the main food groups, including fruits, vegetables, whole grains, lean proteins and healthy fats. A diet rich in these provides the essential vitamins, minerals and antioxidants that our brains need to function optimally. While studies have shown that diets high in refined sugars, trans fats and processed foods are associated with increased inflammation in the body (which can increase the risk of depression and anxiety), diets rich in anti-inflammatory foods, such as omega-3 fatty acids (found in fish and flaxseed), can potentially provide therapeutic benefits for mental health conditions.

The Mediterranean diet has the largest evidence basis for its mental health benefits.[6] This diet, which emphasizes whole grains, fruits, vegetables, legumes, nuts and olive oil, has been associated with lower rates of depression and better cognitive function. The landmark study published in 2017 found that a 12-week Mediterranean-style dietary intervention significantly reduced symptoms of depression compared to a control group receiving social support.[7] However, the Mediterranean diet may not appeal to someone who has grown up with a very different culinary tradition. In these cases, it's important to support your loved one to identify the principles of a healthy diet within the context of their cultural background. This means focusing on nutrient-dense whole foods that are familiar and accessible, rather than imposing an entirely new way of eating.

TWO SIMPLE STEPS TO A HEALTHIER DIET

- Since our brains are 73 per cent water, even mild dehydration can affect mood, concentration and energy levels. We should aim for eight glasses (minimum) of water each day.
- Appropriate supplementation can also support mental health. For example, we know that low levels of vitamin D are associated with depression. And a lack of zinc and essential fatty acids has been found in those with eating disorders. If you suspect a vitamin deficiency, hormonal imbalance or other underlying health issue is at play, encourage your loved one to get their blood work done, and ideally their saliva and stools sampled, too.

Nutritional psychiatry is a burgeoning field that focuses on the gut microbiome's influence on our brain chemistry and behaviour. Often referred to as our "second brain", it's estimated that around 95 per cent of our neurotransmitters, including serotonin, are produced in the gut.[8] This means that altered gut microbiota or gut dysbiosis (an imbalance of microorganisms in the intestines) is linked to a range of psychiatric and neurological disorders, such as anxiety, depression and schizophrenia. To support a healthy microbiome and restore balance to the gut and brain, we need to consume a variety of prebiotic and probiotic-rich foods, such as fermented foods like yogurt, kefir, sauerkraut and kimchi.[9] A new class of probiotics, known as "psychobiotics", has also shown promise in improving mood and reducing anxiety.[10] These are live organisms that when ingested can produce health benefits in patients affected by mental illness by releasing neuroactive substances like GABA and serotonin. If your loved one is on SSRI antidepressants (selective serotonin reuptake inhibitors) or coming off them, taking these can be particularly beneficial.

There's often no exit plan for medication, which points to the need for personalized treatment plans to manage withdrawal symptoms effectively. Studies show that up to 55 per cent of individuals discontinuing antidepressants endure substantial withdrawal symptoms, while 27 per cent report feelings consistent with addiction.[11] Amino acid supplements, vitamins (in particular B12) and minerals can all be used to support neurotransmitter synthesis and overall brain health during the tapering of antidepressants.[12, 13]

Quality Sleep

Sleep is a period of intense neurological activity when the brain removes toxins that accumulate during the day, consolidates memories and processes emotions.[14] It also has an impact on endocrine regulation, energy metabolism and even responses to vaccines.[15] Sleep and mental health share a bidirectional relationship, each profoundly influencing the other. Research has consistently shown that sleep disruption is not only a common symptom of mental health issues but can also be a precursor to their onset.[16] Poor sleep quality can exacerbate the symptoms of depression and anxiety, and can even trigger mania, hallucinations and psychosis. Therefore, it's vital to recognize the signs of sleep disturbances and take proactive steps to address them promptly. A holistic approach to sleep includes learning progressive muscle relaxation, and practising yoga or meditation, to help align the body's natural rhythms, and focusing on foods that naturally support sleep-related hormones such as melatonin. It's also important to create good sleep hygiene practices, such as maintaining a regular sleep schedule, creating a tranquil sleeping environment, and minimizing exposure to screens before bedtime.

Current research points to cognitive behavioural therapy for insomnia (CBT-I) as the gold standard for improving sleep, especially when combined with visualization and ACT therapy (acceptance and commitment therapy).[17] Sleep management should be included in every holistic mental healthcare plan. This might include encouraging your loved one to:

- create a wind-down routine
- track their sleep to identify disruptors or improvements
- begin gentle exercise
- optimize their nutrition by, for example, increasing magnesium-rich foods and decreasing caffeine
- improve their sleep environment
- engage in meditation or sleep visualization
- use CBT-I to explore the relationship between the way they think, feel and behave and how they sleep

Healing Through the Body

Trauma often gets stuck in the body, which is where it needs to be met. It's pretty simple: if someone is in a state of alarm, emotionally dysregulated or burned out, this needs to be managed before any real psychological work can be done. The good news is we can *learn* to regulate our physiology through breathing, movement and touch. So, encouraging your loved one to practise mindfulness or meditation can be transformative.

In recent years, there has been growing interest in the role of the vagus nerve in mental health. The vagus nerve is a key component of the parasympathetic nervous system, which is responsible for the body's "rest and digest" functions. Research has shown that individuals with both depression and anxiety often have reduced vagal tone.[18] If you're interested in finding out more about this, I'd recommend researching vagus nerve simulation (VNS), which is an FDA-approved treatment for drug-resistant depression.

As a psychotherapist, I would like to tell you that talking therapies will only get you so far; the mind–body connection cannot be ignored and is central to healing. So, if your loved one does opt for therapy, aim to find an integrative therapist, who works somatically as well as psychologically.

Here is a list of other mind–body practices that have shown some efficacy in treating mental health issues, which you might want to look into. Many of these are key for the reduction of stress, depression and anxiety, which you may be experiencing yourself.

- tapping, also known as emotional freedom technique
- self-havening touch and facial acupressure
- eye movement desensitization and reprocessing (EMDR) to process traumatic memories
- yoga for relaxation and insomnia
- acupuncture, including for hormonal imbalances
- biofeedback, which measures specific physiological functions (such as heart rate, breathing)
- tai chi and qi gong for managing stress
- breathwork to regulate the body's response to stress and anxiety
- aromatherapy for influencing the area of the brain responsible for emotion
- animal-assisted therapy to increase levels of oxytocin and reduce cortisol
- guided nature activities to reduce stress

Why not do a little research? Perhaps there's a beneficial activity that you could enjoy together?

Familiarizing yourself with holistic healthcare principles enables you and your loved one to ask informed questions, challenge conventional treatment plans where necessary, and seek out therapies that consider the whole person. I am not suggesting ignoring medical guidance, but rather integrating it into a holistic framework.

The Emotional Pillar

Here's my simplified equation for the emotional pillar (if only emotions were that simple!):

PROCESSING FEELINGS + POSITIVE COPING MECHANISMS = THE EMOTIONAL PILLAR

Processing Feelings

Anger. Grief. Pain. These aren't simply words; they're visceral experiences of what it means to be human. And when someone is struggling with their mental health, these emotions can feel all-consuming. One of the most powerful things you can do is encourage your loved one to express them in a healthy way. This is something you can model yourself and gently guide them toward – which isn't necessarily the same as being the person they speak to!

Let's take anger. Anger is not bad per se. In fact, it can often be justified. And unexpressed anger can be a silent killer, wreaking havoc on the mind, body and soul, and leading to cardiac issues, chronic pain and utter exhaustion. Yet when anger is expelled in explosive outbursts, it can be just as damaging, setting off a cascade of inflammation, skyrocketing blood pressure and overwhelming stress. So, what's the answer? Let your loved one know their feelings are valid and encourage them to find healthy outlets for their anger and pain, be that through exercise or creative expression. Anger is energy; it just needs to be released and channelled well. Some of the great works of literature come from the pens of angry individuals raging against the machine, turning their pain into something profound.

Often beneath anger sits a well of grief. As a society, we don't deal well with grief. So it stays stuck – and so do we – in a sort of emotional stasis. What many of us fail to recognize is that grief signals freedom. When we grieve, we can feel the loss, experience the disappointment, the pain – and then find a new way forward. This, of course, isn't a path that you can take your loved one down; that's the job of professionals. But you can illuminate the path for them.

Psychotherapy offers a safe space for individuals to give voice gradually to stifled emotions. What's important is that your loved one is encouraged to share their story in their own time, in their own way.

When it comes to treating anxiety and depression, cognitive behavioural therapy (CBT) is particularly successful, although I believe that CBT tools are best utilized through work with an integrative therapist who also looks at underlying issues. Above all, CBT can be helpful in identifying and restructuring unhelpful thoughts (cognitive distortions), such as black-and-white thinking, over-generalizing and catastrophizing.

Personally, I recommend MCBT (mindfulness-based cognitive behavioural therapy), which combines traditional CBT with mindfulness strategies, helping the individual to recognize and then disengage from self-perpetuating patterns of rumination.

This section wouldn't be complete without mentioning trailblazing treatments that combine the use of psychedelics like psilocybin and MDMA with psychotherapy. Clinical trials show that psilocybin administered under controlled conditions can result in rapid and substantial reductions in depressive symptoms and anorexia.[19, 20] The mechanism is thought to involve the drug's interaction with serotonin receptors in the brain, which can lead to altered consciousness and potentially provide patients with new perspectives on their lives and emotions.

Positive Coping Mechanisms

Research consistently shows that people who actively cultivate positive emotions and resilience experience greater wellbeing.[21] The good news is that resilience (defined as the capacity to recover quickly from difficult emotional experiences) is a muscle we can all build.[22] That's right, our levels of resilience aren't finite. Yet the application of positive psychology needs to be approached with sensitivity and care when someone is grappling with their mental health. There is a pervasive culture of "toxic positivity", which marks a misinterpretation of positive psychology.

I personally define "toxic positivity" as the overgeneralization of an outlook, where positive emotions and expressions are valued over negative ones to an extent that becomes damaging. Positive psychology itself does not ignore or dismiss negative feelings, but rather encourages a balanced perspective where all emotions are recognized as important. Those people who acknowledge and accept their negative emotions without overly dwelling on them tend to recover more quickly from stressors and exhibit fewer depressive symptoms, compared to those who either ignore their problems or fixate on them (there's more on this in Chapter 6 on ambivalent feelings).

We know that increasing resilience can improve mental health outcomes, too. But practising daily gratitude, identifying one's strengths, participating in enjoyable activities, and engaging in positive reframes and empowering affirmations might seem daunting or unfeasible to someone struggling with their mental health. Yet I'm here to tell you that these valuable tools, along with many others, can still be adapted to *meet someone where they are*. It just requires careful consideration and patience.

While expecting someone in the depths of depression to keep a daily gratitude journal might be unrealistic, you can still highlight small, everyday positives in casual conversation, encouraging them to recognize these moments without making it a formal task. Try to do this, because extensive research from Virginia Commonwealth University has revealed that practising gratitude significantly reduces the likelihood of developing major depression, generalized anxiety disorder, various phobias, as well as nicotine, alcohol and drug dependencies.[23]

Self-compassion is another practice that can offer immense benefits, particularly for those who are harsh on themselves. Studies have shown that self-compassion leads to lower levels of anxiety and depression.[24] You can aid in cultivating self-compassion by modelling this behaviour yourself. The bottom line is through showing kindness and understanding for both yourself and your loved one, emphasizing the universality of suffering, and still remaining committed to being happy, you can play a crucial role in shaping their mindset and adaptability.

The Intellectual Pillar

At the heart of intellectual wellbeing lies the concept of lifelong learning and ongoing cognitive engagement across varying levels of capacity. After all, we are all in a perpetual state of becoming. Here's my equation for the intellectual pillar:

**ONGOING LEARNING + HAVING GOALS
= THE INTELLECTUAL PILLAR**

Ongoing Learning

Cognitive activity has been proven to influence mental health significantly. Research like the Rush Memory and Aging Project shows that active mental engagement in later life reduces the risk of cognitive decline and maintains a positive sense of self.[25] For everyone, especially those with neurocognitive challenges such as dementia, engaging the mind isn't just about staving off decline; it's about nurturing a continuous sense of self-evolution.

For loved ones who are lucid and fully capable, intellectual engagement might involve reading stimulating books, learning new skills or participating in special interest groups. For those with more severe cognitive impairments, engagement could look like sensory activities, puzzles or enjoying stories and music that resonate with them. Listening to music activates most regions of the brain, and may enhance the efficiency of brain cells in processing information and supporting the brain's adaptive capabilities.[26]

The bottom line is intellectual wellbeing is not about achieving a certain level of brilliance or reaching a final destination; it's about the journey of continual growth and learning as a human being.

Having Goals

We all need to have meaningful goals that align with our values. Remember, this is also key to recovery. Not only can you model this yourself (which is a central theme in Part 2), but you can help your loved one identify their passions and interests, and encourage them to pursue activities that bring them fulfilment. This could be through work, volunteering or hobbies that offer structure, learning and social interaction.

At the end of this chapter, we'll cover practical ways for you to help your loved one set SMART goals. First, though, I'd like to share the experience of Vera, 67:

> As the mother of a daughter with bipolar disorder and ADHD, I often ask her what she wants to do with her life and tell her that she is capable of doing whatever she wants. I try to encourage her to dream big and then later we think together about ways that she might be able to achieve her goals – one small and manageable step at a time. I show her role models. What would I say to other parents in a similar situation? Push them a bit but not too hard.

By nurturing her daughter's gift for art, Vera helped her find a path that combined her passion with a meaningful career. Her daughter became an art teacher and later an art therapist, specializing in working with those with bipolar disorder and other psychotic disorders.

The Occupational Pillar

Vera's daughter found a way to share her talents and experiences with others in the form of her occupation. In her case, her purpose emerged from her greatest challenges, which brings us on to the next pillar:

PURPOSE + MEANINGFUL WORK
= THE OCCUPATIONAL PILLAR

Purpose

Purpose is our primary motivator; it instils hope and drives our actions. In Victor Frankl's masterpiece *Man's Search for Meaning,* he depicts the necessity of finding purpose and a reason to exist even in the bleakest of circumstances, namely a concentration camp. Certainly, in my clinical experience, the pursuit of purpose is the most effective antidote to depression, inertia, loneliness, low self-esteem and existential angst. This is why my therapeutic approach focuses on how individuals engage actively with the world around them – in other words, what they *do* to contribute to the world and find meaning in their lives, whether voluntarily or through employment.

Research has shown that having a sense of purpose is associated with better mental health outcomes. Helping your loved one connect with theirs could be their lifeline. There's also a 65 per cent chance of completing a goal if you tell someone else about it.[27] However, it's important to remember that purpose means different things to different people – from self-realization and creative expression, to work success.

Meaningful Work

There is a difference between our "job" and our "work". Sometimes we don't need to change our external circumstances (that is, change our actual job), but to imbue it with "our work". Visualization can be a powerful tool in helping us to imagine what such a transformation might look like. When someone is depressed, sometimes the creative imagination can offer the possibility of something else. In time, these inner imaginings or visions might be translated into valuable goals.

Studies repeatedly show that decent work improves mental health and promotes recovery by offering financial independence, a sense of purpose and social interaction.[28] The reality is that most people are eager to work, even if they have a more complex mental illness.[29] This is where supported employment comes in.[30] In essence, supported employment is a tailored approach that helps individuals with significant disabilities find and keep meaningful jobs. This model believes that with the right support, anyone who wants to work can do so. It emphasizes equal pay, safe working conditions, and career advancement opportunities like those offered to other employees.

If your loved one has a severe mental health condition, introducing them to supported employment could be transformative. It begins with vocational profiling to understand their skills and job preferences, and includes forming partnerships with employers to overcome traditional recruitment barriers. To find out more about supported employment and how it might benefit your loved one, consider reaching out to local community mental health centres or searching online for resources and agencies that specialize in this employment model.

Perhaps confidence is the main blocker in your loved one's life when it comes to work. This is something I would recommend is addressed with a cognitive behavioural therapist, with the emphasis on setting achievable goals that motivate change. My personal motto is: opt for courage, not confidence. By taking courageous steps – even when you don't feel confident – and living through the experience, you build a case against your inner critic. And, in turn, build confidence.

We all need a reason to get up in the morning and, for most people, that's having something meaningful to engage with in their day. Some people may be able to work full-time in a fulfilling career, while others may benefit from part-time work, volunteering or group activities that provide structure and social interaction. The key is to help your loved one find work that aligns with their abilities and interests, and to provide encouragement along the way.

The Social Pillar

Research has consistently shown the profound impact of robust social support and connection when it comes to mental health outcomes. A notable 2010 meta-analysis found that individuals with strong social relationships had a 50 per cent increased likelihood of survival compared to those with weaker ties.[31] This influence on longevity is comparable to quitting smoking and surpasses many well-known risk factors, such as obesity and physical inactivity. Here's the thing: mental distress and the associated feelings of shame thrive in isolation. Connection is the antidote. Here is my equation for this pillar:

$$\text{SUPPORT NETWORKS} + \text{MEANINGFUL RELATIONSHIPS} = \text{THE SOCIAL PILLAR}$$

Support Networks

Many people who find themselves in a supporting role tell me their loved ones resist additional support networks, preferring to rely on them instead. This creates a huge strain on both parties, potentially trapping the caregiver and amplifying the sense of isolation for the person being supported.

If you take one thing away from this chapter, it should be this: a robust care plan consists of many different types of support, which minimizes dependency on a single person. Four layers of support are optimal for creating a comprehensive and balanced network.

Layers of support for your loved one might include:

- **Engaging other family and friends:** This might include providing practical and/or emotional support. For example, other family members might take turns calling or visiting.
- **Utilizing peer support:** Connecting with others facing similar challenges can offer a unique sense of belonging and validation that someone is *not alone in this.* Mentors, whether in a formal or informal capacity, can offer guidance, advice and perspective based on their experiences.
- **Social activity/hobby groups:** Whether it's returning to a once-loved hobby or discovering a new interest, activities (especially group ones) bring joy, purpose and an opportunity to meet like-minded people.
- **Accessing volunteer or befriending programmes:** These can provide companionship, the chance to engage in activities together, and offer respite for you as the primary caregiver.
- **Accessing educational workshops or community resources:** These might include local mental health organizations, online forums, workshops or educational materials – which also overlaps with the intellectual pillar as a means for personal growth.
- **Participating in religious or spiritual groups:** This can provide a sense of belonging and shared identity. (See also the spiritual pillar.)

If your loved one is hesitant – or refuses – to engage with external support, here are some strategies to consider:

- **Gradual introduction:** Resistance to support often stems from a fear of the unknown. Gradually introducing the idea through casual conversations might help. Share positive examples of how external support has helped others.
- **Empathy and active listening:** Feeling thoroughly understood can make a person more open to suggestions. Acknowledge their feelings about receiving help from others and ask about their concerns. This can provide you with insights on how to address their fears or reservations.
- **Leverage familiar faces:** If possible, introduce support from people your loved one already knows. Seeing a familiar face can reduce the anxiety associated with receiving help from "strangers".
- **Incremental support:** Start with minimal and non-invasive forms of support that do not feel overwhelming or threatening to your loved one's autonomy.
- **Highlight the benefits for both:** Explain how external support can benefit not just your loved one's health and wellbeing, but also improve the quality of your relationship by reducing stress and dependency. Make it clear that your suggestion comes from a place of love and a desire to strengthen your relationship.

Meaningful Relationships

Andy, 52, told me how opening up his mother's support network through introducing more close family members into it not only reinforced their relationship, but created more meaningful connections in her life:

My elderly mum is increasingly anxious and is now facing cognitive decline. We were always close and, in some ways, I was more like a partner to her after Dad died. It hasn't been easy and I've carried a lot of responsibility on my shoulders. It got too much for me recently and I decided to finally reach out to my other siblings and my own kids about how I was feeling. My kids suggested we take turns to call her every day. Now we have a rota, with different members of the family calling her on different days. It's just 30 minutes out of their day once a week, but I can't tell you what a difference it's made to my mental load – and hers. She loves the fact that she now gets to regularly speak to some of the younger members of the family, too.

If your own support network is able to give you more time for yourself, you're likely to feel less put upon and bring your best self to your relationship with your loved one, which will enable this to become more meaningful and authentic in turn. At the end of this chapter, you'll be encouraged to help your loved one create their own, multi-layered support network.

The Spiritual Pillar

I've intentionally kept this section short, as spirituality is a deeply personal matter. For some, it may involve faith and religious practice, while for others, it may be a sense of connection to nature and something greater than oneself. Regardless of how it is defined, spirituality can be a powerful source of strength, resilience and hope. Here is my equation for this pillar:

$$\text{TIME FOR SELF-REFLECTION} + \text{HIGHER WISDOM} = \text{THE SPIRITUAL PILLAR}$$

Time for Self-Reflection

In the chaos and noise of daily life, it's easy to lose touch with our inner selves. This is especially true for those who have experienced abuse or neglect, which might have closed them down in some way. Taking time for introspection, whether through prayer, meditation, journaling or simply sitting in silence, can allow us to tune in to ourselves. It provides a space for us to process our experiences, gain insight into our challenges and connect with our deeper truth.

Higher Wisdom

Ultimately, this pillar is about finding connection to a higher state of consciousness. It's about recognizing that we're more than our struggles, and that there is a deeper source of strength available to us. Ample evidence shows that individuals receiving mental health and addiction services consider spirituality a crucial aspect of their recovery.[32] As you support your loved one on their journey, remember to attend to this often-neglected dimension of wellbeing.

The Financial Pillar

Research shows that financial stress has a profound impact on mental health. For example, people with depression who are in debt are 4.2 times more likely to still have depression 18 months later than those who aren't in debt.[33] What's more, 49–64 per cent of care recipients are financially dependent upon their family and friends.[34] You might find yourself in this position. Perhaps you've lent money to a loved one, which is not protected and regulated in the way consumer credit would be.

Many people with mental health issues choose to borrow money informally because they're out of other options, find the application process too stressful, or are in a desperate situation that requires immediate relief.[35] While this may provide a lifeline in the short term, it can create entanglement and even lead to coercive control by either the borrower or the lender. It nearly always has a negative effect on both parties' mental health over time. I've heard from many people how being indebted to friends and family has heightened their stress, feelings of shame, guilt and worsened their depression and anxiety. Be mindful of this.

PROMPT: If you find yourself offering money to your loved one, even when they haven't asked for it, it may be worth considering why you're doing this, and whether controlling behaviour is at play.

Clearly, it's important to find a balance between supporting your loved one's financial needs and maintaining your own financial stability. This may involve setting clear boundaries and expectations around financial contributions through contracting with them thoroughly, as well as encouraging your loved one to take an active role in managing their own finances to the extent that they're able. With that in mind, here's my equation for the financial pillar:

LIVING WITHIN YOUR MEANS + FINANCIAL STABILITY = THE FINANCIAL PILLAR

Living Within Your Means

A key principle of financial wellbeing is living within our means. If you suspect your loved one is struggling with financial issues that they're keeping secret, it's crucial to cultivate a space for open and supportive dialogue. Financial troubles are often deeply intertwined with feelings of shame and fear, so express your concern in a way that centres on their wellbeing and avoids accusatory language. Encourage them to share their experiences and struggles, assuring them that you're there to listen and support rather than to judge or reprimand.

If they're open to it, you can suggest exploring resources and approaches together, such as:

- creating a realistic budget that tracks variable expenses and fixed costs
- opening bills instead of ignoring them
- dealing with priority debts first (such as the mortgage, tax or court fines)
- going cardless and paying for everything in cash (which can make money seem less abstract)
- defining life goals (short, mid and long term) and understanding what money is required
- contacting a financial advisor who specializes in debt management
- attending workshops and support groups that focus on financial literacy

Compulsive spending can be a symptom of underlying emotional distress. CBT therapy can provide strategies to help manage the behaviour and address the emotional aspects driving it. The main work is around managing impulse control and finding other ways to get the dopamine rush that spending brings. Throughout this process, it's important to help your loved one to recognize their own ability to regain control over their financial situation, which can significantly reduce feelings of helplessness and anxiety.

Financial Stability

Some mental health issues such as addiction, bipolar disorder and borderline personality disorder can cause unpredictable financial behaviour. If it's an area you have genuine concerns over, you might consider setting up a durable power of attorney for finances. This legal document allows a trusted person to manage financial decisions on behalf of the individual when they themselves aren't in a position to do so responsibly. It's important to discuss this option with your loved one when they're in a stable state, to ensure their wishes are respected and understood. As part of this, you might consider shared monitoring of bank accounts and credit cards. This enables you to keep an eye on spending patterns and intervene if necessary. Many banks and financial institutions offer alerts that notify you of high spending activities or low balances.

The Environmental Pillar

The environmental pillar recognizes that our surroundings aren't just a backdrop to our lives, but an active force that shapes our mental health:

SAFE SHELTER + FEELING CONNECTED TO PEOPLE AND PLANET = THE ENVIRONMENTAL PILLAR

Safe Shelter

Feeling unsafe, whether that's due to financial struggles, interpersonal conflicts or inadequate personal space, can significantly heighten mental health symptoms, impede recovery and send just about anyone over the edge.

Many people who struggle with their mental health often experience a sense of being unwanted or burdensome to their families, even if this perception doesn't align with reality. This is something to be mindful of, as you might wish to actively reassure them they are wanted at home. For those experiencing PTSD, adapting to a new environment, even if it's safer, can still feel overwhelming and isolating. The experience of displacement and cultural adjustment can contribute to feelings of anxiety, loneliness and alienation.

Separately, the wrong environment or somewhere that's not conducive to health can massively impact outcomes. Here's Benji, 31, talking about how moving into the countryside helped his mother get off drugs:

> After we'd thrown so much money at rehab, we knew she couldn't stay in London anymore, where the drug dealers were just around the corner. In the middle of the countryside there was no access to drugs, and eventually alcohol became her drug of choice. But as a family, that was the lesser of two evils. The change in setting meant we had some years of more peace – even if she stayed in bed most of the day, as a kid I could still enjoy playing in the open space.

By cultivating spaces that are safe and reflective of our unique needs, we can create a foundation of resilience and support that sustains us through life's challenges. If you have a loved one of adult age who lives with you but it's within their reach to live independently, make this the ultimate objective. Offer support by helping to identify what adjustments are needed to give them independence. Down the line, this might include meeting up at neutral locations, rather than making home visits. This will not only reinforce their ability to operate independently but frame your relationship as one between equals.

Above all, help your loved one to identify elements that enhance their sense of security within their living space. Support can also extend to exploring local resources such as domestic violence shelters, housing assistance or community safety programmes.

Feeling Connected to People and Planet

Connecting deeply with both people and the planet forms a fundamental component of holistic health. Access to green spaces and natural environments has been linked with better mental health outcomes. If your loved one struggles to go outside, incorporate natural elements into their home, such as houseplants or nature-themed artwork. However, it's also worth noting that indoor pollution can be much worse than outdoor pollution, due to limited air flow.[36] Therefore, regular cleaning, ventilation and air purification may be necessary. Addressing indoor air quality is a critical aspect of environmental health and it also improves respiratory health, mental clarity and energy levels.

If your loved one struggles with SAD or other climate-related mental health challenges, it may be helpful to explore treatments such as light therapy or vitamin D supplementation, or even to consider moving to a more suitable climate (easier said than done, of course).

How Does This Model Apply to Severe Mental Illness?

The eight-pillar holistic approach can counteract the often-dehumanizing treatment of those with severe mental illness. It places quality of life at its centre – something everyone deserves.

When possible, rely on any advanced directives or expressed preferences about healthcare and lifestyle choices. If your loved one is unable to identify areas of their life that require attention or articulate their treatment needs, empowerment can take the form of advocacy for adjustments that align with their known preferences and values, even if they're currently unable to voice them. This may mean simply observing their reactions to certain activities or therapies and adjusting accordingly.

Ultimately, it means being a thoughtful, informed and compassionate steward of another person's wellbeing, always striving to enhance their quality of life in ways that honour their individuality and humanity. By empowering yourself with knowledge and being proactive in your loved one's care strategy, you can make a significant difference in their life.

When introducing any new routine or therapies, it's important to do so incrementally and monitor responses over time. It's generally advisable to monitor a new approach over the course of three to six months, and adjust as needed. Here's Maureen, 39, talking about the things she has done to support her sister, who remains in full-time psychiatric care:

> Despite the challenges my sister faces with her psychotic disorder, being in a long-term hospital setting doesn't confine our approach. They don't offer her anything in the way of holistic healthcare, so I've educated myself about what we can do. For example, I bring in art supplies during my visits, so she can paint the people and places that inhabit her mind. I've spoken to the nurses about engaging her in gentle exercise routines, which significantly helps with stress reduction. With her doctor's approval, we've also introduced fish oil and vitamin D (which is much lower in those with schizophrenia) supplements into her regime.[37] This tailored approach helps her thrive in her own way, despite the severity of her condition.

Accessing Care

Let's face it, navigating a holistic approach to healthcare without substantial financial resources can be challenging and can require a bit more research into what's available.

In the UK, the NHS does provide some complementary therapies, although availability can be limited and varies by location. Additionally, the NHS sometimes refers patients to social prescribing services, which connect individuals to nonclinical services, ranging from health and fitness programmes to community activities.

In the US, the situation is more complex due to the varied landscape of state regulations, insurance providers and the coverage they offer. Some insurance plans cover certain alternative therapies like chiropractic care, acupuncture or nutritional counselling. And some medicine practitioners and integrative health clinics offer services on a sliding scale based on income, which can make treatments more accessible.

On both sides of the Atlantic, local community centres, charities and support groups may offer some free or low-cost services that align with holistic care principles, including yoga, meditation classes or nutritional education. Apps and the internet also provide a wealth of free, or low-cost, resources. Additionally, schools where professionals train in holistic practices like massage therapy or acupuncture usually offer services at reduced rates.

Ultimately, holistic health emphasizes lifestyle changes, such as improved diet, increased physical activity and better sleep habits, which don't always require costly interventions. Considering the current challenges in mental healthcare, what creative solutions can you implement to help build at least four layers of support for your loved one (aside from you)? How can existing resources and community connections help you create a resilient support network?

Helping Your Loved One Get Started

At the right time, you might want to introduce the concept of holistic health to your loved one if they're not already familiar with it. Simply sharing what you've found interesting and/or relevant in this chapter can plant a seed. Below is an example of the type of thing you might say:

I've been reading a bit about holistic health, which is an approach that looks at a person as a whole, rather than just focusing on their symptoms. It's made me reflect on how different aspects of my life, like sleep and nutrition, impact my own [insert health challenge, for example back pain] – how some things contribute or alleviate my symptoms. For example, if I sleep badly my pain is worse, but when I eat anti-inflammatory foods and practise my Pilates exercises I feel it improves. I'm wondering if exploring this perspective might be helpful for you, too. I'd be happy to share some resources if you're interested in learning more.

Note the tone: curious, reflective and inviting, rather than prescriptive. You're opening a dialogue, not pushing an agenda. And you're directly connecting it to your own experiences. If they express an interest or willingness to think more holistically about themselves and their lives, you might suggest the following exercise.

TABLE OF BEHAVIOURS

This process of self-reflection can provide valuable insights and a starting point for making changes.

1 Draw a table for your loved one that has three columns. In the first column, list the eight pillars of health. Give the next column the heading "Things that support my health" and the third the heading "Things that challenge my health". (See page2 128–9 for an example of a completed table.)
2 Suggest they fill the table out for themselves. This is something they might wish to do in private or with your support; either way is fine. The important thing is they reflect on the factors that help or hinder them for each pillar.

Setting SMART Goals

Based on their completed table, the next step is to encourage your loved one to identify SMART goals that align with their values and aspirations, which stands for goals that are:

Specific
Measurable
Achievable
Realistic
Timely

To illustrate how to go about this, let's consider Jessica, 36, who works in the media. She attends networking events several times a week, which fuels her drinking and cocaine consumption. She is ambitious and takes on more and more responsibility, leading to high levels of anxiety. When we meet, she is close to burnout. Separately, she is running up debt, when she should be saving up to buy a home. She knows she needs to start making healthier choices for herself, but doesn't know where to start as her issues are all entangled. Here's how Jessica completed the table from the previous section:

Pillars of Health	Things that support my health	Things that challenge my health
Physical	I feel a lot less anxious when I cut down on drinking, and when I do yoga twice a week, acupuncture for anxiety, sleep tracking.	Too much alcohol consumption, partying in the week. Poor sleep as a result of drinking. No down time from work.
Emotional	Speaking to a therapist weekly.	When I avoid my emotions and drown my sorrows through drinking. Toxic relationships with certain friends.

Pillars of Health	Things that support my health	Things that challenge my health
Intellectual	Reading books about personal development. Starting a graphic design course.	Excessive scrolling on social media, especially before bed.
Occupational	No emails post 7pm; focusing on long-term work goals, not short-term networking at parties.	Work events that fuel my drinking. Pressuring myself to perform better so I get a promotion.
Social	Spending more time with my nan; being more selective about who I hang out with; volunteering fortnightly at the food bank.	Feeling like I need to drink or do coke when I hang out with certain people. When I speak to Mum too much.
Spiritual	Forest bathing and long weekend walks; becoming aware of my spiritual hole.	For example, filling my emptiness with addictive behaviours.
Financial	Investing in my savings, so I can work toward buying a flat. Living within my means.	Not buying everyone drinks I can't afford so they like me.
Environmental	Spending time in the countryside and feeling more connected nature,	Living in the city which means I go to more events, where I drink.

Here's a step-by-step framework that helped Jessica set a SMART goal, based on assessing the pillars of her life:

1 **Identify the most pressing issue.** In Jessica's case, this was addressing substance use. However, she wasn't ready to go there, so we started off by focusing on another key (but highly related) area: financial management.

2 **Set one overarching, broad, long-term objective connected to this.** (More than one goal can overwhelm someone.) In Jessica's case, the goal tied to financial management was to start saving toward a deposit for her own flat.

3 **Know the value underpinning the objective.** In Jessica's case, the idea of laying down a sturdy foundation was deeply important to her sense of stability.
4 **Transform this into a SMART goal.** For Jessica, that meant:
   - Defining exactly how much needed to be saved – making it *specific*.
   - Setting a benchmark for savings, such as a monthly savings goal – which was *measurable*.
   - Ensuring the monthly savings goal was realistic based on her income and expenses, so budgeting was required – meaning it was *achievable*.
   - Connecting the goal to personal values and long-term aspirations, like homeownership leading to financial stability and independence – which made it *relevant*.
   - Establishing a deadline, like aiming to save for a down payment within three years – which made the goal *time-bound*.

   In Jessica's case, she set herself the SMART goal of saving $350 every month by cutting unnecessary expenses.
5 **Review and Adjust Regularly:** For Jessica, this meant setting up regular check-ins to discuss progress and challenges, and adapting goals as necessary to remain aligned with her evolving needs and circumstances.

Through redirecting the money she would usually spend on alcohol, drugs and socializing into savings, Jessica began to make tangible progress toward her dream. This not only boosted her self-esteem but also lessened her reliance on substances for emotional fulfilment. The act of saving became a daily reinforcement of her ability to control and enhance her life, laying a solid foundation for tackling her substance use. As her savings grew and her spending on short-term highs diminished, she found herself more equipped and motivated to address the deeper issues surrounding her substance abuse. The financial discipline she cultivated helped to reveal the profound impacts of her habits, not just on her finances but on her whole life.

This approach proved pivotal for Jessica. It allowed her to engage with her addictive behaviours from a position of strength rather than vulnerability, eventually leading to a more holistic recovery journey. This underscores the principle that sometimes, addressing secondary issues first can create a more conducive environment for tackling primary challenges, especially if someone is not yet ready. But if appropriate, why not introduce your loved one to the concept of SMART goals and suggest you each come up with them for yourselves?

Creating a Holistic Care Plan

If your loved one is open to the idea, use the ideas in this chapter to create a holistic care plan with them (or they could do this solo, or with someone else). Remember, the ownership of such a plan ultimately rests with them. It's their road map to wellness, and they should be in the driver's seat, with you (and potentially their healthcare providers) alongside them.

If it helps, my equation for an effective holistic healthcare plan looks like this:

PERSONALIZATION + EMPOWERMENT + EIGHT-PILLAR APPROACH + FAMILY SUPPORT + CONTINUOUS ADAPTATION = ROBUST TREATMENT PLAN

Here's the key:

- **Personalization:** Each person's unique mental, emotional, physical and social factors – and needs – should be considered.
- **Empowerment:** The patient should be involved in decision-making processes. This also leads to better outcomes.

- **Eight-pillar approach:** A person should be treated in their entirety through a range of modalities.
- **Family support:** Engagement and education of family members/friends to provide emotional, logistical and sometimes medical support is essential.
- **Continuous adaptation:** Regular reassessment and modification of the treatment plan is required to reflect changes in the individual's condition and circumstances.

It's useful to consolidate all the information in one place, both for your loved one and anyone they might want to share it with.

I've included a very simple holistic care plan template on pages 269–70, which you might like to share with your loved one. It's important to know this is a living document and should be viewed only as a flexible roadmap. In fact, there may be times when despite your best efforts, the wheels come off completely – and that's when you need an emergency plan, which we'll look at next.

CHAPTER 5
CREATING AN EMERGENCY PLAN

"When my son goes missing, I have made a vow to always find him. I always tell him just to go to the hospital first. Because if the streets get him, we'll never get him back."

Margaret, 64

Let's turn our attention now to what to do in a crisis, how to know if you're in one and how to assess risk. In this chapter, we will explore strategies for "crisis preparedness" and cover the necessary steps to ensure safeguarding is in place. Finally, we'll touch on how best to navigate the delicate post-crisis phase of recovery and healing.

The notion of planning for a crisis may seem alien to you, and you may even question its necessity. While it's true that predicting a mental health emergency is often beyond anyone's capability (particularly the first time it happens), taking a proactive approach to planning is less about predicting the future and more about preparing for it. The midst of a crisis is not the time to figure things out, so it makes sense to do some thinking ahead of time. A safety plan can help dispel some of the panic, disorientation and indecision you may experience, enabling you to act with clarity and purpose when every moment counts. Hence, I'd suggest reading this chapter when things are calm.

For your loved one, a crisis plan can stand as a testament to the power of your love and emotional support. With prepared responses and processes at the ready, there may be a deepened sense of mutual trust. Above all, it empowers the individual at risk – allowing them to contribute to their care plan *when they can*.

Why Warning Signs Matter

Mental health crises are rarely monolithic events, but rather a series of urgent situations that can manifest in different ways. Very often, a crisis is predicated by a trigger of sorts, be that substance use, hormonal changes (including becoming pregnant or menopausal), sleep interference, a life stressor, changes in circumstance, relationship conflict or resurfaced trauma. Even if a trigger cannot always be identified, usually there are some warning signs that a crisis might be on the horizon. It's important to familiarize yourself with what these might be, as timely intervention could prevent a crisis from escalating.

Through providing timely support, the right resources and effective management strategies, the likelihood of self-harm or suicidal behaviours lessens. This proactive approach not only helps to stabilize the individual more quickly but also minimizes the risk that hospitalization will become necessary, or that the person will go on to be arrested.[1] What's more, early intervention facilitates a faster recovery process and can help prevent an untreated condition from becoming chronic, or secondary problems (like substance abuse) from developing.[2] With early intervention, someone is also more likely to engage with treatment plans.

Let's focus on recognizing the signs of psychosis, addiction relapse and severe, acute depression. Remember, symptoms can manifest differently in everyone; the key is to observe any significant changes in behavior, particularly those that appear abruptly and without explanation.

Recognizing Signs of Mania

A manic episode can be difficult to spot at first, as the individual might appear to be super productive and firing on all cylinders. However, when someone's behaviour becomes increasingly frantic, they're much more talkative than usual, have insomnia, racing thoughts, are uncharacteristically excitable or irritable, have grandiosity of thought and are engaging in risky behaviour, like compulsive spending or dangerous driving, it's possible they're slipping into mania (which can lead to psychosis).

Now, I'm not for one moment suggesting that whenever someone is excitable they're about to experience mania – life is full of highs and lows, and it's a wonderful thing to be fully alive to these experiences! But the fact is that when someone is entering mania, or a mixed episode (when someone feels both high and low), their behaviour starts to deviate wildly from their baseline. Recognizing these precursors might help prevent a full-blown psychotic episode from taking place.

Be a stable influence by encouraging them to eat (for example, prepare simple food that can be eaten easily), sleep (short naps can have a big impact) and keeping spaces calm.

Recognizing Signs of Psychosis

Psychosis is when a person finds it hard to distinguish between reality and non-reality. They experience delusions, disordered thinking, paranoia and hallucinations, such as hearing voices. Not everyone with bipolar disorder experiences psychosis; it can happen during a depressive episode, but is more likely to occur with a manic episode. Psychosis is also a key symptom of schizophrenia, but it can happen to anyone – here are several other causes:

- stress
- drug or alcohol misuse

- a traumatic experience
- giving birth
- head injury or physical conditions, such as a brain tumour
- side effects of prescribed medication

With psychotic disorders, early treatment, particularly during the first episode, can result in significant improvements and a reduced likelihood of future episodes. Early warning signs for psychosis involve social withdrawal, a decline in self-care, trouble thinking clearly, a deterioration in functioning, suspiciousness of others and a subtle change in perception.

If your loved one shows these signs but retains some self-awareness, now is a good time to encourage them to put safeguarding measures in place, such as to adopt restorative sleep patterns, adhere to their medication regime, stop any alcohol or substances and speak to a therapist. There may be other more personal safeguarding steps that help to ground them, such as reaching out to specific peer support or listening to music. This is also an opportune moment to help them to reflect on past experiences so as to manage the current one more proactively; for example, to consider what helped or didn't in the past at such a time. During these moments of lucidity, your loved one might process guidance and take steps to manage their symptoms better. Therapy can provide a safe space for someone to share their impulses before they take action and find ways to express their "psychotic side" in healthier ways. I cannot state this enough: just like with physical illness, early treatment of psychosis leads to better outcomes.

If your loved one is unresponsive, highly distressed or their symptoms rapidly escalate, involving their physician or care coordinator – preferably with their consent – is the next step. The important thing is never to challenge someone's delusions or beliefs when they're in this state.

Even if the psychosis is a pleasurable, spiritual experience for your loved one (many people report feeling as though they were in communion with the Divine), never attempt to break the psychosis. Instead, focus on their safety and on gently guiding them toward professional help, all the while respecting their experience. And remember, if someone is at risk of harming themselves, or others (including you), contact emergency services immediately.

De-escalation

De-escalation tactics aim to prevent a situation from worsening and help all individuals involved feel safe and supported. A lot of the tips in Chapter 2, on communication, broadly apply, so you might want to re-read it. I have summarized some key de-escalation strategies below:

- **Remain calm:** This means speaking in a soft, low tone and avoiding displays of frustration or anger.
- **Use clear and simple language:** Ask what they feel or need at the moment.
- **Don't take things personally:** Sometimes people behave out of character and we need to learn to let it go.
- **Create a safe environment:** Remove any potentially harmful items and ensure the space is quiet.
- **Be an ally:** Show empathy and build on the trust you have already built so you can partner together.
- **Respect personal space:** Avoid crowding your loved one and maintain a respectful distance to prevent them feeling threatened or trapped.
- **Allow time for reflecting:** Set the slow pace and let them know decisions do not need to be made in haste.
- **Set clear and straightforward limits.**
- **Do not enter into a power struggle:** Rather, bring their attention back to the current predicament.
- **Offer choices and give control:** When asking a question, offer options, and give the positive choice first.

- **Don't focus on facts:** Never address delusions. Instead, address how the person feels and demonstrate understanding through repeating back what they say.
- **Plan an exit strategy:** If you're unable to de-escalate the situation, leave the area and call for professional help.

When there is no ability to reason or reflect, being admitted to a psychiatric hospital might be necessary for your loved one (more on this coming up). At present, the only treatment available during an acute phase of psychosis are antipsychotics, which are typically administered as oral pills. It is, of course, wholly possible that your loved one may refuse to take these – again, we will cover what would then happen.

Recognizing Relapses

Relapse in addiction can be devastating for family members who have been actively encouraging sobriety. In reality, though, relapses are often a necessary part of the recovery process. A crisis is marked by the intensity and speed with which the person falls back into old patterns of substance abuse, or addiction. For example, those who have maintained long-term abstinence from drugs or alcohol are at a high risk of overdose, or even death, if they consume the same amount as they used to. That's because they will have lost the tolerance they once had. However, with proper medical attention and management, withdrawal symptoms and risks can be controlled.[3]

Addiction can take many forms, from shopping to sex, to name a few. For our purposes now, let's focus on substance abuse, as it's associated with the highest levels of risk. Having said that, the following framework would apply to any sort of relapse, or return to self-destructive behaviours.

Emotional relapse is typically the first phase, often prompted by a life event, but not always. Sometimes self-destructive impulses can emerge when someone feels more settled and like they need to disrupt the peace. (This is particularly true for those with BPD.) Common signs of emotional relapse include irritability, mood swings and anxiety, coupled with erratic eating and sleeping patterns. During this stage, engagement with support networks may diminish, weakening the commitment to recovery. Behavioural changes, like increased isolation and loss of interest in hobbies, are early warning signs that are crucial to detect. Timely intervention at this point could pre-empt further progression into the second phase of relapse, which is mental relapse. This is where an individual might start to romanticize their past substance use and reflect positively on their drug-using days. These memories can entice someone toward using again. They may also have a false sense of control, whereby they believe they can use casually without repercussions. Conversations around controlled use often signal an impending relapse.

Once mental relapse sets in, the transition to physical relapse often follows swiftly. Even a one-off instance of using can rekindle strong cravings and risk a return to old ways. If your loved one starts re-engaging with old friends and distancing themselves from sober peers, this might highlight the need for vigilant support and proactive care. We know that social interactions play a critical role in relapse prevention, so getting the right peer support in place is crucial. Often, people may exhibit "dry drunk" behaviours – actions that mimic those of their drinking days – before they return to the substance. When these signs emerge, it is important for the right person to engage in an open dialogue, posing direct questions that prompt reflection on the repercussions of returning to drink, like: "What are the benefits and drawbacks of having a drink?" Encouraging your loved one to catalogue the costs that drinking has incurred in their life can be a potent reminder of the stakes. However, delivering an ultimatum is rarely the best move and should only be considered as a last resort.

Recognizing Depression

It's not easy to detect depression in people who are adept at concealing their feelings. Men, in particular, may display anger rather than sadness. An increase in outbursts or an unusual display of aggression can be indicative of underlying depression. Depression can manifest physically, too, so movement might become sluggish and eye contact poor. Severe depression is when a person's symptoms stop them from performing even simple daily tasks. Weight loss can be prominent due to loss of appetite, personal hygiene may become poor and there may be a complete withdrawal from social interactions.

Ultimately, the best way to support your loved one is to encourage them to become mindful of their own symptoms when they are well, so that they, too, can spot the onset of a major depression before it takes hold. Many people find that regular journaling helps them to do this, as well as daily mood logging, which also considers factors such as menstrual cycle, sleep and diet. Certainly, sleep patterns are often a barometer for mental health, and can alert you both to any disturbances that may need addressing.

It's also smart for your loved one to be aware of any person, event or situation that potentially makes them feel worse – so if warning signs do appear, they can actively avoid them for the time being.

Risk of Suicide

When your loved one is struggling with their mental health, the fear of suicide may be an ever-present shadow. This can be highly distressing, complex and stressful; I'm deeply sorry if you're going through this. Know that your feelings, though nuanced and possibly enduring, are valid, and seeking therapeutic support for yourself could be your salvation. Give yourself permission to process and understand all your own feelings (see Chapter 6). Your journey through this is as important as the support you extend to your loved one.

Understanding the scope of suicide globally helps us to recognize its prevalence and the critical need for timely support. Each year over 700,000 people worldwide take their own life, with many more attempting suicide and more still contemplating it.[4]

Being aware of the warning signs of suicide and knowing how to act can make a difference. Signs can include significant mood changes, withdrawal, expressions of hopelessness, or changes in behaviour that indicate despair. Engaging in open conversations, providing emotional support, and connecting your loved one with professional help are vital steps. Familiarize yourself with local mental health resources, including crisis intervention teams and crisis hotlines.

In my view, it is imperative nationally and internationally to elevate the conversation on suicide, to dismantle the taboos, and to foster an environment where prevention can thrive. The same is true for the way you approach the subject matter in your own life. Yet addressing the risk of suicide can feel like an overwhelming and frightening responsibility. Understanding the distinction between suicidal ideation and intent is key. Suicidal ideation is an umbrella term for thoughts about self-harm, which can range from passive wishes about not waking up to more active imaginings of one's own demise. These ideations can be fleeting or persistent, vague or detailed, but they share a common thread: they're thoughts, not actions. Often, they reflect a deep-seated pain or a desire to escape from insurmountable struggles. Sometimes they may come about because of intrusive and obsessive thoughts stemming from anxiety. As a therapist, I work with people's shadow material all the time, including thoughts of self-destruction, and know this is part of the human experience. While these revelations are to be taken seriously, usually they do not signal an imminent risk if there is no plan or intent to act on them.

Suicidal intent, on the other hand, signifies a shift from contemplation to planning and preparation. Intent carries with it specific strategies, means and a timeframe, turning the ideation from a passive to an active state. It is a strong predictor of a possible suicide attempt and therefore warrants immediate attention. A common misconception is that depression alone leads to suicide. In reality, depression can certainly bring about thoughts of wanting to end one's life. However, it is often when these feelings of depression are combined with other conditions – those that involve restlessness or difficulty controlling impulses – that there might be a higher risk of someone actually attempting suicide.

Of course, predicting the moment someone may attempt to take their life is rarely possible. In fact, sometimes a suicidal person is particularly upbeat in the run-up to it, as they have resolve and a clear purpose. This is something to be mindful of: if your loved one, who has been very unwell and without hope, suddenly becomes very optimistic, it could potentially signal something to this effect. You might want to ask them what has brought about this change. Ultimately, you need to work with – and learn to trust – your own instincts, as people often deny feeling suicidal as a defence against getting help.

If you suspect your loved one is suicidal, listen extra closely to their words. Overwhelming fatigue or expressions of hopelessness such as "everyone would be better off without me" can be clues. Try not to disregard such comments, even if they are simply a cry for attention.

If you take one thing away from this chapter, let it be this: contrary to the misconception, discussing suicide openly does not increase the risk of it happening; it creates a space for intervention and can pave the way for crucial support. Your sensitive enquiry won't initiate suicidal ideation or instigate anyone to act who wasn't already planning to. Instead, it may reveal the issues that need to be addressed to alleviate their despair. Encourage your loved one to describe what they're going through, how long they've been feeling this way, and how pervasive their thoughts are. Ask them kindly but directly if they've contemplated self-harm or ending their life, assuring them that you're asking from a place of love and concern, not anger or criticism. Invite them to share their struggles with you, but understand if they'd rather not. Above all, let them know you are there for them, and encourage them to seek professional support, such as therapy. Offer to help them find a therapist or to make an appointment.

If a loved one expresses direct thoughts of suicide or has a plan, it is crucial to take this very seriously. Encourage them to call an emergency suicide prevention hotline. These hotlines are staffed with trained professionals who provide immediate support. Offer to be there with them while they make the call, or make the call yourself if they're unable. We know that interventions that swiftly follow the first signs of suicidal thoughts or behaviours can drastically reduce the risk of an attempt.

When someone is imminently at risk of doing something, they may feel detached from others, their environment and their emotions, often without visible distress. To help, engage them in conversation with simple, present-focused questions, which can reconnect them with the world around them. Two examples are, "Describe in detail something you can see" and, "If you could eat anything right now, what would it be?" Try to ensure their safety and do not leave them alone.

Self-Harm

We have discussed the distinction between suicidal ideation and intent. But what about self-harm? The motives behind self-harm can vary widely, but it does not usually signify a wish to die. And contrary to popular belief, it is almost never done for attention, but is a deeply private act.

Understanding self-harm is not easy and the natural impetus and advice would always be to remove any potential weapons. However, it can be beneficial to understand where it stems from, as this can also help us to reframe the type of support we provide. Non-suicidal self-injury (NSSI) usually develops as a coping mechanism for intense emotional pain, or conversely, it becomes a way to break through a feeling of numbness. I think of self-harm as a form of nonverbal communication – so it becomes about connecting with the underlying emotional message, rather than merely addressing the physical manifestations of a loved one's distress. (This is similar with eating disorders and addictions, too.) This may involve improving communication, family dynamics and conflict resolution skills.

It's also important to realize that removing this coping mechanism without offering an alternative can intensify feelings of helplessness, anxiety and emotional turmoil, potentially leading to more severe mental health crises or increased risk of suicidal behaviour. Alternative coping mechanisms might include suitable distraction techniques such as:

- listening to music or playing an instrument
- snapping an elastic band or squeezing a stress ball
- holding ice
- eating something with an intense flavour, spicy or sour
- smelling something that's pleasant or evokes memory
- punching a pillow
- going out for a walk or run
- doing something creative
- making a lot of sound or screaming
- practising mindfulness
- journaling or writing down their feelings

These are just some ideas; what's important is your loved one is supported in finding something that works for them. CBT can be very helpful in facilitating this.

It would be remiss of me not to inform you that self-harm, while not always indicative of suicidal intent, does significantly increase the risk of future suicide attempts. This is because a type of desensitization can occur when someone is habitually exposed to self-inflicted pain and fear-inducing scenarios, inadvertently priming them for more severe future self-harm or a suicide attempt. This is why the Samaritans believes that reducing self-harm can help suicide prevention.[5] Escalation in the frequency, intensity or method of self-harm all increase the risk (see below for a framework on assessing risk).

If you believe your loved one is self-harming, it is crucial to encourage them to speak to someone they can trust about their feelings. Never press them for specific details about their injuries, nor give ultimatums, as these tactics simply push behaviour underground.

Framework for Assessing Risk

One of the most recognized frameworks for assessing risk of suicide, and the one I use, is Joiner's model.[6] The theory integrates two core psychological experiences – thwarted belongingness and perceived burdensomeness – which many of us might be able to relate to on some level. Thwarted belongingness speaks to social isolation, while perceived burdensomeness is the feeling that you're a burden to others. Risk of suicide is higher in people who experience both of these, and feel hopeless about these states improving. Therefore, any early interventions and prevention efforts should focus on addressing the feelings of disconnect from others and of the world being better without them.

Help your loved one to foster social connections, utilize peer support and discover the importance of their contributions. You might wish to encourage and facilitate involvement in community activities or interest groups, anything that nurtures a sense of belonging. Promote the idea that their contributions are valued, no matter how small they may seem. Remind them that their presence in the world enriches the lives of others.

Below is the Joiner's model checklist. It's important to say that while assessment tools can provide valuable insights, they're not infallible. A negative response on a questionnaire does not unequivocally rule out risk, so vigilance and continuous support remain key.

JOINER'S MODEL CHECKLIST

The more these elements are present and entrenched, especially when they're accompanied by a sense of hopelessness, the higher the risk of suicide. Mental health professionals use these indicators qualitatively, considering the intensity and interplay of these factors.

Psychological experience of:

- **Thwarted belongingness:** Assess for signs of social isolation, lack of meaningful relationships or feelings of not fitting in anywhere.
- **Perceived burdensomeness:** Look for feelings of being a burden to others, expressions of self-hatred or beliefs that others would be better off without them.

Capability for suicide:

- **History of painful experiences:** Determine if there is a history of exposure to physical pain or emotional trauma, which could include prior suicide attempts.
- **Fearlessness about death:** Evaluate the individual's fearlessness regarding pain and death, which could manifest in behaviours like engaging in risky activities or showing a lack of self-preservation.

- **Practical considerations:** Check if the individual has made preparations or has access to the means to commit suicide (for example, firearms, medication, agricultural equipment, etc.), indicating a higher level of capability and planning.
- **Hopelessness about belonging and burdensomeness:** Establish whether there is a sense of hopelessness about these states changing – for example, whether there is a persistent and static viewpoint.

Ultimately, it's vital to understand that the weight of your loved one's choices is not yours to bear. You can offer support, unconditional love and understanding, but you cannot walk anyone else's path for them. It has taken me a while to grasp that fully myself, and I'm still learning the importance of balancing care with handing responsibility back to the individual. Your best efforts come from a place of hope, but finding the right path to healing is ultimately down to the individual.

PROMPT: Stand strong in the knowledge that, while you walk alongside your loved one, their decisions aren't a reflection of your love or the help you provide. Your role isn't to save, but to support – to offer light in their darkest times. Let this be your guiding principle.

Before we move on, I'd like to share the transpersonal perspective on suicidal ideation, since it offers a unique and compassionate lens through which to view the inner turmoil that can drive someone toward thoughts of ending their life. This perspective suggests that such thoughts might not be a desire for the end of all existence, but rather a deep yearning for transformation – the death of an old self that is suffering, in the hope that a new, more whole self can emerge. It recognizes the pain but also acknowledges a profound possibility for renewal and change; as if you are seeking the "death" of a part of yourself that cannot find peace or fulfilment in its current form. This view is not intended to trivialize the pain or the gravity of suicidal ideation – far from it. Instead, it opens a door to the possibility of rebirth: the emergence of a new self that can experience life differently, with renewed purpose and vitality. The path of transformation is challenging and intricate, yet within it lies hope for a renaissance of the spirit.

This does not in any way diminish the real danger of suicidal ideation, nor does it place the responsibility for healing solely on the individual experiencing these thoughts. It does, however, offer a compassionate framework for understanding and supporting someone in their journey through darkness, toward the possibility of finding a new dawn within themselves.

Crafting a Crisis Plan

A crisis plan should outline clear steps to be taken should someone not be able to make decisions for themselves. It should be created collaboratively between an individual living with mental illness and their support network, which may include family, friends and healthcare professionals. Such plans not only empower the person struggling, but also provide direction for loved ones and healthcare providers during a crisis, potentially reducing the need for involuntary measures. The responsibility for this crisis plan does not lie on your shoulders alone.

Not just a document, it ought to be a living conversation, evolving as circumstances change. Therefore, it requires an open, empathic and ongoing dialogue. This might include understanding your loved one's preferences for hospitals, treatments or the nomination of a trusted individual to make decisions on their behalf.

Navigating this path requires sensitivity, clear communication and a deep understanding of the person's wishes, the legal landscape and the reality that sometimes, despite everyone's best efforts, emergency measures might need to be taken.

Although this won't be relevant to everyone, here are a few benefits of making a crisis plan:

- **It empowers your loved one to have a say in their care**, even when they might not be able to communicate their needs.
- **It may prevent situations from escalating** to the point of requiring involuntary measures, such as being sectioned under mental health laws.
- **It ensures there is a clear understanding** among all parties about preferences for treatment, support and care.
- **It's very important for someone who's mentally unwell to have a few places of trust** they can go to, whether that's family members or even a police station, which can become a place of safety. It's all about having a structure in place that everyone knows about.
- **It can build trust** between an individual, their family and their healthcare team.

Here's a step-by-step guide on how to support your loved one to make a crisis plan, if they're unable to do this with a therapist:

Step One: Start the Conversation Early

It's important to discuss the creation of a crisis plan when your loved one is well, or as well as they can. Make it clear to them that this is a precautionary protective step, and hopefully something that will never need to be utilized. Before you do this, consider if you're the best person to have this conversation with them. Whoever does so should approach the subject with sensitivity, emphasizing that the plan is a form of self-care and a step toward empowerment. Give that assigned person this chapter to read.

Step Two: Involve the Right People

It's worth discussing with your loved one who else should be a part of the conversation – such as mental health professionals, other family members or friends. However, if you suggest adding a certain name to this list and your loved one disagrees, it's important you respect their wishes. They need to be comfortable with everyone included on their crisis plan.

If no one else is involved, it might suggest that a wider, more robust support network needs to be established (see page 117). This can even include a local church, police station, café or hospital that might extend a welcoming hand, providing prior contact has been made.

Step Three: Identify Crisis Signs

Together, list the signs that might indicate your loved one is entering a crisis phase. These could be changes in mood, behaviour, thought patterns or daily functioning. This will be harder to predict if a crisis hasn't happened before, but it's still possible to brainstorm what could happen. Recognizing these early signs can lead to de-escalation. This exercise also helps build self-awareness for the individual, so that they can learn to self-manage their symptoms better.

Step Four: Establish Support Actions

Detail the support your loved one finds helpful during difficult times. This list should be driven by them and might include:

- specific coping strategies, such as listening to music or practising mindfulness
- reaching out to mental health professionals, such as therapists, psychiatrists or support groups
- social interactions, including phone calls about day-to-day chit-chat, or arranging a meet-up
- help with daily tasks

If your loved one is very unwell, you might consider:

- having them share their location with you via suitable phone apps, or even putting a tracking device on their car with consent
- keeping a spare key, so you or another trusted individual can get into their home if necessary

Step Five: Pinpoint Protective Factors

Help your loved one to identify protective factors that reduce the potential for self-harm and serve as reminders that life is worth living. These might include positive personal relationships, a cherished pet, religious beliefs, focusing on future hopes or something they feel responsible for in the community. Encourage your loved one to write these down and refer to this list during a crisis.

Step Six: Encourage Them to Create a Comfort Box

A comfort box is a personal toolkit that can help soothe and distract someone from distressing thoughts. It might include:

- meaningful items, such as photos, letters, or mementos that remind them of happy times or loved ones
- digital assets such as videos of fun times and happy memories, which they might want to keep on a USB stick or in a designated folder on their phone

CARING FOR YOUR LOVED ONE

- music (such as a specific playlist that lifts their spirits)
- sensory objects that can calm the senses, like scented candles, soft fabrics or stress balls
- notes or cards with positive affirmations or encouraging words to read during tough moments
- favourite snacks, as sometimes a familiar taste can be very comforting

Step Seven: Make a Record of Treatment Preferences

What treatments have been effective in the past? Consider together whether there are specific medications that should be used or avoided. What about hospital preferences or the use of alternative therapies? This section of the plan should reflect your loved one's preferences regarding medical interventions and support. It should also include an up-to-date record of current medications. It is prudent to involve a medical professional in this step.

Step Eight: Define Emergency Contacts

Who should be called in a crisis? Provide a list of names and numbers, perhaps in order of emergency. It's worth including opening hours here, too. Have it all in one accessible place, so your loved one doesn't have to start scouring the internet should they become distressed. This list should include contact details for:

- friends and family members
- professional support (such as their doctor and/or psychiatrist)
- hotlines run by volunteers
- specialist organizations
- emergency services (including the address of their nearest ER)

Step Nine: Think About Legal Considerations

When creating a crisis plan, it's important to consider any legal documents that can support your loved one's wishes regarding their care. Two significant instruments are advance healthcare directives and power of attorney, where preferences for psychiatric treatment can be documented, as well as who can make decisions on behalf of the individual if they're unable to do so.

Copies of the completed documents should be given to all key individuals.

LEGAL DOCUMENTS

The requirements can vary by jurisdiction, but many regions have statutory forms that can usually be found through healthcare providers or local government websites. Some forms may need to be witnessed or notarized to be legally binding.

Advance healthcare directives are legal documents in which your loved one can specify their preferences for medical treatment.

A healthcare power of attorney (HCPA) is a type of advance directive whereby someone can appoint another person, called an agent, to make healthcare decisions on their behalf, should they themselves become incapable of making decisions. The document will usually detail how much power the agent has over decisions and may include instructions for specific scenarios.

A mental health power of attorney is similar to a HCPA but is focused on decisions regarding psychiatric treatment.

Step Ten: Keep This Plan Accessible

Not only should this plan be reviewed regularly, especially if your loved one's situation or treatment changes, but it should be easily accessible. Consider keeping both a written and digital copy that can be shared instantly if needed.

A crisis plan is about reducing risk and ensuring the dignity of your loved one is respected, even in the most challenging of times. Above all, it's about facilitating them to think about ways they can help themselves *in the moment*, should they be in a crisis. This is not thinking you can do for them.

Law Enforcement During a Crisis

If your loved one is in the throes of a mental health crisis, the first concern is their immediate safety and yours. An ambulance is often the best first call if a person is primarily a risk to themselves and not acting aggressively toward others. Paramedics can provide medical care and transport the person to a hospital where they can receive psychiatric treatment. While this may understandably feel daunting to do, it's the safest way to ensure your loved one receives immediate care that could be life-saving.

If the person poses a significant threat and requires restraint, or is in a situation where a crime has been or might be committed, calling the police may be necessary. Some regions have specialized mental health crisis teams that can be dispatched in these situations. These teams typically include mental health professionals trained to de-escalate crises. Find out if such services are available in your area by contacting local mental health services and doing your own research.

If law enforcement is called, they will assess the situation to determine the best course of action. Police officers are generally not there to arrest the person in crisis, but to ensure everyone's safety and facilitate access to appropriate care.

When you contact emergency services, clearly state that it is a mental health crisis and request responders trained in crisis intervention or ask for a mental health crisis team, if available. As mentioned in Chapter 1, it's important to address the fact that racial inequalities exist in mental healthcare and law-enforcement responses. This knowledge can understandably increase anxiety about seeking help during a crisis. If you're concerned about this, say so, and inform law enforcement of any concerns you have about racial bias and reiterate the need for a compassionate, nonviolent approach.

As part of a crisis plan, it might be helpful to research local mental health advocacy groups or services that understand and work to counteract such biases.

In any interaction with emergency services, try to remain as calm and clear in your communication as possible. If it feels safe and appropriate, inform the responders of your loved one's mental health history and any de-escalation techniques that have worked in the past. Remember, your role as an advocate for your loved one is critical. If law enforcement must be involved, ask about the process, what will happen to your loved one, and ensure your loved one is informed about their rights. It is usually permissible for a relative or friend to accompany someone who is being detained under mental health laws to a place of safety. Legally speaking, a place of safety is a hospital, and not a police cell. However, due to critical shortages of hospital beds and varying local practices, this ideal is not always achieved. Involving a mental health advocate or legal representative, if possible, can provide an additional layer of support.

When all is said and done, the prospect of your loved one being arrested during a mental health crisis is distressing. If this occurs, seek legal advice immediately. A lawyer specialized in mental health law can help navigate the system and advocate for the rights and proper treatment of your loved one. These steps won't eliminate systemic issues, but they can help in upholding fair and compassionate treatment.

Different Treatment Outcomes

The landscape of mental health treatment and hospitalization varies greatly depending on the needs of the patient, as well as the legal and medical framework of the country in which care is provided. Understanding these nuances is important for both you and your loved one.

Rehab Clinics

Voluntary treatment and rehabilitation centres are facilities that individuals enter willingly to receive treatment for mental health issues, substance use disorders or both. These centres are often quite diverse in terms of the services they provide and the philosophies they follow. Residential treatment programmes are designed to remove individuals from potentially triggering environments and provide a safe space where they can focus solely on recovery, while outpatient services offer flexibility, allowing individuals to maintain their daily routines such as work or school while receiving treatment. They provide intensive, structured treatment during the day, but allow patients to return home in the evenings.

Financially, voluntary treatment centres can vary significantly. Many are private and require payment, which can be substantial. Some may accept insurance, but coverage details and out-of-pocket costs will depend on individual policies and the centre's billing practices. There are also publicly funded facilities and community-based programmes that offer services at low or no cost, although these might have longer wait times or fewer resources.

Sectioning

Acute hospital care typically occurs in emergency circumstances. This may be due to severe psychosis; a suicide attempt, where immediate intervention is required to preserve life; violent outbursts that may lead to harm; or a significant relapse or destructive behaviour in the context of an underlying mental health condition. In the UK, the process known as "sectioning" under the Mental Health Act allows for individuals who are experiencing significant mental health crises and pose a risk to themselves or others to be hospitalized for treatment, typically without their consent. This is intended as a last resort when other avenues of voluntary care are insufficient. The process involves assessments by health professionals and requires the agreement of multiple parties to ensure it is justified.

Involuntary hospitalization can be deeply traumatic for both the patient and their loved ones. Being forcibly admitted strips an individual of their autonomy, an act so profound that its echoes can be felt for many years. Yet, paradoxically, it can also be a lifesaving intervention.

If your loved one is hospitalized, they will likely feel scared and vulnerable. When it comes to providing reassurance, be specific about your commitment to them. Instead of a vague "I'll be here for you", try saying, "I'm planning to visit again tomorrow afternoon and on Saturday. Would those times work for you?" This provides a concrete timeline that your loved one can look forward to. It shows that you're organized in your efforts to support them, which can be comforting in a setting where they may feel they have little control. Regular check-ins and follow-up visits are important. They help you stay informed about any changes in their condition or treatment plan. Being in the loop allows you to be a more effective advocate for your loved one's needs and wishes, especially in a medical setting where they might feel overwhelmed or side-lined.

Amidst the hustle of doctors and the incessant beeps of machines, creating a semblance of comfort for your loved one becomes a critical aspect of care. Think about ways that you can make their stay as comfortable as possible through bringing familiar and comforting items from home, photos of loved ones, a favourite blanket, small plant or well-loved pillow. Give them access to things they enjoy, such as music, magazines or books. As strange as it may sound, encourage them to use the exercise facilities if there are some available.

Encourage your loved one to express their needs and concerns, and relay these to the caregiving staff. In times when they cannot speak for themselves, you may need to become their voice, ensuring their preferences aren't overlooked in clinical routines. Above all, advocate that your loved one needs to be spoken to, explained what's happening (they will be deeply confused) and treated as a human being. They may be under constant surveillance, have items removed from their possession, and feel their life is under threat; Find every way you can to give them back their dignity.

As hard as this will be for you, attempt to maintain a sense of normalcy through routine. If they enjoy a particular TV show, arrange to watch it together at the usual time. If they like reading the morning newspaper, make sure they have one each day. These small actions can make a significant difference in their mental wellbeing. Let them choose their meals when possible, decide on leisure activities, or set a schedule for family visits. A sense of control can alleviate feelings of helplessness.

If spirituality or religion is a source of solace for your loved one, facilitate access to these services. Whether it's arranging visits from a local spiritual leader or providing access to religious texts, support their faith practices. Use technology to help them stay connected with friends and family who can't visit in person.

Ultimately, engage your loved one in their care by discussing daily goals and progress. Celebrate small victories to build confidence – and plan for the future together. Talking about post-discharge plans gives them something to look forward to, instils hope and reinforces the temporary nature of hospital.

Community, or Outpatient, Treatment Order

Community treatment orders (CTOs) typically come into play after someone has been sectioned and subsequently discharged from hospital. Its legislation is designed to ensure that the individual continues to receive treatment when they return to the community, which commonly includes regular psychiatric appointments and medication adherence regimes. The nature of treatment can vary, but it usually entails meetings with multi-disciplinary teams for ongoing assessment, relevant therapeutic interventions, and the involvement of a coordinating case officer. The order typically lasts for six months but can be extended.

Noncompliance can sometimes lead to the individual being readmitted to hospital for further treatment under the order. It's important to note that their use is subject to legal requirements and ethical considerations, which are often points of debate in the field of mental health. Their application raises significant issues regarding personal autonomy and the rights of those with mental illness. It's advisable for those under a CTO, or their loved ones, to seek advice from a mental health advocate or legal professional if needed. There are processes in place for individuals to appeal against their community treatment order if they believe it's unwarranted.

After Linda, 48, was released from hospital, where she refused to take her medication, she received a community treatment order:

> Antipsychotic injections (antipsychotics) changed me into someone I didn't recognize – I put on almost three stone, neglected my appearance and withdrew from life. My energy deteriorated; a simple walk was too much. I was like a zombie. I'm not going to lie – it was the worst nine months of my life. But in the end, they stopped. However, it did highlight the need for me to take ongoing mood stabilizers and find ways to

actively self-manage my illness. So, in some ways, the experience has reinforced the need for me to look after myself, so I never have to go back to that place.

Other Avenues

Choosing the right path can be complex, but it should always be a collaborative effort orbiting around your loved one's needs and prognosis. There exist diverse methodologies to manage mental health crises, particularly those dealing with addiction and substance use. Programmes such as Alcoholics Anonymous and Narcotics Anonymous advocate for total abstinence and ongoing peer support, while harm-reduction programmes are predicated on the philosophy of minimizing the harmful outcomes associated with drug use, rather than insisting on complete abstinence. As mentioned, an example of this approach is Insite in Canada, where individuals can use substances under the watchful eye of medical professionals. This non-traditional approach underscores the need to care for individuals non-judgementally who are trying to navigate the turbulent waters of life in their own way without judgement.

Post-crisis Debrief, Recovery and Healing

In the aftermath of a crisis, the path to recovery may seem daunting. However, it is in these moments that the foundation for healing can be laid. Studies show that psychoeducational family interventions reduce relapse and rehospitalization rates of schizophrenic patients by up to 20 per cent, but I'm confident this is the case for other mental illness as well.[7]

These structured programmes improve a family's understanding of an illness, enhance communication skills and provide strategies to support the patient's treatment and recovery. Additionally, holding a structured family debrief that reflects on what happened and what could have been done differently is key for future planning. This is not about assigning blame but about gaining clarity. It requires an honest appraisal of the resources available and the gaps that need to be filled.

Modifying a crisis plan might mean altering medication, adjusting therapy schedules or even redefining emergency contacts and support networks. However, this should only be done once the dust has settled.

Recovery from a crisis is a deeply personal journey, often punctuated by moments of both clarity and confusion. The path to reclaiming oneself after such an ordeal is not simply about returning to a state of prior normalcy, but rather about the transformative process that can arise from making sense of what happened. For the person who endured the crisis, recounting the experience might be painful, yet it can also be a cathartic release, shedding the weight of unspoken fears about the breakdown of their sense of self. Your love and support may act as their only anchor in these early days. In time, the hope is that they become the protagonist in their own story of healing. In doing so, they not only reclaim their power but also guide the hands of future psychiatrists and mental health services in how best to assist them. They become their own most trusted expert.

Psychosis can sometimes be akin to a spiritual awakening, and change the course of someone's life; for example, some people may become religious or spiritual afterwards. Allowing a loved one to assimilate their discoveries and experiences is important in helping them to integrate healthily back into the world. This should be done gradually.

Healing, as much as it is a personal journey for the one who has weathered a crisis, is also a communal passage for those who stand by them in the brunt of the storm. Ricky, 34, describes his experience:

I can't fully grasp what [my family] go through, I admit it. I experience a rush from psychosis, but for them, it's the worst kind of hell. They're hit with this deep darkness that I don't see – the constant worry, the intense stress, and how it throws off their whole life. The full force of my own struggles with psychosis is quiet now, kind of lost in the mists of my mind. But for the ones I love, watching me battle through must be something else – a really overwhelming, haunting thing to see. Something they can't forget.

Healing is about the collective. Sharing experiences with others who have walked similar paths can dismantle feelings of isolation. It's in these shared narratives that everyone can find coping strategies, encouragement and, importantly, the reassurance that they are not alone.

Furthermore, engaging in joint activities can reinforce familial bonds weakened by crisis. Be it through shared meals, walks in nature, or collaborative projects, these are more than activities; they're threads rewoven into the fabric of family life, repairing and strengthening it bit by bit.

It comes down to embracing a forward gaze. Building a vision for the future that includes the loved one in recovery as an active participant. Set collective goals, celebrate each victory and plan for a future that, while acknowledging the past, isn't anchored to it. Remember, the crisis is a chapter, not the entire narrative of your – and your loved one's – story.

PART 2
CARING FOR YOURSELF

CHAPTER 6
MESSY FEELINGS OF AMBIVALENCE

"As I sat with my husband, who was riddled with early-onset Alzheimer's, I found myself shovelling cake down his throat. Part of me wanted him to choke to death while the other part just wanted him to relish every last bit."

Trisha, 52

It's rare to experience one pure emotion. We can feel tired when we're happy, or find ourselves hungry when we're sad (grieving, even). Or feel a combination of arousal and fear both at the same time. Emotions are complex and multifaceted. So why do we still berate ourselves for these overlapping messy feelings, which are simply an intrinsic part of being human?

I'm here to reassure you that whatever mix of emotions you're feeling right now, as you're reading these words, is okay. And whatever you felt yesterday, or will feel tomorrow, is also okay. They show you're alive. So, congratulations on that major achievement!

In this chapter, we will address some of the feelings you may be experiencing as someone supporting a loved one with their mental health. These may include anger, irritation, powerlessness, fear, guilt, shame, resentment, desire or even apathy. There's space for them all. Of course, there are lots of emotions I'll fail to mention too – and that's part of it – since your feelings are deeply nuanced and personal to you. Besides, sometimes a feeling can't be named.

Above all, we'll think about why embracing and processing difficult feelings will actually make you far happier than avoiding them.

Feelings Schmeelings

Feelings are bandied around *all* the time, but what on earth are they, in fact? I propose they are subjective experiences influenced by:

- our primary response to internal or external events (such as happiness, sadness or anger)
- our core beliefs (such as personal ideas about the way things should be)
- our unconscious processes (such as the things we haven't yet consciously understood)
- our environment and circumstance (such as where we are and how we feel about it)
- our physical sensations (such as racing heart or sweaty palms)
- our level of somatic awareness (such as more subtle internal bodily sensations)

So, yes, your feelings aren't straightforward; lots of factors – some conscious and some unconscious – are influencing them all the time. Which is why you may sometimes struggle to put your finger on what it is you're feeling at any given moment! And to make matters even more complicated, we know there is an interplay between these various factors, too. For example, emotions can trigger physical responses, like when fear leads to a racing heart. Conversely, physical states can influence emotional experiences: if you're exhausted, you don't need me to tell you you're likely to feel irritable. What's more, emotional states like anxiety can significantly heighten our body's somatic sensitivity – which is why we often have all sorts of physical sensations, and mystery aches and pains when our body is in fight-or-flight mode.

Further along in this chapter, we'll discuss practical and holistic techniques that can support us in the midst of big or confusing feelings.

Emotional Polarities

Every object that interacts with light casts a shadow – and the same is true for us, and our feelings. In other words, every emotion has a counterpart, which is why emotions don't exist in isolation, but as part of a spectrum. The person you love the most in the world might also be the source of the most intense frustration or resentment, because the depth of your bond amplifies your emotional response and level of expectation. Similarly, moments of joy can sometimes heighten our awareness of sadness due to the transient nature of life. It's why people cry at weddings and laugh at funerals.

Too often, we deny certain experiences or feelings, thinking they belong to others and not us! This is when we project the rejected parts of ourselves onto others – for example, blaming others for being rude, when *really* we're the one with offensive thoughts that we can't face. Or priding ourselves on always being measured, while other people are "angry". The reality is that if you are measured you are also angry, it's just you don't find it acceptable to express anger. This doesn't make you a better person, it makes you a more repressed person. Avoiding or suppressing one side of any polarity actually leads to emotional imbalance, and keeps you smaller and more restricted than you need to be. After all, you're a whole, full, rich, wonderful human being.

The concept that *we are not human beings on a spiritual journey, but spiritual beings on a human journey* rings true to me – so why deny yourself the experience of what it means to be human?

Just like the weather, we can't be sunny all the time. I mean, imagine a world where the sun is always shining, the sky is perpetually blue and no drop of rain ever falls. While this might seem like an idyllic paradise on the surface, the reality is it would be a barren, lifeless landscape. Without rain, plants wither and die; without storms, the air remains stagnant and polluted; without the chill of winter, ecosystems lose their balance. Just like nature relies on a variety of weather patterns, humans depend on a spectrum of emotions for psychological and spiritual growth, and survival. Emotions are not innately good or bad. But the meanings we ascribe to them can make them so.

Why It's Important to Do the Emotional Work

My work as a psychotherapist generally involves:

1 helping a client to process their emotions, which often entails an ending of sorts
2 gently guiding them to uncover the hidden wisdom or gift in a situation
3 offering tools and frameworks to help them move forward with fortified resilience

My point is that we need to *feel feelings*, otherwise we can't move to stages 2, 3 and beyond. Jumping straight to those stages is akin to toxic positivity or spiritual bypassing (like when people repeatedly take drugs to make them feel better so that they can avoid working through complicated emotions or psychological issues).

It's only once we have given space to whatever comes up, that we can then realize, "I am not my thoughts. I am consciousness, I am awareness."

Take the bottom of the ocean; it's always down there – but it requires a lot of effort and safety measures in place to reach it without harm. If you free-dive straight to the bottom of the ocean, you die. Therefore, I invite you to put time and effort into getting to know yourself – and discovering your own depths – slowly and deliberately. We can only tune out of our minds once we have enough self-awareness to do this.

And in turn, the more we accept and understand ourselves, the more we can learn to accept and understand others, as Oliver, 31, explains:

> Recognizing that sometimes I have negative, problematic thoughts has made me realize that there's a little bit of darkness in all of us. My mother's came out in a different way, of course, through addiction. But I think through being honest with myself about my own feelings I gained a more in-depth understanding of what being a human is.

Beautiful Rage

Anger, often viewed negatively, can be a powerful force that signals when something is wrong; when boundaries have been crossed and action needs to be taken. Constructive anger can drive social change and ignite the desire to overcome obstacles. It's a natural and necessary emotion that, when effectively released, can contribute to our emotional and physical wellbeing. The problem isn't the anger, it's the way it's managed and expressed because of the stories we layer over it. That's when we end up being passive-aggressive, huffing and puffing, saying nasty things under our breath, or suddenly exploding in a fit of rage and being physically violent. The impetus isn't wrong, but so often our response to it is.

When we're angry, our cortisol levels spike, so we need to release this energy safely to get back to healthy levels. In short bursts, cortisol can be beneficial, providing the impetus to deal with immediate challenges. However, chronic high levels of cortisol can lead to a range of health issues, including cardiovascular problems, immune issues and weight gain.

Therefore, we need to learn to release intense emotion, but do so constructively through physical release or creative expression (there's more coming up on this in Chapter 7). In my research for this book, I've spoken to countless individuals like Beth who felt they had to suppress their own joy or success to make their loved one feel better about themselves. That would make anyone angry. Beth, 26, explains:

> All I've ever wanted was a dog because my partner and I know we won't have kids. But I ended up creating a separate WhatsApp group to share puppy photos with my family because I didn't want to upset my sister, who was struggling with her depression and a little jealous of my new dog. I was hypersensitive about how she'd feel, but if I'm honest I was also pissed off with myself for doing this. So in the end, I just turned my anger in on myself.

Beth did what felt right at the time – and who's to say any of us would have done any differently? She was being incredibly considerate to her sister. However, the fact that she had such a strong emotional reaction when doing it suggests that she went against herself (that is, she kind of betrayed herself) to do it. I would argue that the root issue was not admitting to herself the frustration she felt toward her sister in the first place. Denying this led her to behave in a way that wasn't aligned with her truth – so she suffered as a result.

Now, I'm not suggesting Beth should have expressed her anger to her sister, not at all. But I am suggesting that if she could have *admitted her feelings to herself*, she could have decided to honour them in a way that felt appropriate at that time. Even if the action ended up being the same. Alternatively, she could have acknowledged her feelings and, once they had subsided, have an open communication with her sister, where she expressed her own excitement about the dog and her wish to share this joyful news with her. Encouraging her sister to respect her state of mind and needs may even have created a healthier dynamic and helped the sisters to recognize *each other's* boundaries.

Jealousy Works Both Ways

According to studies, around 65 per cent of mothers and 70 per cent of fathers exhibit a preference for one sibling over another.[1] However, there's something particularly unique about sibling relationships where one sibling has a mental health issue. These dynamics can stir up all kinds of sibling rivalry. The one in the supporting role may feel jealous of the attention their sibling commands because of their struggles, thinking, "Well, what if I want to lose my shit and go crazy?" I've heard this from umpteen individuals who, while their "sick sibling was babysat", act out through promiscuity or substances, reasoning that if they couldn't get their parents' attention, at least they could get attention from others.

Conversely, the one who is struggling may feel jealous of their "perfect" sibling, who seems to have it all *sans* the mental health issue. They may forever be comparing themselves to their sibling and always feel that they come up short. These unspoken dynamics can take on a life of their own, which is something we'll look at in more depth in Chapter 10.

Nonetheless, ambivalent feelings such as these are wholly natural and valid. How we are treated by our parents in the sibling hierarchy can have a tremendous impact on our self-worth and the way we form relationships later on. Sometimes, people tell me about severe abuse they encountered from a sibling who was mentally unwell or unhappy. When this goes unrecognized by parents, it sends a clear message to the individual that the world is unsafe and that they don't matter. Abuse might start subtly but can escalate to severe physical or emotional harm. It takes tremendous resilience, and often considerable therapy, but such victims can end up learning to honour their experiences and feelings, and speak out. Over the years, I've met many inspirational people who were neglected or abused, and who later became strong advocates for justice.

Feelings Toward the Narcissist

Ambivalent feelings extend beyond sibling dynamics, of course. If we have a parent or other close family member who we perceive to be narcissistic and draining, the complexity of emotions only deepens. Jessica, 34, described to me how her mother's anxiety, accompanied by her narcissism, meant that she was always the one who everyone worried about. Even as a child, Jessica's needs were secondary to ensuring that her mother was okay and well-attended to. The effects on her were sizable and, as a result, she felt like she missed out on much of her childhood; she could never be naughty, or claim attention for herself – something every child should rightfully do. In addition, she felt overly responsible for never doing anything that made her mother even more anxious, which cut out a lot of sports and things she might have enjoyed. Whether or not her mother realized it, the whole family revolved around her, and Jessica's self-worth depreciated as a result. She internalized the belief that she wasn't important and needed to subjugate her own feelings and needs. This made her intensely shy and self-loathing; yet she also found it hard to separate from her mother for fear of what it would do to her. She felt trapped in her love and care for her. Maybe this is a familiar feeling to you, too?

The reality is that when someone doesn't feel well a lot of the time, they occupy a lot of the space and take the oxygen for themselves. And everyone else responds to this differently. Some people might find a way to illicit attention for themselves through honing a special gift or skill, while others like Jessica might shrink in stature.

Jim Carrey, whose mother was addicted to painkillers, has talked openly about the abandonment he experienced because of her often being high. He took it upon himself to become the funny guy and entertain her through comedy. Luckily for him – and the world – he got great at doing that and turned it into a glittering career. But who might he have been if he hadn't internalized the need to play the entertainer?

If You've Stopped Caring ...

Your bandwidth will ebb and flow throughout life based on whatever you're experiencing at that time. When we have little capacity left, we often just stop caring. Not because we're awful people, but because it's the psyche's way of shutting down and protecting itself (read more about hypoarousal in Chapter 7, on burnout). Pete, 42, describes how he put up emotional blockers to survive:

> I've come out of the situation with my bipolar mother relatively unaffected. I think the only negative thing is that it perhaps brought out a slightly sociopathic, narcissistic side of my personality where I became less empathic to people who are going through tough times. Maybe because I almost consciously don't put myself in the shoes of someone who's going through a negative experience because I don't want to feel it all over again. I just find myself protecting myself from that sort of negative emotional loop. Which is something I still need to work on because I want to be more empathic for my wife.

Pete's response is perfectly natural and not to be judged. The emotional toll of supporting a loved one who is struggling with their mental health is exhausting. I'm sure we've all shut off parts of ourselves to survive (which is smart, if you think about it). However, if this tendency goes unchecked, we can end up *cut off from ourselves*. And this can be a breeding ground for anxiety and/or addiction issues. We may end up always looking for ways to numb our own feelings.

Often, this sense of detachment is accompanied by a type of guilt, since society often pressures us to be endlessly patient; but this is an unhealthy construct. When addiction is in the picture, there's also a pervasive worry about what might happen next. You might even wish the nightmare would end, which can result in feelings of shame. But adding a layer of guilt on top of our feelings is paralysing, leaving us stuck in a cycle of self-criticism.

To break this cycle, it's crucial to acknowledge and process guilt. Ignoring it allows it to fester and therefore become an unconscious driver. By confronting apathy, guilt and the whole gamut of our feelings, and understanding their roots, we can release their hold on us.

Navigating Change and Loss

Mental health challenges can sometimes alter a person in profound ways. While their physical appearance (sometimes) remains the same, their behaviour and personality might shift, making them feel unfamiliar. It's natural to experience a sense of loss for the person they once were, and acknowledging these feelings is an important part of the healing process. In therapy, we recognize that the loss of one aspect of life can bring up feelings related to other losses or disappointments, making the current situation feel more overwhelming.

Participating in rituals that facilitate letting go, such as writing letters and burning them, or creating a piece of art to symbolize a transition, can be very healing. In the therapy room, we often use chair work, which is when we get to have an imaginary conversation or interaction with someone, which can help us find closure or greater understanding. This is a method from Gestalt therapy, and something you might want to explore more for yourself.

> **PROMPT:** Reflect on whether there's anything you need to do to process a change in your loved one – or in your relationship. Is there a type of grief that needs to be experienced and assimilated somehow?

If your loved one has survived a suicide attempt, you might be experiencing a whirlwind of mixed emotions. There may be profound relief that they're alive, mingled with rage, disapproval and guilt. The fear of a future attempt may loom large, creating a constant undercurrent of anxiety. When someone you care about attempts suicide, it can shatter your perception of them. Their illness may have transformed them in ways that are difficult to comprehend. You may find yourself mourning the life and relationship you once had.

If someone later does kill themselves, the emotional complexity intensifies. Alongside grief and sorrow, there might even be a sense of respite. Such relief is often shrouded in guilt and shame, as societal beliefs about death and love conflict with this. It's essential you know that your feelings do not diminish the love you have for them. They simply highlight the immense pain and helplessness you felt watching them struggle.

Unconditional love is tested in the most profound ways in these situations. One person shared with me, "I think it's taught me a lot about what unconditional love actually means, as cheesy and cliché as that sounds. There were definitely times I hated her, and times... I feel so guilty saying it, but the honest truth is there were moments where I thought maybe it would be easier if she didn't come back." This raw honesty acknowledges the unbearable tension between love and pain, hope and despair.

Such feelings do not make you a bad person; they make you human. The extreme stress and emotional turmoil of caring for someone who is suicidal can bring out these reactions. It's essential to find a way to process these feelings, whether through therapy, support groups, or confiding in trusted friends or family. Healing involves accepting these messy emotions as part of the journey and understanding that they're a natural response to an extraordinarily challenging situation.

The way through this emotional landscape is not linear. There may be days of intense sadness, moments of peace, and times of acute anger. Allow yourself to feel these emotions without judgement. Each feeling is a testament to the depth of your love and the impact of the loss.

Remember, you are not alone. Many have walked this path and found ways to navigate life alongside the pain by continuing to honour the memory of their loved one. Seeking help and connecting with others who understand your experience can be invaluable. In time, you may even find a renewed understanding of what it means to love, even in the face of immense pain.

Actions Matter, Not Feelings

We've spent most of this chapter talking about the importance of processing emotions; that the only way out of them is to go through them. However, I'm also here to share that the content of your feelings doesn't actually matter: what matters is the way you relate to them.

Emotions are rooted in biology. They are complex physiological and psychological responses designed to help us navigate our world. They're not there to make us happy, but to keep us alive. They do not carry inherent value judgements of being "good" or "bad". Instead, they're simply experiences that provide information. Sadness, for example, signals a loss or unmet need, while anger can indicate that a boundary has been crossed. Every person experiences a wide range of emotions, and this diversity is a normal aspect of being human. According to the University of Berkeley, people experience an average of 27 distinct emotions daily.[2] Hopefully that stat makes you feel a little less alone! It also proves how fleeting emotions are.

My point is that it's your beliefs and the stories you layer onto your emotions that can either cripple or free you, not the emotions themselves. For example, feeling anxious before a presentation isn't wrong or strange, but depending on the story you tell yourself about the anxiety, it can lead to feelings of inadequacy or a fear of failure that can be debilitating. Conversely, the anxiety could be interpreted as nervous excitement. Therefore, it's not the feeling of physical sensation that matters, but how we respond to it that can lead to positive or negative outcomes. Constructive responses involve acknowledging and understanding feelings, and using them as a guide for appropriate action or inaction, whereas destructive responses involve suppressing feelings, reacting impulsively or allowing them to dominate our behaviour.

Clearly you can't and shouldn't attempt to work through all 27 fleeting emotions, but if there are certain feelings that are prominent and stick around, it's no good ignoring them and hoping they'll just go away. Unfortunately, it takes effort for something to effortlessly go. And that's called mindfulness.

If you take one point away from this chapter, let it be this: we live in fear of our feelings overtaking us, but *feelings do not have to control our actions.* However, they're more likely to do so if they're suppressed, as that's when they become distorted.

When we accept our feelings they lose their power, and actually they tend to go away pretty quickly. Taking a sledgehammer to them does no good. In fact, it often breeds the absolute opposite response, which is resistance. You know the drill: if I tell you *not* to imagine a pink elephant, it's all you will be able to think of.

Through acknowledging the shadowy parts of ourselves, we discover the ability to choose how we live. When we understand that we sometimes struggle with hateful thoughts and rage, we can choose to decide how to respond to them when they surface. We can then learn to soothe the raging parts of ourselves, connect with our bodily signals on a deeper level, and not be afraid when the heat rises in us, because we will know this aspect of ourselves and how to meet it. But if we deny this aspect, we live in fear of it surfacing. That fear will then dominate our thoughts and in the end our actions. And the only thing that really matters at the end of the day is our actions. Besides, the more forgiving we are of our own complex feelings, the more forgiving we become of others' complexities.

Management Techniques

Once we have faced our demons, aka our inner turmoil, we can expand our consciousness to realize that the only thing that exists is awareness; everything is filtered through the lens of our awareness. When we know this to be true, we're able to rise above our experience.

Here is my model for fostering self-awareness, acceptance and, ultimately, nonattachment when it comes to feelings. The acronym for the model is easy to remember – it's FEEL – and here's what it stands for.

The FEEL model:
F stands for Focus: Focus on the present moment and the sensations in your body. Take a few deep breaths and allow yourself to focus on whatever is going on for you in the here and now.

E stands for Examine: Examine the emotions that arise without judgement. Notice what you are feeling and whether the sensations in your body change. Be curious and open.

E stands for Embrace: Embrace your feelings with compassion, as though you're giving them a welcoming hug.

Allow yourself to feel whatever arises, embracing it as part of your current experience.

L is for Let Go: Let go of attachment to your emotions and to your preconceived ideas about them. Understand that feelings are temporary and will pass. Release any need to hold on to them with the help of the out-breath.

Everything in the world is whole and exists simultaneously. The task is, therefore, to flow through life and its emotions, while holding on to the fact that we are more than the experience itself. Real love is a bit like this; it encapsulates all feelings, and yet transcends them all. Sometimes that means being angry at someone, sometimes blaming them and, in spite of it all, loving them. That is enduring love. May you find enduring love first for yourself and then for those you choose to bestow it upon. And, as part of caring for yourself, know that it's okay to admit that you have ambivalent feelings. Denying aspects of your experience can lead to burnout, which we'll look at next.

CHAPTER 7
MANAGING BURNOUT AND STRESS

"As I supported my sister through her eating disorder and heard about the abuse she had experienced at the hands of her ex-boyfriend, I became intensely distressed. I started to experience her pain as if it were my own. I found it hard to sleep at night and pulled away from a lot of friends. Eventually, my sister suggested I speak to someone, because my response wasn't helping either of us. Therapy helped me to recognize I was experiencing a type of secondary trauma. Only then could I begin to regain my wellbeing and take the steps needed to truly help her."

CJ, 19

Caring for a loved one with a mental health condition can be physically and emotionally tiring – but would you be able to recognize the signs of secondary traumatic stress or burnout if they came knocking at your door? Some of us become so accustomed to living with high levels of (dis)stress, we do it for years before any crash takes place.

As a society, we're programmed to believe that stress is good for us, and we should just accept it. We often don't leave jobs, or relationships, when they're stressful. Instead, we shoulder (dis)stress like superheroes. And that's okay for a time; admirable even. But here's the thing: the earlier you can intervene, the smaller the crash – and wreckage – usually is. Hence, in this chapter, we'll cover what to do if you find yourself heading toward a collapse.

While the last thing I wish to do is stress you out more, I'll be asking you to take a good, hard look at yourself and evaluate how you're doing. Because while challenging circumstances are often beyond our control, we can choose to (re-)programme our responses. We'll also look to the animal kingdom to see if there's anything we can learn from them about how to deal with stress better. Let's begin by considering what burnout actually is.

Are You Experiencing Burnout?

Burnout is now recognized by the World Health Organization as an "occupational phenomenon", signalling the need for workplace interventions and better stress management. However, this definition is insufficient in my view. It's not something that's only brought on by work, or unemployment. It can be brought on by experiencing any type of prolonged stress.

In the journey of supporting a loved one with mental health challenges, it's easy to cross the invisible line into the realm of burnout without even noticing. Especially when you consider that workforce shortages mean informal carers are left to fill in the gaps – in the UK alone, unpaid family and friends who care for loved ones are the equivalent to four million paid care workers![1] So how can you recognize the signs before it's too late?

Physically, the signs of burnout can be subtle yet persistent. You might experience an unshakable tiredness, a kind of fatigue that lingers despite rest. Changes in appetite or sleep patterns might occur, and your body might speak its stress through frequent headaches or muscle pain. Behaviourally, you might become increasingly irritable, snapping at even the smallest things. There may be self-doubt that wasn't there before, and you might find yourself experiencing feelings of detachment or growing cynicism. Cognitively, burnout can cloud your mind and give you serious brain fog. Concentration becomes a Herculean task, and there's a constant dread about what the day may bring, especially if that involves more demands.

Women are more prone to burnout, as are certain personality types, but it can happen to anyone. Typically, those affected tend to be overachievers and perfectionists, who take on too much and don't ask for help. Privately, they may feel shame that they aren't coping better. If you are that way inclined, be aware that you're more susceptible to burnout. Take stock and make some interventions *today*. Don't let it get to the point where it takes months, or even years to recover.

Burnout is the culmination of unmitigated stress, where the flight-or-fight response is ceaselessly provoked, leaving no room for the restorative rest-and-digest phase. Ordinarily, after a stressful incident, our bodies are designed to return to a state of balance, where cortisol levels normalize and we can enjoy a moment of calm. However, dysregulation occurs when this dance is disrupted – when the rest phase eludes us, leaving us stranded in a state of perpetual alertness, a bit like a relentless fire alarm blaring long after the flames are extinguished.

The result is one of hyperarousal, a state akin to anxiety: jumpiness, tension, breathlessness, decision paralysis, disturbed sleep, chest pains, difficulty concentrating, rapid heartbeat and IBS-like symptoms. This feeling of being on edge might lead us to becoming acutely aware in each moment of someone else's needs, instead of our own. We may continually pre-empt other people's actions as a way of safeguarding against danger.

If this experience lasts too long, our bodies cannot sustain this hypervigilant state and may shift into *hypoarousal* – a state akin to depression. This manifests as sluggishness, hopelessness and numbness. Behaviourally, we might withdraw into passivity, and zone out for hours while watching TV or sleep excessively. In its extremity, this state can lead to fainting or collapsing. Why? Because hypoarousal is characterized by a decrease in physiological and emotional reactivity, often likened to the "freeze" response. This is the body's way of protecting itself, much like how animals play dead in the wild. It could also be considered a mechanism for energy conservation during times of prolonged stress or threat, where fighting or fleeing is not an option.

Studies examining physiological markers, such as cortisol levels and heart rate variability, indicate that both hyperarousal (elevated cortisol and heart rate) and hypoarousal (blunted cortisol response and low heart rate variability) can be present in individuals experiencing burnout. These findings show that burnout can manifest in different ways for different people (also depending on the duration of the stress) – although you might go down the route of getting your own bloods tested to confirm what's going on for you.

My own experience with burnout showed me that it's a profoundly physiological phenomenon. One of the most valuable things I did was to get my bloodwork done and seek out a practitioner of functional medicine to evaluate the results. For those unfamiliar with functional medicine, it typically involves comprehensive testing to understand the intricate interplay of diet, environment and genetics in individual health. It's a smart path for those of us who don't fit into a neat medical box, but who present with more complex and chronic symptoms.

Alongside getting my blood work done (which revealed various deficiencies such as low levels of vitamin C and iron), a saliva test revealed my cortisol levels were alarmingly high first thing in the morning. My body and brain were being flooded with stress hormones from the moment I woke up! I was ready for combat – fight or flight – much less my morning mug of coffee (which I quickly replaced with green tea).

My test results also pointed to some key hormonal imbalances. I was advised to take specific supplements and my body slowly began to regain equilibrium. The impact was profound: not only did I feel more balanced within the space of a month, but my capacity to cope with daily stressors improved significantly.

This experience underscores the importance of learning to listen to your body and catering to its specific needs if you want to bolster resilience.

SYMPTOMS OF HYPERAROUSAL AND HYPOAROUSAL

Here's a quick recap of hyperarousal and hypoarousal and how they're linked to burnout.

Hyperarousal
... is when the body's fight-or-flight mechanisms are persistently activated. Symptoms include:

- anxiety and irritability
- insomnia or disrupted sleep
- hypervigilance (constantly feeling on edge)
- increased heart rate and blood pressure
- difficulty concentrating
- tense body
- overly worrying about others

Hyperarousal is often closely linked to the earlier stages of stress and burnout. When someone is in a hyperaroused state for an extended period, their body and mind are continuously overtaxed, which depletes their energy reserves and resilience.

Practices to explore: yoga nidra, massage, acupuncture, grounding exercises, slowing down the breath, going for a mindful walk in nature, imagining a safe space, body scan, having a warm bath, self-soothing techniques such as firmly stroking down the length of your arms, practising tai chi, softening or closing the eyes, and returning to stillness.

Hypoarousal

... is characterized by reduced physiological and emotional responses. It involves an underactive stress response, often associated with feelings of numbness, disconnection and low energy. Symptoms include:

- emotional numbness or blunting
- fatigue and low energy levels
- depression or lack of motivation
- social withdrawal and detachment
- difficulty initiating and completing tasks

Hypoarousal is more commonly associated with the later stages of stress and burnout, particularly after prolonged periods of hyperarousal. When the body and mind can no longer sustain a high level of stress response, they may shift into freeze mode as a protective mechanism. This can lead to depersonalization (a sense of disconnection from others and the world).

Practices to explore: going for a brisk walk outdoors, rubbing your hands together fast, shaking out the body, using your voice to speak loudly, pushing away the wall, dancing, playing upbeat music, practising the yogic fire breath, increasing your heart rate, and engaging your five senses consciously.

The first step is to identify if you're experiencing burnout and whereabouts in the journey you might be. The best way to ascertain this is through getting your blood and saliva tested. These tests can reveal any underlying issues or deficiencies that may be contributing to your symptoms. Recognizing that you're struggling isn't a sign of failure. It's the absolute opposite: it's the start of healing. Ignoring the signs of burnout can lead to severe health issues, often resulting in emergency hospital visits due to anxiety-induced chest pains mistaken for heart attacks or neglected infections that escalate because people feel they're "too busy" to address them. Continuing down the burnout road only ends one way – with a *CRASH*.

> **PROMPT:** Do you identify with either – or both – of the states described above? Whereabouts on your burnout journey do you feel you are? Does an image come to mind? If so, draw it or jot it down.

Addressing Compassion Fatigue

Compassion fatigue, also known as secondary traumatic stress, occurs when a caregiver becomes deeply affected by the trauma and suffering of those they care for. However, you don't have to be a professional caregiver to experience this. In fact, I believe it's most prevalent when someone we love a great deal has experienced trauma.

It's possible that you're experiencing compassion fatigue at the moment if you're emotionally numb, increasingly anxious, and struggling with intrusive thoughts and a sense of helplessness. In the case of CJ, whose words opened this chapter, her deep empathy for her sister led her into the depths of compassion fatigue. CJ found herself unable to sleep, riddled with disturbing thoughts and images of her sister being abused by her ex-boyfriend. It was as if the trauma her sister had endured had transferred itself onto CJ.

The fact that her sister also had a tendency to disown her pain created a vacuum that CJ, out of love and a sense of duty, felt compelled to fill. This phenomenon where one person energetically absorbs the distress of another is a hallmark of compassion fatigue and secondary traumatic stress.

To navigate a way out of this cycle, both CJ and her sister required individual therapy. I worked with CJ on developing coping mechanisms to handle her intrusive thoughts and anxiety, mostly through distraction. However, what was more fundamental was helping her to establish clear emotional and psychological boundaries (which is what Chapter 8 is all about).

CJ's fixation on her sister's trauma also underscored a critical point that I'd like to make to you now: diving deeply into another person's trauma without professional training can be detrimental to all parties. CJ, despite her best intentions, was not equipped to handle the reality of her sister's past. The fact that she hadn't worked through her own historic issues made her especially unable – and unsafe – to do this with, too.

Strategies to Support Yourself

To keep yourself and your stress levels in check, make self-awareness your goal. Journaling can help you identify unhealthy patterns and triggers of burnout, while mind–body practices can guide your nervous system back to balance. Above all, it's about forming a deeper connection with yourself. The easiest entry point to doing this is via the breath – and the good news is that it's free of charge and something that is always available to you. Here's a simple breathing exercise to get started.

FOUR–SEVEN–EIGHT BREATHING

Breathwork is a powerful tool for self-regulation. I recommend the four–seven–eight breath (developed by Dr Andrew Weil), because it's easy to remember and it's particularly effective for quickly reducing anxiety and promoting relaxation.

1 Inhale for a count of four through the nose.
2 Hold for a count of seven.
3 Exhale completely through the mouth for a count of eight, ideally making a *whooshing* sound.

Once you're familiar with this breathing exercise, you could try placing one hand on your chest and the other hand on your belly while doing it. Form a connection with your body, your skin and your own touch. When we're stressed, we tend to tighten up and shut down, so this is all about softening into yourself and your senses. The more often you do this, the less fearful you will become of your bodily sensations, including the way your body responds to stress (such as with a tight chest or faster heartbeat). That way, you'll be able to bring mindful attention to these sensations and then let them pass through you more easily, trusting that sensations, like feelings, are often transient.

PRIORITIZING SELF-CARE

Since stress and burnout manifest physically, don't underestimate the need to look after the physical pillar of your health (see page 101), paying attention to sleep, nutrition, exercise and somatic healing. Here are a few things you might wish to consider:

- Quality sleep is vital if you're required to be emotionally available for your loved one. If there is a practical requirement for you to remain contactable, set your phone to night mode, or use "do not disturb" settings, with exceptions for specific contacts.
- Stress triggers the body's inflammatory response. Therefore, a diet rich in whole foods, anti-inflammatory spices, healthy fats and antioxidants can serve as a buffer against stress's toll on the body.
- Physical activity makes the body release a cocktail of mood-boosting hormones, including endorphins and dopamine. Even short bursts of activity – such as a brisk walk at lunchtime or practising yoga – significantly boost mental and physical wellbeing.
- Invest time in finding physical methods to bring yourself out of fight, flight or freeze mode. See pages 184–6 on hyperarousal and hypoarousal to try to work out what your body needs.

Learning from the Animal Kingdom

Before we complete this chapter, I thought I'd take you somewhere unexpected – and that's out into the wild. The animal kingdom centres on survival, which is mighty stressful! Some species "play dead" as a survival strategy, mimicking hypoarousal. However, beyond this freeze response, animals employ a range of dynamic stress management techniques that offer more proactive strategies for humans. Here are some key insights that might be useful…

Lobsters: shedding the old shell

Lobsters become uncomfortable when they outgrow their shells, so they have to shed them to form new, larger ones. This process, called moulting, is stressful and leaves the lobster vulnerable for a period of time, as their big new shell is initially softer than the old one. That's when they retreat to a hiding place, like a rocky cave, to avoid potential danger, while their new shell hardens.

The lesson: Stress can help us to grow, but only up to a point. Then it's time to take a pause, retreat and rejuvenate. If you don't give yourself the time to do this, you risk injuring yourself – or others – when you're under-resourced to cope. Rather, through learning to take a step back, we can recover and come back stronger. Professional carers experience the need for renewal, too, whether through taking time off, going on vacation, replenishing their reserves through hobbies, or just relaxing, for example.

Ducks: shaking off stress

After a stressful encounter such as a confrontation, ducks engage in a vigorous shaking or flapping of their wings. This is known as a "displacement activity" and is done when conflicting motivations or stress are experienced. This physical release helps them to find an outlet for their nervous energy, so that they can then return to a calm state.

The lesson: Engaging in a physical activity, such as shaking out the body, dancing or tapping fingers immediately after a stressful event, can prevent stress from building up and becoming chronic and more harmful.

Elephants: social support

Elephants are known for their strong social bonds and communal living. For example, when faced with a threat, they collectively form a protective circle around the more vulnerable members of the group. Similarly, they exhibit mourning behaviours when a member of their herd dies. They gather around the deceased, touching and smelling the body, and show signs of distress. This collective mourning helps the herd cope with the loss.

The lesson: Offering and receiving help within the community and building a supportive network reduces the impact of stress on the individual. This also ties into research that shows actively seeking support for yourself fosters resilience and better adjustment, including in young carers.[2]

Zebras: living in the moment

Zebras are constantly under threat from predators. When a predator is detected, they flee as a herd. This rapid response ensures their survival but involves a significant stress response characterized by increased heart rate and adrenaline release. However, once the threat has passed, zebras have an incredible ability to quickly return to a state of calm. This rapid down-regulation of their stress response prevents the build-up of chronic stress.

The lesson: Taking decisive action in the moment can help manage immediate stress and prevent a situation from escalating. Afterwards, finding ways to consciously regulate our stress response is key – be that through techniques such as deep breathing, progressive muscle relaxation or mindfulness meditation.

Bees: structured routine

Bees, particularly honeybees, exhibit remarkable strategies for managing stress through their highly structured social organization and routine. Effective communication and coordination are essential for the smooth functioning of the bee colony. For example, bees work together to maintain the hive's temperature, either by clustering together to generate heat or by fanning their wings to cool it down. Similarly, they perform the waggle dance to communicate the location of food sources to other members of the hive.

The lesson: Sharing resources and responsibilities to distribute the workload prevents burnout and builds strength in numbers. This might include delegating tasks, reorganizing workflows or creating new opportunities for expansion and process improvement. Yes, that's right, ensuring you have at least four layers of support in place for both your loved one and yourself is essential.

So, there it is: if the body is stressed, meet it where it is. And that means working somatically to calm down your nervous system, heal and make way for change. In the next chapter, we'll look at some of the changes you might want to make to preserve your energy and create space for yourself through setting boundaries.

CHAPTER 8
SETTING AND HOLDING BOUNDARIES

"My boundaries used to be about as solid as a wet paper bag. If someone needed something, I'd cave, no matter what it cost me. It was like I was open 24/7, a walk-in store with no locks on the doors. It took me a long time to realize I was the one who needed to flip the sign to 'closed' once in a while."

Mike, 45

Boundaries are the invisible structures that shape our interactions. They help us to discern what belongs to us and what belongs to someone else. Let's think of them as the guardians of our inner peace. In this chapter, we will explore how to set and hold your own boundaries, as well as how to recognize if you're in a codependent relationship.

If you don't yet know what your boundaries are, that's okay, too. We will start to map these out through considering your needs and values. In understanding our boundaries, we understand ourselves and in setting them in place, we are set free.

Where Do Our Personal Boundaries Come From?

The demarcation lines we draw around us are largely etched during the first seven years of our lives. That's when we unknowingly absorb from our caregiver/s a sense of what behaviour is acceptable versus unacceptable. For example, consider your childhood dinner table – a microcosm of boundaries in action – where ideas about manners, food and conversation created a shared understanding of what mealtimes are. I'm always struck by how many of my therapy clients (regardless of their background) didn't regularly sit down for a family meal. Instead, they were taught to heat up microwave meals while Mum and Dad were absent. This lack of a clearly delineated mealtime, where food was prepared and enjoyed together, had a marked impact on many of them. Some developed eating disorders, while others have struggled to accept nourishment in other ways.

Similarly, our relationship to our bodies is often tied to our family's approach to personal space, nudity and physical expressions of love. One family's comfort with openness may contrast with another's emphasis on privacy, each setting a distinct "boundary norm" for the infant. The list goes on: the way money was handled; how chores were divvied up; how tantrums were managed; and so forth. These all form "boundaries blueprints" for the way we later operate.

You see, from the moment we're born, we create an internal image of ourselves and the significant people in our lives. These "internal objects", as they're known in therapy, become templates that can govern our future if we're not careful. Therefore, the way a caregiver respects or violates a child's boundaries will influence that child's ability to set and respect their own boundaries (as well as other people's boundaries) later in life, unless it's something they're acutely aware of. My point is that when we have a better understanding of our blueprints, we can do a better job at setting boundaries in the present day. Why's that? Because around 90 per cent of what we perceive about our current environment is based on past experience. With that in mind, we're now going to take a brief look at your early life.

GET TO KNOW YOUR BOUNDARIES BLUEPRINT

Please reflect on the following questions and write down your answers in your journal.

1 How did your caregivers demonstrate boundaries? Were there clear rules and expectations, or were boundaries ambiguous and fluid?
2 Identify childhood moments when your personal space or autonomy was disregarded.
3 Think about how discipline was handled in your home. Was it consistent and fair, or unpredictable and harsh?
4 Recall how emotions were expressed and dealt with in your family. Was there space for all family members to express their feelings openly, or were there unspoken rules about what emotions were acceptable?
5 Identify any repeated phrases or messages about decision-making and saying "no" that you received growing up.

To be clear, most people have issues with setting boundaries and today's "always on" culture (thank you, smartphone) has done nothing to quash this. I think many of us do things we don't want because we're too afraid to put a much-needed boundary in place. Hopefully the previous exercise allowed you to identify your own personal reasons for this.

PROMPT: Can you think of a time when you didn't set a boundary with your loved one when you needed to?

Act or Pay

If you feel used, angry or guilty a lot of the time, it's an indication that you need to set some boundaries. Simply knowing your boundaries blueprint isn't enough. Boundaries should be thought of as dynamic forces that propel us toward healthier behaviour. They are all about action, momentum and response, requiring proactive management and continuous reinforcement.

It's also important to recognize that most of us don't change our behaviour without a forcing function. We only change when the discomfort associated with staying the same outweighs the apprehension of trying something new. I call it "act or pay", because the price of inaction costs more than the price of change! Transformation only occurs when we accept this to be true.

DO A LIFE INVENTORY

We're going to start to evaluate the cost of your boundaries – or lack of them.

In your journal, jot down how a lack of boundaries might be contributing to each of these aspects of your life.

- **Physical health** (including energy levels, blood pressure, attending your own medical appointments, pre-existing conditions, diet). For example, "I never schedule my own check-ups even though I've been told I'm pre-diabetic."
- **Mental health** (including your sense of peace, stress levels, cognitive wellbeing, resilience). For example, "I'm on anti-anxiety medication and often feel pulled in every direction, but I still can't say no."

- **Financial health** (incl. your savings, spending, whether you're owed money). For example, "I can't trust my partner with his spending, and we have a joint account, so some months we can't pay our bills, including food."
- **Other relationships** (incl. friends, family, other meaningful relations, your social life). For example, "My wife is anxious and likes me around a lot, so I've stopped meeting up with my friends."
- **Work commitments** (incl. your productivity, sick days, ability to concentrate, relationships at work). For example, "I haven't chased a promotion or pay rise in five years, both of which I really want, because I need to clock off early every day."

It might now be worth considering how much of what you have written down is directly correlated to supporting your loved one. It can be easy to point the finger and "blame" another person, or situation, for your own lack of self-care. And sometimes it is absolutely the driver. But perhaps the underlying issue is your own lack of boundaries with yourself?

You know the drill: you'd never miss someone else's health appointment but struggle to schedule one for yourself. You sometimes forget to eat but always feed your family. And so on. I have found this behaviour tends to correlate with people who experienced neglect in their childhood. The belief gets internalized that somehow they don't matter; whereas, "If I pin my existence on looking after someone else, I matter."

The tendency to put oneself last is especially prevalent amongst women, who end up in supporting roles both professionally and personally. For example, women do three times more unpaid care work than men.[1] And those who do find themselves in leadership positions are far more likely to experience imposter syndrome than men (75 per cent of female execs across different industries report feeling like a fraud).[2]

Whether this applies to you or not, it's possible that you can identify with the feeling of being in the shadows. And here's the thing: the more you learn not to make a fuss, the more likely you are to end up in codependent relationships. Why? Because when we suppress our own needs and desires to avoid conflict or attention, we inadvertently set the stage for a dynamic where taking care of others becomes our primary way of connecting with them.

Is It Codependency?

Let me be clear: just because you find yourself in a supportive role, this doesn't mean you're in a codependent relationship. Codependent relationships are characterized by a chronic pattern of lost selfhood and over-reliance on the other person. In these relationships, one person typically sacrifices their needs, desires and health to meet the needs of another. Quite often, they're not even able to distinguish their own needs from those of the person they're supporting.

Let's consider Mike, 42, who's a very successful entrepreneur. However, he doesn't really feel worthy and has a lot of guilt about his privilege. Partly that's down to his personality and innate brilliance, which have meant that things have come fairly easily to him. But it's also down to the fact that he has a severely disabled younger brother, who he's always needed to support. He can now afford to provide round-the-clock care for both him and their elderly mother, who raised them singlehandedly. However, Mike has also always attracted friends, in particular romantic partners, who "need" a lot from him. Two of his previous girlfriends experienced eating disorders, addiction issues and self-harmed, and he rescued his current girlfriend, Lottie, from an abusive relationship. He loves Lottie very much, but it's clear this relationship is based on him continually coming to her rescue, be that through money or sorting out her legal and emotional issues. I asked him to consider whether he has a saviour complex, based on his upbringing.

Saviour complex, also known as the "white knight" syndrome, is when someone has a compulsive need to save others, which often stems from an unconscious desire to feel needed or to distract oneself from one's own issues and vulnerabilities. For this reason, saviours may seek out, or be attracted to those who are in vulnerable or precarious situations. It was only when Mike's younger brother tragically passed away and he himself needed support for the first time (and couldn't be as present for Lottie and her problems) that he finally saw the nature of their asymmetrical relationship.

Features of saviour complex include:

- **Attraction to unstable situations**: gravitating toward relationships where the other party is seen as helpless or in distress, requiring intervention.
- **Self-esteem tied to helping**: deriving self-worth predominantly from the ability to help, fix or save others.
- **Resentment over time**: although the initial desire to help is genuine, resentment may build if the saviour's efforts aren't appreciated or reciprocated as expected.
- **Neglect of own needs**: individuals may neglect their own emotional or physical wellbeing because they're focused on helping others.
- **Chronic disappointment**: frequently disappointed when their saving efforts don't lead to the expected changes, leading to cycles of frustration.

People with a saviour complex often end up in codependent relationships, which traps both individuals in assigned roles: one person is the "fixer" and the other "needs to be fixed".

"Fixers" are scared to let go of being indispensable. Often, these individuals assumed responsibility in their family from a young age and cared for other members. Over time, their deep-seated need for approval becomes an adaptive survival strategy – since being useful kept them "safe", or loved. So they continue to go above and beyond for others to ward off the anxiety of being abandoned; whereas the one "looking to be fixed" may be stuck in a cycle of not taking responsibility for themselves, instead outsourcing their problems to others.

My belief is that the driver for both individuals is their search for a secure base (aka a reliable place of safety), which is ideally achieved in childhood through a secure attachment to a parental figure.

Relationship addiction can occur when you fear the relationship ending so much that you're willing to lose or betray yourself to keep it going. It looks like two people who aren't exploring their individuality but are clinging on to each other – and inadvertently holding one another back. In these relationships, issues of control play out. The first step is to become honest with yourself if this is the case. Very often the dynamic fluctuates between the extremes of either controlling the other person, or allowing them to control us.

Still wondering if you're in a codependent relationship? Here's a checklist:

- **Self-sacrifice**: Are you constantly setting aside your own needs for your loved one?
- **Approval seeking**: Do you feel a compulsive need for their approval and fear their rejection?
- **Responsibility for others**: Do you often take on their responsibilities as your own, feeling responsible for their happiness and wellbeing?

- **Boundaries:** Is it challenging for you to set and maintain boundaries with your loved one?
- **Self-worth:** Is your self-worth heavily influenced by your ability to "solve" their problems or by how much they rely on you?
- **Neglecting other relationships:** Have your relationships with other friends and family deteriorated?
- **Obsession with relationship:** Do you obsess over this particular relationship at the cost of your own interests, hobbies or wellbeing?
- **Difficulty communicating:** Are you afraid to express your true feelings and needs to your partner?
- **Fear of abandonment:** Do you maintain the relationship as it is because you're afraid of being alone?
- **Resentment:** Do you harbour feelings of resentment because of the imbalanced nature of your giving and their taking?
- **Control:** Are decisions made through mutual agreement and respect for independence, or are they often dictated by one person's demands, fears or anxieties, leading to a cycle of compliance?
- **Lying:** Do you lie for your loved one, and regularly find yourself making excuses for them?

If you identify strongly with more than three of the points on the checklist above, especially if they're having a negative impact on your wellbeing, then this may suggest a codependent dynamic. This is something that is best addressed through both relationship and individual therapy, but, as a starting point, if you identify as a "fixer" you might like to try to reflect on the ways in which this could be keeping you or your loved one stuck.

While we all have certain personality strengths, if we get stuck in a role, we can't grow. The "fixer" doesn't get the opportunity to learn to be vulnerable and receive support. And the person "looking to be fixed" doesn't get the opportunity to realize their own capacity for problem-solving. It takes a lot of effort and mutual desire to untangle from the roles we play in life. The same is true if you repeatedly lie or cover for your loved one. In those instances, you're engaging in "silent rules" and enabling their behaviour (more on this in the section on coercive control). *Even when someone is a victim of mental health or their circumstances, it doesn't mean they get to behave however they want.*

Take it from me, it's possible to create a healthier blueprint for your relationships through recognizing the role you might be stuck in. As I advise clients: *"Let it begin with me."* In other words, mind your own actions and attitudes first, instead of pointing fingers. We must admit that we're powerless over other people.

Above all, be kind to yourself throughout this process. It's about slowly learning, and then unlearning, entrenched behaviours, which likely go way back.

The Challenge of Changing Behaviours

Putting new boundaries in place often means learning to tolerate discomfort and anxiety. It requires finding ways to self-soothe. We can discover how to do this through utilizing the breath, touch and movement (see Chapter 7). Please invest time in discovering practices that work for you. Otherwise, you may always end up taking the well-trodden path in a bid to avoid difficult feelings and scenarios.

Let's face it, society leads us to believe that caregivers should be selfless and always available, which can make boundary-setting feel taboo – as if asserting your own needs somehow makes you selfish or is indicative of a lack of commitment. In many cultures, there's also the expectation that familial duties should come before personal needs. This can place enormous pressure on family members to conform to roles that might not align with their personal wellbeing or life goals. In addition, many of us may worry that by asserting our wishes, we might provoke conflict, damage relationships or even cause the other person to leave. In the case of mental health, there may be a genuine worry that establishing a boundary could precipitate a crisis.

While understandable, this concern can be paralysing and lead to a cycle where boundaries are continually sacrificed to avoid potentially negative outcomes. In CBT, we label unhelpful thought patterns that lead to unhealthy behaviours as "cognitive distortions". Let's look at the three most common cognitive distortions in the context of supporting someone with mental health issues:

1   **Black-and-white thinking**: This distortion involves seeing things in absolute terms, without any middle ground. It's the "all or nothing" mindset where situations are viewed as either perfect or disastrous, with no room for nuance. For example, you might think, "If I set a boundary to have some time for myself, I'm a bad caregiver." This leaves no room for the healthier view that taking time for self-care enables you to be a more person caregiver.

2   **Over-generalizing**: This is the tendency to take one instance and generalize it into an overall pattern. It often involves using words like "always" or "never", and can lead to a skewed perception of events or behaviours. For example, if your loved one reacted negatively to a boundary once, you might think, "They're always going to react badly when I set boundaries", even though this may not be the case.

3   **Catastrophizing**: This involves expecting the worst possible outcome to occur. It's when you magnify the potential negative consequences of an action to the point of becoming paralysed by fear, even if the scenario is improbable. For example, you might worry, "If I tell my partner I need to go away on a work trip, they'll spiral into a crisis." While being sensitive to their needs is important,

it's equally important to assess this belief critically and recognize that people often have more resilience than we give them credit for.

The goal is to reshape such thought patterns into ones that are more balanced and realistic.

That way you might even reframe your role and see that setting boundaries is not a rejection of the other person, but an important aspect of a sustainable and mutually respectful relationship. In short, when an unhelpful thought takes hold, don't just believe it. Instead, learn to recognize and interrupt cognitive distortions, and actively reframe them.

Here's a CBT process that helps reframe unhelpful thoughts following an activating event. It might be useful to do when you feel a boundary has been violated. Grab your journal and work through each step.

1 **Challenging situation:** What scenario played out?
2 **Emotion or feeling:** How does this make you feel in yourself and your body?
3 **Automatic thought:** What thoughts or beliefs do you automatically have about the situation?
4 **Associated behaviour:** How do you act as a result?
5 **Evidence for the thought:** What facts support the truthfulness or validity of the thought?
6 **Evidence against the thought:** What facts suggest this thought may not be entirely true or accurate?
7 **New thought:** What new thought takes into account the evidence for and against the original thought?
8 **New behaviour:** What new, healthier behaviour can you implement?

Here is an account from Pete, who was an only child and experienced his mother being manic on and off since he was four years old. Although they enjoyed plenty of happy times, he ultimately decided he needed to create some healthy separation in order to build his own life.

> When Mum was manic and trashing the house, I'd come in and make sure she was safe. But it got to a point where I couldn't bring myself to clear up after her anymore. I would be so, so thankful that one of her best friends would come and sort out the mess. As her son, it was a boundary I needed to put in place. We were codependent for a long time, and there were these knock-on effects for my wife and others. I realized later I was putting responsibility on my wife, saying, "You need to fix this as well." But actually she didn't; it wasn't her responsibility.

Being Good Enough

The term "good enough mother" was coined in the mid-20th century by the British paediatrician and psychotherapist Donald Winnicott.[3] He used it to describe a mother who provides a responsive and nurturing environment for her baby, yet who gradually allows her growing child to experience frustration and disillusionment, to develop the qualities of resilience and autonomy. Winnicott emphasized that what's crucial in parenting is providing an environment that facilitates a child's transition from total dependency to independence.

I'd suggest taking this approach in relation to your loved one, too. As the "good enough" friend/relative/partner you cannot – and should not – strive to meet every one of your loved one's demands, or heal every pain. The attempt to be a perfect caregiver is not only unrealistic but counterproductive, as it prevents the other person from developing their own coping strategies and sense of agency. Just as the "good enough mother" balances her availability with necessary absence, you ought to find a healthy balance between support and space.

The phrase "detach with love", used in some contexts by the spouses of alcoholics, is a beautiful idiom to hold on to. By not always being available or solving all problems for your loved one, you allow them the space to find personal strength or other resources. Ultimately, it comes down to accepting our own limitations. Below is a list of steps to help you examine your output and limitations objectively:

- **Make a list of the support you provide** (for example, "I spend four hours weekly assisting my brother with tasks and managing his appointments").
- **Assess impact on you** (for example, "I often feel I have little time for exercise or relaxation, which makes me irritable with my partner").
- **Rate how sustainable it is from 1 to 5: 1 = completely unsustainable, 5 = completely sustainable** (for example, "2 – I'm also starting to fear my partner might leave me").
- **Acknowledge your limits in a written statement** (for example, "I accept that I cannot manage all of his appointments alone anymore").
- **Create a positive permission written statement** (for example, "I give myself permission to reduce the hours I assist my brother to two hours weekly and to prioritize my self-care").

Stepping Out of the Drama Triangle

The drama triangle is a model created by psychologist Stephen Karpman, which illustrates unhealthy relational dynamics.[4] However, I'm sharing this with you because I think it vividly illustrates the pitfalls those in supporting roles can face, particularly when their boundaries are weak or undefined. In short, the triangle is made up of three points: the Victim, the Rescuer and the Oppressor.

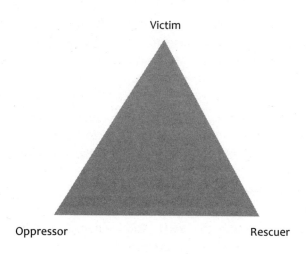

The drama triangle

Does this triangle sound familiar?

Perhaps, as the caregiver, you often find yourself in the Rescuer role, compelled to intervene and solve problems. Occasionally, you might find yourself cast as the Oppressor, especially when frustration peaks and you express critical judgements to manage a tricky situation. Maybe, deep down, you feel more like the Victim, overwhelmed and powerless in your predicament.

The drama triangle is exhausting, and while participants often shift roles, they're rarely able to find a way forward. Why? Because *they need to find a way to step out of it entirely.* The missing point of view in the drama triangle is the Adult perspective. The Adult is the part of us that can assess a situation objectively, make decisions based on current information, and interact with others in a respectful and assertive way. All of which is necessary for healthy boundary-setting.

To make the transition from any of these roles to the Adult state, we need to learn to practise RACT:

- **Recognize** if you're becoming a rescuer, oppressor or victim.
- **Ask** yourself what the adult perspective would be.

- **Communicate** clearly your needs and boundaries, explaining their necessity for the health of the relationship.
- **Take** responsibility for your own choices and actions.

By fostering our Adult mind, we can step out of the exhausting cycle of the drama triangle and move into a more balanced, equitable mode of interaction *in the moment*. This shift allows for the creation and maintenance of healthy boundaries.

Guilty or Not Guilty

The drama triangle can be fuelled by complicated feelings such as guilt, as Natalie, 35, describes:

> There was a bargaining phase when I'd try to bribe my sister. She was so off the walls, addicted to meth, I'd tell her I'd pay her rent just so she would come over.
>
> When she was evicted, I took her in, despite the fact I was living with two other flatmates, who had their own lives and schedules. Her erratic behaviour continued; she regularly brought strangers into our home and even stole from me. One explosive night, when I confronted her, she broke a lamp over my head. She had nowhere to go, but I knew I had to kick her out.
>
> Before long, she'd show up at my window, tearfully apologizing and begging for help. Each job I helped her get; she'd lose. Giving her money felt like the right thing to do – I wanted to know she was sleeping safe and eating. But later, I'd feel guilty and foolish, realizing I was just perpetuating the problem.
>
> Not giving her money tormented me, too. I started thinking I was fucking crazy. There came a point when I think I had to disassociate, splitting her identity in my mind into "my Phoebe" versus "bad Phoebe", who was a stranger to me.

Natalie's story is a powerful one, testimony to a loving and devoted sister. Her intention to ensure her sister's safety was pure-hearted, but unfortunately her support inadvertently enabled her sister's drug addiction – and overruled her own boundaries again and again. Now, hindsight is a beautiful thing and it sounds like Natalie was doing an amazing job, holding down a hell of a lot of responsibility. However, let's consider some things she might have done differently if she had used the RACT method outlined above.

She might have *recognized* that she was about to step in and play the Rescuer right before she gave her sister money for the umpteenth time. This would have required pausing, slowing down her heart rate (because adrenaline is always pumping in emergency situations) and *asking herself what her Adult mind* would say. Perhaps she could have demonstrated her support in other practical ways, or tied any financial support to clear conditions related to her recovery efforts, such as contributing to counselling sessions.

Then she might have *clearly communicated* this to her sister with love in her heart. This is where consistent messaging is so important.

The final part is arguably the hardest, which is to *take responsibility* for your choices and actions. Very often, we step in to avoid experiencing guilt. While this is completely understandable, it isn't the best course of action.

So, what if we learned to reframe our uncomfortable feelings instead? And started valuing their purpose? When we constantly sidestep them, we rob ourselves (and our loved ones) of the opportunity to grow. By continuously rescuing loved ones from the consequences of their actions, we might unintentionally prevent them from reaching their own pivotal moments of realization. When we cushion or shield someone (including ourselves) from hitting rock bottom, we might inadvertently be stopping that person from reaching a point where genuine reflection and change are possible. In essence, learning to sit with discomfort, to understand its origins and implications, can pave the way for personal growth and the potential growth of those around us.

The reality was that Natalie felt guilty whether she did or didn't give her sister money. There was no "perfect" decision. This is a confronting reality, but ultimately one that offers perspective. Setting boundaries *will lead* to an internal tug of war – and that's to be expected. Remember, our feelings are there to keep us alive. Not happy.

Guilt is painful and complex. Discerning between "appropriate" and "inappropriate" guilt can be very helpful. You'll find some features of both in the table below.

Another useful framework is to consider whether something is "constructive" or "destructive": constructive guilt can motivate positive change, while destructive guilt merely weighs one down without leading to beneficial action. Ultimately, we don't need to feel guilty or afraid, but if we do, we are still entitled to set a new boundary.

Appropriate Guilt	Inappropriate Guilt
• Arises from actions or decisions where an individual intentionally harms, betrays or acts unjustly against another. For example, stealing from a loved one, or repeatedly cheating on your partner. • Serves as a moral compass, pointing toward a need for reparation, apology or change. • Tends to be transitory, decreasing once corrective action is taken. • Motivates positive change or reparative actions.	• Stems from societal pressures, or the perceived needs of others that conflict with our own best judgement. For example, saying "no" to lending money to a drug-addicted relative. • Lacks a corrective purpose. Instead, it burdens the individual. • Often lingers, without any clear path for resolution, creating chronic stress or anxiety. • Can result in self-sacrificial behaviour, reinforcing negative patterns and boundaries.

I also wanted to briefly touch on Natalie's concept of "my Phoebe" versus "bad Phoebe", as it's an important one. It indicates the struggle of reconciling the memory of a loved one before and after their addiction. Accepting the duality and understanding that the person's core identity is unchanged but clouded by addiction, or mental illness in general, can be a profound realization – and crucial in the process of asserting boundaries. It helped Natalie to disassociate herself temporarily from her feelings of tenderness for her sister, which was actually important. Her own safety and the safety of her housemates had to take precedence, so Natalie's psyche created a smart way of being able to make tough decisions. That's how disassociation from trauma works; it's a helpful mechanism at the time. But if it carries on, and you stay in the state of paralysis, numbness or, conversely, over-activation, that's when it turns into PTSD or anxiety. After the threat has ended, the adaptive state needs to end, too. This usually requires somatic (physical) practices, or integrative psychotherapy that involves bodywork.

Before we conclude this case study, I thought you might be interested to know how Natalie and Phoebe's story ended. After doing everything possible for Phoebe, including taking her to a rehab facility in Melbourne which she escaped from, Natalie and her family were out of options. It was a subsequent relapse, which led to Phoebe being sectioned and placed in a state-ordered mental health facility, that eventually sparked a change. Natalie explained, "She hadn't 'liked' her experience there, and saw she needed to do a certain amount to have the control to avoid that situation again." After she was finally released, Phoebe took significant steps to rebuild her life. She got married and went back to school to complete her master's degree!

The critical takeaway here is that sometimes stepping back allows those we love to step up. It was when the responsibility for her recovery shifted from her loved ones to herself that Phoebe finally began to harness her resolve to heal.

A Quiet Reckoning with Ourselves

When it comes to boundary-setting, the critical work often happens internally, away from the heat of conflict or the sway of another's presence. And since boundaries are inherently abstract, it can be useful to try to give them form. To make them more tangible in your mind's eye. To do this, I'm going to invite you to do a visualization that will help you to design your own boundary, and find a space that you can retreat to when things become too much.

BOUNDARY VISUALIZATION

Read this aloud to yourself and then repeat the exercise in full, remembering that when visualizing something, it's important to see it as vividly as you can.

1 Close your eyes and take a deep, grounding breath. Let the air fill your lungs slowly, hold it for a moment, and then release it, letting go of any tension with your exhale. Do this a few times until you feel a sense of calm wash over you.

2 Now, picture a space where you feel completely at ease. This is your sanctuary, a place designed by you, for you. Start to build this space from the ground up, noticing the details that make it uniquely comforting and secure. It can be somewhere new or familiar.

3 Within this sanctuary, begin to visualize the boundaries that define and protect this space. Consider the material of your boundary. And the entry point to your sanctuary space. How do you – or others – get in?

4 As you visualize this boundary, feel its strength, its presence. It's a manifestation of your need for personal space and wellbeing. It protects without isolating, it

defines without constricting. Take a moment to walk along this boundary in your mind, feeling a sense of gratitude for the protection it provides.

5 When you're ready, take a deep breath in, inhaling the strength and stability from your visualization. As you exhale slowly, bring your awareness back to the present, carrying with you the image of your personal boundary.

6 When you open your eyes, remember the feelings your visualized boundary provided. Hold on to them, and know that you can revisit and reinforce this mental construct whenever you need to reassert your boundaries in real life.

Visualization can be a powerful tool when we want to create emotional space; for example, it can be useful to imagine washing yourself down after a challenging interaction, or to imagine stepping inside a golden egg filled with light – nothing can get in or out other than golden light. If you're a sensitive person, you might easily absorb someone else's feelings or experiences; in which case, try to imagine holding an oversized sponge that's absorbing their energy instead of you doing it.

Implementing Boundaries

So far, we've looked at what boundaries might mean to you and why they're necessary. Now we're going to get practical about the best ways to put them into place. Boundaries should be introduced gradually rather than bluntly imposed. This allows the other person (and you) to adapt without feeling overwhelmed or cornered.

For example, if you wish to limit the amount of time spent discussing stressful topics, start by gently steering conversations away and gradually reducing the time spent on these subjects. The fact is that when it comes to setting boundaries, explanations aren't always necessary or beneficial. If your loved one is highly reactive or personality-disordered, offering too many justifications can lead to fights or manipulative counterarguments. In such cases, the focus should be on the boundary itself, not on the rationale behind it. However, if you feel your loved one has the strength to hear your perspective, simply share why this is important to you and avoid any blaming statements. Also try not to speak about actual "boundaries" as this word can be emotionally triggering. Rather, simply state a need you have and the action that will follow.

If you're concerned about, say, switching off your phone at night or putting some parameters in place around your availability, share the importance of your sleep in helping you feel healthy and function better. And share that you're going to switch off your phone after, say, 9pm. Let your loved one know who to contact in an emergency outside of these times. Discuss anything around that boundary – but not the boundary itself. If appropriate, you might want to provide a written reminder or a visual cue for your loved one, clearly stating your non-available hours, emergency contacts and reassurances of when you will be available again. If your loved one is in a residential facility, consider having a separate caregiver pager or setting specific ringtones for certain contacts. This can balance the need to be reachable with the need to disconnect and rest.

Introducing one boundary at a time is essential. It allows for a period of adjustment and assessment, and provides a singular focus, reducing the potential for confusion. So, it's worth carefully considering what that first boundary you're going to introduce is. Settle on something that is meaningful but also achievable. Start off on a positive note, if you can. Once you have both adapted well to a boundary (watch out that you're not the one breaking it) and there's a semblance of stability, introduce another.

Revisiting Boundaries

If you're facing resistance or ongoing challenges in asserting your boundary, you will likely feel exhausted. This is a tough road. Unfortunately, the question of how long to persist may be complex, since it's a balance between consistency and flexibility. If a boundary is repeatedly being violated, it might be time to reassess its realism or the approach in enforcing it. Sometimes, a slight modification can make a boundary more attainable and still serve its purpose. Remember, a boundary isn't set in stone. And you're not failing if it needs adjusting.

Start off by determining the primary reason behind the boundary. Ask yourself what the non-negotiable elements are. And reflect on exactly where and why the boundary is being broken. Is it too rigid? Is it being communicated effectively? Or does your loved one simply not understand its importance? Pinpointing the conflict helps in making precise modifications. Then, instead of completely removing a boundary, make small tweaks.

When modifications are made, and the boundary is respected, offer positive reinforcement. In general, it's a good idea to use positively phrased language (i.e., speak about what you *do* want, rather than what you don't want). Even with adjustments, consistency in how you enforce and respect the boundary is crucial. This sends a clear message that while you are flexible and understanding, the boundary still serves an important function.

One particular case that comes to mind is of Emma, a loving mother, whose 19-year-old son, Alex, struggled with debilitating depression. She set a clear boundary with Alex: no swearing during their conversations. She explained, "It's a long story, but due to my own childhood, I find swearing particularly difficult and unacceptable. So it's important that when we interact we do so respectfully and without resorting to using harsh language that's insulting."

Initially, Alex agreed, understanding this boundary to be a sign of mutual respect. However, his compliance was sporadic, and during his darker days swearing became prevalent, leaving Emma feeling disrespected and emotionally drained. During our sessions, Emma expressed her frustration and the emotional toll it was taking. She felt unheard, but she also understood that Alex's mood disorder often made it difficult for him to control his outbursts.

Together, we explored the boundary she had set. It was clear the boundary was essential for Emma but equally clear that Alex was not able to adhere to it consistently. We worked on modifying the boundary. Instead of a zero-tolerance policy on swearing, we introduced a softer approach. Emma would calmly acknowledge Alex's struggle and remind him of the boundary by simply saying, "I know it's tough, but let's try to keep our conversation respectful." If the swearing continued, she would gently but firmly end the conversation, stating, "I'm here for you, but I need to step away until we can talk without swearing." This slight modification acknowledged Alex's struggles while reinforcing Emma's needs. It wasn't about punishing Alex but about safeguarding the emotional space for both of them.

Over time, this adjusted boundary proved effective. Alex began to catch himself mid-swearing and would apologize, trying to rephrase his thoughts. Emma felt more in control and less emotionally fatigued. She was grateful for the change, and their communication improved significantly.

During our sessions, when she was forced to revisit her boundaries, we would go back to the boundary visualization and Emma would tend to her broken wall. I would guide her through a process where she imagined fixing it – putting bricks back in place that had been kicked down, planting ivy along it to bring it back to life. There was something deeply healing about envisaging herself repairing the damage and making the area safe again. Over time, her wall even changed:

sometimes it was more rigid and at other times she brought in more malleable material.

The more we engage with our boundaries, the less daunting and abstract they become. Each effort to assert or implement a new boundary builds our confidence and our competence. The initial discomfort ebbs away, replaced by a newfound strength in the simple yet profound act of saying "no", or "not now", or "not like this". This isn't an act of punishment but an act of self-preservation that ensures you can continue to provide care without losing yourself in the process.

Knowing Your Work

As we hone the craft of setting healthy boundaries, a transformation unfolds within us. We begin to acknowledge the sovereignty we hold over our lives, and in doing so, we learn to respect the sovereignty of others. We tend to our garden, so to speak, and recognize that our neighbours have their own gardens to tend. This mutual respect for personal space and responsibility fosters not just independence, but a collective harmony where each is empowered to address their own issues with autonomy and dignity.

By committing to the practice of healthy boundary-setting, we learn a vital aspect of self-care. We begin to understand that resolving our own concerns is our responsibility, just as others are responsible for theirs.

I want to end this chapter with something I say a lot to my clients – and would now like to say to you. In life, there is "Your Work, Their Work and God's Work". You don't have to be religious to believe this; allow me to explain. "Your Work" is everything that is within your control – so perhaps take a moment to consider what those things are (it's different for us all, depending on our situation). "Their Work" is your loved one's reactions and the things within their control, which you have no control over. Finally, "God's Work" is everything that is outside of anyone's control – those force majeure moments, acts of nature and unforeseen events like Covid. When we can accept this model and ultimately relinquish control outside of anything that is not "Your Work", we open ourselves up to the possibility of greater happiness and even miracles to occur.

> **PROMPT:** For the next week, whenever you find yourself stressed or anxious, ask yourself which category the issue belongs to. If it falls under "Their Work" or "God's Work", practise mentally releasing it and focus on what you can do within "Your Work".

CHAPTER 9
RECLAIMING YOU

"I hid behind my son's diagnosis because it kept me busy. Every day, I occupied myself with something he needed doing. It meant I didn't need to look at the state of my own life – and put any effort into changing things. Except as his mum, I wasn't inspiring him to recover. Since finding a job I enjoy, I'm just as available for the things that matter. For the rest of the time, I'm busy and much happier."

Tammy, 40

This chapter is all about reclaiming you. To find the right starting point to go on that journey, I would like you to consider your life, based on the eight pillars of holistic health we explored in Chapter 4. You've already considered how the pillars apply to your loved one, but now we're going to look at how they apply to you. As a reminder, they are:

1 **Physical pillar:** diet, sleep, physical health and healing
2 **Emotional pillar:** processing feelings, positive coping mechanisms
3 **Intellectual pillar:** continued development, learning, personal growth
4 **Occupational pillar:** career and having purpose
5 **Social pillar:** support network, family and friends, recreational time
6 **Spiritual pillar:** self-reflection and meaning
7 **Financial pillar:** financial stability, disposable income

8 **Environmental pillar:** physical environment, safe shelter, nature

I'd like you to take a moment now to consider these eight pillars of holistic health in more detail.

REFLECTING ON YOUR NEEDS

This exercise will help you separate out the different areas of your life, and see which pillar of holistic health requires the most attention.

1 Copy the pie chart below into your journal and score the different pillars (1 = least happy, 10 = most happy) by shading in the segments of the circle.

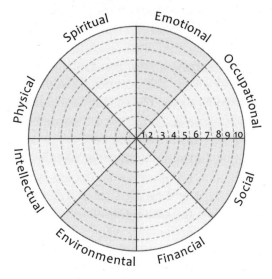

2 Pick the area where you'd most like to experience change – where your needs are consistently unmet, either by yourself or others.

3 Brainstorm up to five ideas that could improve this area's score. For example, if your intellectual score is low, you could learn a new language, travel or try a new activity that pushes you out of your comfort zone.

4 Now just pick one idea to start that will give you maximum impact.

5 Decide on a small step you can take immediately to address your main intention; for example, "I'll take a creative writing class to aid my writing ambitions." (Refer to the section on SMART goals on page 128 to help plan this.)

6 Afterwards, set a reminder in your calendar for 30 days' time to review the progress you've made (for example, have you applied to any courses?). Committing to this new action for at least 30 days is crucial; after that, you can always swap or add something else into the mix.

Facing Resistance

If you found the last exercise a little overwhelming, please know that you're not alone – and we did dive straight into it! It's common to feel resistance when venturing into unfamiliar territory, or before enacting change. Remember, resistance appears differently for everyone and, like any emotion, the key is to recognize it and give it space. I think of it as the unconscious fighting to remain that way. Much like how a dog suddenly becomes "deeply asleep" the moment you mention a bath! It's as if he's thinking, "If I can't see the bath, the bath can't see me", perfectly mirroring our own mind's attempts to avoid facing change.

As a therapist, I've learned we can't just rush in and try to demolish our defence mechanisms; instead, we need to approach them with love and understanding, gradually easing their grip.

WHERE DO YOU FEEL RESISTANCE?

This exercise will help you identify the areas in your life where you feel resistance.

1 Find a quiet space where you can reflect without interruption.
2 Bring awareness to any defences that might be coming up for you. These might be internal obstacles, external obstacles or a combination of both.
3 Just allow whatever comes up to arise. Then, in your journal, complete the following statements:

    1. My resistance feels/sounds like ...
    2. When I tune in to my resistance, the following images and/or memory comes to mind ...
    3. Despite my resistance, the things I have some control over are ...
    4. If I carry on as I am doing, I avoid looking at ...

When I ask clients the fourth question, they usually express an avoidance of the unknown. You see, when we focus our energy on fulfilling a role for someone else, in some ways, we stay in our comfort zone. We have a purpose – not one we might have originally chosen for ourselves, but a purpose all the same.

Don't panic if your resistance is tied to low self-esteem. Some of the most impressive people I've met are racked with self-doubt behind the scenes. It's simply that they don't let it dominate their lives. After all, it's your actions – not your feelings – that matter. So, how to take action when you lack confidence? You forget about finding confidence and opt for courage instead. Courage is a far more tangible and important metric than confidence, which can be faked. When you take courageous action (even if it's small), you're building a case against your inner critic and confidence tends to follow. You see, we all have different brain systems that want different things. It comes down to choosing which part of yourself you'd like to strengthen.

If guilt toward your loved one or other family members is holding you back, you might find it useful to research family systems theory, which posits that individuals should always be viewed as part of their wider family system. This means that when we invest in self-care, or in other areas of our lives, we simultaneously enrich the collective. This is supported by research on caregiver burnout, which shows that caregivers who practise self-care report lower stress levels and provide higher-quality care for others.[1]

The fascinating theory of quantum entanglement (bear with me here!) also backs this up. It states that two particles remain connected despite the distance between them. In other words, even when we're not *with* a person, we can affect them in a positive or negative sense through the *way we are*. It's like that saying: "When you see the world differently, the world itself starts to change." So, consider if through modelling new behaviour that makes you happier, you might even be able to impact your loved one's mental health positively.

Setting Yourself Up for Success

The concept that we're all in a perpetual state of becoming is central to existential philosophy. It emphasizes the ongoing process of self-discovery, which requires us to engage with the world and other people, even if that means we sometimes experience friction, or make mistakes! Besides, the greater our self-awareness, the better we can become at course-correcting (should we need to do so).

To support you in the process of taking positive action, you might consider getting yourself an accountability buddy. Research shows that committing to another person can increase your chances of achieving a goal by up to 65 per cent, and scheduling regular accountability appointments can raise this success rate to 95 per cent![2] A trusted friend or peer can also provide a useful mirror through regular planned interaction and feedback.

Areas of Impact

While the previous exercise hopefully helped you to zero in on your life and unique circumstances, research indicates that people in supporting roles benefit most from investing in two key areas:

1 finding support for themselves (which ties to the social pillar)[3]
2 finding a purpose that is all theirs (which ties to the occupational, intellectual and/or spiritual pillars)[4]

This is because, as I said in the introduction, *loneliness increases caregiving stress, whereas having a sense of purpose reduces it.*

So, for the remainder of this chapter, we'll spend a bit more time exploring the vital role of building your own support network, and helping you to realize your purpose in life. The goal is to empower you to reclaim your time – and rediscover aspects of yourself that may have been overshadowed by your caregiving responsibilities.

This isn't straightforward to do. But I know it's possible because I've witnessed remarkable transformations again and again: people entering therapy amidst a crisis, or exhausted by a relationship dynamic in their life, which ultimately leads them to a personal breakthrough.

Getting Support for Yourself

Actively seeking support is vital for your happiness and mental health. Consider who is supporting you, and how. You can think of this concept in terms of concentric circles. That's when two or more circles have the same centre point, like this:

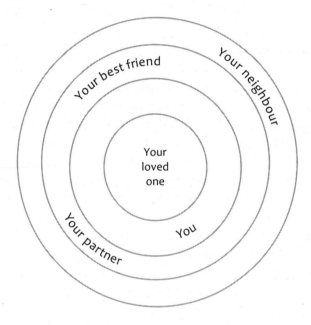

I like to think the world is made up of billions of concentric circles of support, all overlapping! For argument's sake, let's say the circle in the middle is your loved one, the person currently struggling with their mental health. Then you are the circle that directly surrounds them. What you need is for the circle that surrounds you (such as another appointed loved one) to focus on *your* needs, rather than the needs of the person two circles away from them. This may sound obvious, but rarely is. So often, we're primed to offer support to the one we perceive as being the most in need.

You see, we all need to establish concentric circles of support (and notice it's plural, not a singular circle) to maintain our wellbeing and resilience. By establishing these circles, the person in the supporting role can find solace, guidance and strength, which enables them to provide more effective care in turn. This is how community is built and how "problems" are shared.

Mental healthcare professionals like me also benefit from having their own concentric circles: all therapists are required to be in supervision, and their supervisor also has a supervisor. And so the circles of supervision – and support – continue. This makes for a system that's far more robust.

Establishing your own support network doesn't mean betraying your loved one, but ensuring you have the capacity to provide the support they need. Too often, shame, guilt and secrecy are associated with admitting that someone we love has a mental health issue. And, even more so, if we're finding it too much. But these barriers must be demolished.

I'd like to share Sheila's story with you, as it neatly illustrates the importance of seeking the right type of support – which sometimes comes from unlikely sources. Sheila (48) has a husband who has been diagnosed with clinical depression, while her widowed father has dementia. She loves them both very much, but often feels overwhelmed by her circumstances. The overriding feeling she has is one of resentment, and sometimes she daydreams of upping sticks and starting all over again, even though she knows she won't do this. In moments of solitude, she wonders if other people ever feel the same way.

It's then that Sheila remembers a friend of a friend, Lynn, whose partner had a chronic illness that took up a lot of her time and energy, which meant she stopped attending social events. While their situations aren't identical, the emotional landscapes they navigate may be similar, so Sheila decides to reach out to Lynn through Facebook. After exchanging a few messages, Sheila invites Lynn to meet for a coffee. She admits that she doesn't want advice, but would love for them to share their experiences.

As they talk, Lynn opens up about how she has grappled with her own resentment. She shares that what helped her most was a shift in perspective gained through journaling. This allowed her to express all her pent-up emotions and make sense of her feelings. Over time, she began to seek out small windows of time just for herself, like early morning walks or rediscovering her love of pottery through local classes. As Sheila listened, she found solace. Lynn didn't offer direct solutions or advice but instead simply shared her own story. Through Lynn's narrative, Sheila realized that while her journey was hers alone to navigate, the themes of human experience echo universally. Plus, she heard about some strategies that had worked well for Lynn. When we met afterwards, Sheila explained:

> What most benefitted me was finding someone key in my support system who wasn't a key person in my husband's or father's life. With Lynn, that meant going a little further afield, but it means I now have a unique type of support that's all mine and there's no risk of confidentiality issues arising.

Let's consider some other more structured ways of finding support next. By evaluating your needs and the unique nature of your situation, you can choose the most suitable form of support for you.

Community Networks

Community networks provide a broad spectrum of support through shared interests and backgrounds. These can range from creative arts workshops to broad-based groups centred around shared interests. They might include neighbourhood associations, professional training bodies, hobby-based groups or cultural study groups.

Support Groups

Support groups are tailored to specific issues, where members share a common challenge. Examples include Codependents Anonymous (CoDA), or Carers Trust (UK), or Family Caregiver Alliance (US). These groups offer a safe space to share experiences, offer and receive advice, and learn coping strategies specific to the shared challenge. The solidarity found here can be a powerful tool in managing personal struggles.

Group Therapy

Group therapy, while similar in format to support groups, is facilitated by a mental health professional and follows a structured approach. Sessions are designed to encourage individual sharing, providing each member with insights into their behaviours and thought patterns through feedback and observation. Our role within the family can often be neatly mirrored within the therapy group, inviting room for exploration.

One-to-One Therapy

One-to-one therapy offers a private and confidential setting to process personal experiences, with a therapist guiding the exploration of your thoughts, feelings and behaviours. Part of the therapist's role is to hold you accountable to yourself. In practice, that means not spending all the session talking about someone else, but engaging in self-enquiry and learning to navigate your emotions, potentially leading to a more profound sense of closure and acceptance.

Finding a Purpose

I've said it before and I'll say it again: *While loneliness increases caregiving stress, having a sense of purpose reduces it.* So, let's dive into connecting with our purpose now. To do this, we're first going to mine insights about ourselves from both our childhood and today. And then we'll use these insights to create a vision for the future.

We can learn a lot from our younger selves. Why? Because we're all born with a built-in understanding of what we need (such as food, sleep and care) and a toolkit of internal resources to meet those needs. However, we lose touch with our primal selves over time. So, this is an invitation for you to reconnect with who you once were and what you wanted. Just like a tree or plant needs the right conditions to grow, so do we humans. That's why life sometimes requires us to prune our broken branches and repair our torn bark. I think of it as stripping back layers of unhelpful conditioning to get back to our pure essence.

In the hustle and bustle of everyday life, the dreams we had, the hobbies we loved, the friendships we treasured, the natural instincts we possessed often get buried under layers of "adulting". But imagine if you could garner valuable insights for your present and future by looking at your past? This means revisiting who you were and the things you loved as a kid.

LOOKING BACK TO LOOK FORWARD

I'd like you to take a moment now to reconnect with your younger self.

1   Find a photo of yourself as a kid (ideally under the age of seven) that you're particularly drawn to.

2 Spend time looking at this photo over the course of several days and start to notice what innate qualities or traits you detect in your younger self.

3 Reflect on what your dreams, passions and sensibilities were. What came naturally to you?

4 Keep this photo where you can look at it frequently.

PROMPT: Your past self isn't a stranger. They're simply an earlier version of you, brimming with dreams and untainted passions. When you revisit your beginnings, remember that you're not regressing but reconnecting with a part of yourself you might have lost along the way.

Rediscovering hobbies, interests and connections from your past can reignite your zest for life. With that in mind, let's look now at what you know to be true for you today.

LOOKING IN THE MIRROR TODAY

I'd like you to reconnect with whatever lights your fire today. To do this, reflect on and answer the following prompts.

1 When was the last time you felt truly engaged and absorbed in an activity? What were you doing?

2 Think about a time when you felt proud of yourself. What were you doing and why did you feel so proud?

3 What gives you a sense of meaning in life?

4   If you had unlimited time and resources, what projects or activities would you pursue?

Having now reflected on yourself, both in the past and today, the next step is to integrate what you've learned in a vision for the future.

CREATE YOUR VISION BOARD

The goal of this exercise is to create a vision board that reflects your purpose, aspirations and values today. This visual representation can include images, words and symbols that resonate with you.

1   **Gather materials**: Collect magazines, markers, scissors, glue and a large board or piece of paper.
2   **Identify themes**: Think about themes that represent your motivations, such as creativity, adventure, learning, helping others, etc.
3   **Select images and words**: Cut out or draw images and words that symbolize these themes. Arrange them on your board in a way that feels meaningful to you.
4   **Reflect**: Spend time reflecting on your vision board. What patterns or themes emerge? How do these elements align with your core values and interests?
5   **Look at it daily**: As visual creatures, we absorb information most powerfully through visual mediums. This sends messages to the conscious and unconscious, which encourages our behaviour to align.

Let this vision board be a daily reminder of your intentions – and how rich your inner and outer world is.

Living Out Your Potential

One of the greatest antidotes to existential meaninglessness and loneliness is the inexorable pursuit of purpose. Purpose is our primary motivator; without it there is no hope. Holocaust-survivor Victor Frankl's amazing book *Man's Search for Meaning* proves the necessity of finding purpose and a reason to exist even in the bleakest of circumstances. And it is the *pursuit* of purpose, rather than necessarily the realizing of it, that is so vital.

When I spoke to Pete (who we met briefly in Chapter 6) about his relationship with his bipolar mother, he explained how his coping mechanism as a child was detachment through focusing on his schoolwork. He also became a bully, publicly shaming other kids who weren't as capable as him. When he later realized the distress he was causing others, he redirected his energy into learning about positive psychology and personal development. His growth mindset, along with reading about human consciousness, ultimately healed him and took him down a different road.

Shortly after the death of his mother, he met a woman who was running a charity for children with rare forms of cancer, having lost her own son to the disease. He explained to me:

> I'm really inspired and motivated by people like that because I think they're the best examples of humanity. They remind us that any tragedy, no matter how hard, can be our superpower of impact in the world. My whole business drive now is to help people become healthier versions of themselves – I've channelled my experiences and it's why I'm doing what I'm doing. In a way, I feel like it was what I was meant to experience.

On some level, Pete knew that his mother wasn't going to be able to provide for him, as much as they loved one another

– so he went off and did it for himself. Pete's safety mechanism was to become emotionally distant for a while, and instead become staggeringly self-reliant. In many ways, he's a self-made person. The kids of parents who've had mental health issues often are.

I've spoken to others who have described how their work helped them maintain their sense of self – and separation. For example, 22-year-old Beth's sister was on suicide watch in the room next door when Beth started her dream job. Although this was an incredibly stressful time for Beth, when she logged on to those work calls, she could be the Beth who still had a life, was a professional and who was able to escape for a bit. In these uncertain times, finding daily meaning and purpose is more important than ever. We cannot always depend on our political and religious leaders, but we can take the lead in our own lives. And often, our purpose is right under our nose; it's just a matter of fully opening our eyes to it.

Finally, I will leave you with this thought: each day, a staggering number of our cells (estimates suggest tens of billions) undergo a process of death and replacement. This cycle is a natural part of our body's complex system of maintenance and renewal, known as cellular turnover or apoptosis.[5] It's a reminder that change is woven into the very fabric of our biological existence. Just as we're biologically wired to renew, we're psychologically equipped for continuous transformation and growth, at any stage of life, both individually and together.

CHAPTER 10
CARING FOR YOUR RELATIONSHIP

"At the start, I saw my partner as my knight in shining armour. I hid my flaws, like the fact that I was depressed and had chronic fatigue. When I later found out he wasn't the guy I thought he was, I was forced to confront myself. In projecting onto him, I missed seeing the real person before me – equally flawed yet brilliant, and uniquely neurodivergent. Through dropping my mask, I learned to appreciate both his and my own complexities. "

Olivia, 38

In Part 1, we looked at caring for your loved one, and in Part 2, we've focused on caring for yourself. Now, I'd like to look at caring for your relationship with your loved one, whether it's familial, platonic or romantic. When two people come together, their personalities, attachment styles, unconscious material, energies and histories collide. And the closer those people get, the messier that shared space can become.

Relationships are inherently complex. When mental health issues are part of the mix, things become even more nuanced. The concept of intersubjectivity helps to explain the shared, mutual reality created in relationships. This shared space is shaped by each person's perceptions, feelings, experiences and their assigned meanings. A therapist might consider the intersubjective field or relational space that is created with their client to better understand the dynamics at play.

To help you reflect on the various influences impacting your relationship, I will be asking you to imagine it as its own solar system. We will then explore what losing strategies look like and how to replace them with win–win solutions. Finally, we'll give some thought to the nature of romantic relationships, and the unique challenges they present.

It's said that we never truly know what goes on between two people behind closed doors. But here's the thing: often neither do they! Much of our behaviour is unconscious and, while it remains that way, it results in a stalemate. This chapter aims to help you gain a better understanding of your relationship and determine whether a system update is necessary.

Your Relationship is its Own Solar System

In the vast universe of human connections, relationships can be visualized as intricate solar systems. Each system consists of various celestial bodies – planets, moons, comets, stars and so on – each playing a unique role in the gravitational dance that unfolds. The dynamics within each solar system are influenced by a complex array of personal traits, shared experiences and external forces.

Just as celestial bodies maintain a delicate balance of forces to keep their orbits stable – to avoid collisions or drifting apart – relationships require a similar balance of emotional give and take, along with continual adjustments to stay on track. I like this analogy because it reminds us that relationships are dynamic and responsive systems that need ongoing nurture and adaptation, based on the unique internal and external forces at play.

The way two (or more) people orbit each other in life is influenced by:

1 **The personal:** Each individual brings their own preferences, history, background, biochemistry and personality traits

into the relationship. Think of yourselves as two unique planets, each with distinct characteristics and terrain.

2 **The shared field:** This represents the mutual space and connection between you, encompassing shared memories, joint ventures (including offspring), communication styles and levels of trust and intimacy. These shared experiences act like gravitational forces that define your orbits around each other. A scarcity here can also be indicative of the nature of the relationship.

3 **External influences:** Factors outside the personal and shared realms that either support or strain the relationship, including societal norms, family dynamics and cultural references. These can either stabilize or disturb your orbits, impacting the relationship's trajectory and condition.

The solar system represents the relationship ecosystem, where each component's movements and interactions affect the whole. To illustrate this, let's consider it as a Venn diagram (as shown below, with details for each section on the following page), which I think makes it clearer to understand!

The relational solar system

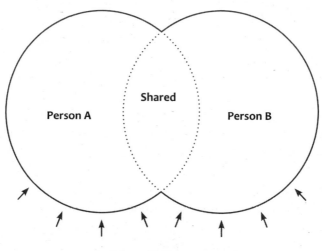

Person A

Shared

Person B

External Influences

Person A

Temperament ★ Family background ★ Significant events
Relationships ★ Religious or spiritual beliefs ★ Likes and dislikes
Physical and mental health ★ Hopes, dreams and fears

Shared

Nature of relationship ★ How well/long you've known each other
Shared memories ★ Mutual hobbies ★ Shared assets
Common goals ★ Communication ★ Co-creations

Person B

Temperament ★ Family background ★ Significant events
Relationships ★ Religious or spiritual beliefs ★ Likes and dislikes
Physical and mental health ★ Hopes, dreams and fears

External Influences

Geographical factors ★ Prejudices ★ Housing and living situations
Other family and friends ★ Institutions and local community

Mental health issues can alter the gravitational pull within a relationship. However, it's important to see that such challenges are but a single influence in your relationship's expansive solar system. And just like every star and planet in space, nothing stays still and remains the same. Through mapping out your own relational solar system, you may become more aware of:

- **Multifaceted impacts**: Relationships don't exist in a vacuum. They're shaped by everything from deeply personal experiences to broad societal influences. In creating your own solar system, it's possible you'll consider factors and perspectives you'd not considered before.
- **Who your loved one is beyond their mental health**: Every individual is more than their struggles; they're influenced by a myriad of things.

- **Shared treasures**: The process may illuminate the shared field and gravitational forces that bring you together! You may rediscover cherished memories, mutual pastimes and shared dreams.

Now it's time to create your own relational solar system diagram. Before you start, check out the example venn diagram below, filled in by Diane, who is struggling to cope with her eldest son Michael's depression.

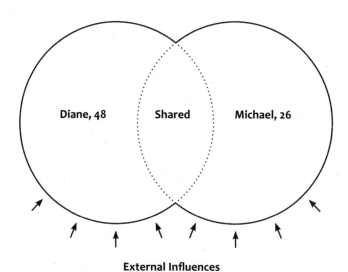

External Influences

Diane, 48

I am a single mum to two boys in their twenties ★ Christian faith is important to me ★ My dad was Nigerian and absent ★ My Spanish mum raised me ★ I love Michael but want him to move out ★ I hope to find a partner in life and have a happy relationship

Shared

Mother and eldest son ★ Lives together with young brother (16) ★ Michael pays some bills but owes Diane money (scared to ask for it) ★ Shared history of absent fathers ★ Mutual love of animals

Michael, 26

Now has a job he loves in the media ★ Starting to earn money ★ Has a history of drug-taking, depression and anger issues ★ On antidepressants ★ Atheist ★ Overweight ★ Smokes weed ★ Didn't know his dad

External Influences

Live in London in a cramped flat with little space to breathe ★ Diane is anti-drugs (Christian influences) ★ Racial separation and "otherness" pervades – both experience the colonizing shackles of whiteness

DRAW YOUR OWN RELATIONAL SOLAR SYSTEM

This exercise should be done alone, but try to consider the other person's perspective too.

1 Grab your journal and draw three conjoining circles.
2 Fill in the left circle with information about yourself based on the cues I've provided. Bullet points are fine.
3 Fill in the right circle with information about your loved one. You might go back and forth between the two circles, and that's okay. The important thing is that the information you write down is objective and factual. Add as much detail as you can.
4 Then write down all the significant things you share in the middle section. Remember, this is ever-evolving, so this is just a snapshot of how things are at this moment.
5 Finally, in the space surrounding the circles, write down all significant "external influences".
6 At the top of the page, write the heading "our relational solar system" and reflect on the full picture of your relationship.

Don't worry if you don't capture everything. Just jot down what seems important. Ultimately, it's about taking a step back and considering the things that may be noteworthy about you both as individuals and in your relationship, both positive and negative.

Once you've completed this, you may become aware of the things that both bind and separate you from your loved one, whether those are differences in culture, race, beliefs or personality traits. Perhaps you've become aware that you share more similarities than you might have realized. Be curious about what you've written and consider any new findings as they present themselves.

For example, look at your relational solar system diagram and consider a current challenge within it:

- **Orbital stability:** Is this issue primarily influenced by mental health concerns or does it stem from another dynamic? How does understanding its origin alter your perspective and approach to resolving it?
- **Recurring orbits:** Reflect on any patterns within your solar system. Are there recurring orbits or trajectories that regularly influence your relationship's path? Identifying these can help predict and manage future cycles.
- **Core influences:** If you were to identify a core gravitational force or fundamental issue in your relationship, what would it be? What creative strategies could you employ to adjust this force or redirect it to ensure a smoother path?

Distinguishing between influences directly caused by mental health and those that are downstream effects can profoundly influence how relationships are managed. Typically, issues directly caused by mental health challenges often manifest as behaviours directly linked to the condition's symptoms.

For example, a person with anxiety may exhibit increased neediness or frequent requests for reassurance, impacting how they interact within their relationships.

However, downstream effects are the subtler, often more complex matters that evolve over time. These might include a breakdown in trust due to inconsistent behaviour, long-term resentment from a perceived lack of empathy, or a general erosion of communication. These issues are not symptoms of the mental health condition itself, but are responses to the stress and strain it places on the relational dynamics.

Identifying the difference between direct impacts and downstream effects can be helpful in guiding more appropriate responses. When issues are recognized as direct effects of a mental health condition, it may prompt those involved to seek specific therapeutic or medical interventions. In contrast, identifying issues as downstream calls might call for different strategies, such as mediation, enhanced communication techniques, or therapy focused on relationship dynamics, rather than individual treatment. This discernment can help in treating the root cause of relationship issues.

Attachment Styles

Your respective attachment styles also play a fundamental role in shaping how you and your loved one relate to one another. Attachment styles develop early in life based on our relationship with our caregivers. These become our blueprint for relationships throughout our lives. Here's a brief overview of the primary attachment styles:

- **Secure attachment:** Those with a secure attachment style tend to have a positive and stable view of themselves and their relationships. They feel comfortable with intimacy and are usually warm and loving. In relationships, they're reliable, adaptable and able to handle conflict constructively.

- **Anxious attachment:** Those with an anxious attachment style often worry about their relationships and crave closeness, but they fear that others might not reciprocate their feelings. This can lead to behaviours perceived as needy or clingy. Anxiously attached individuals are often very sensitive to their partner's emotional cues but may require constant reassurance and attention.

- **Avoidant attachment:** Those with an avoidant attachment style often value their independence to the extent that they may feel uncomfortable with too much closeness. They tend to keep their distance emotionally to avoid getting hurt and might seem aloof. In relationships, they often maintain their autonomy at the cost of intimacy.

- **Disorganized attachment:** Those with a disorganized attachment style, sometimes known as fearful-avoidant, desire closeness but fear getting too close. This can result in mixed signals and erratic behaviours, causing confusion in their relationships. Those with marked disorganized attachment have usually suffered some form of abuse in childhood.

> **PROMPT:** Reflect on how your own attachment style might push your loved one further into theirs. By recognizing and moderating your own tendencies, you can encourage a healthier balance in the relationship.

Too often, we have the same argument again and again, and it usually comes down to attachment styles (for example, "Come closer. I fear losing you." Or, "Leave me alone, I need some space.") I would highly recommend researching these styles more deeply to understand better how they may be impacting your relationship dynamics.

Shared Field

So far, we've thought about what makes up the shared field in very practical terms. However, there are also intangible influences. The fact is most of the time we are sending and receiving unconscious thoughts. Learning to harness intuition can, therefore, help us to connect on a more subconscious level. Intuition often speaks to us most clearly when we're in a state of stillness, free from the usual distractions of our busy minds and lives.

It's during such times that our intuition can reveal insights (including about our relationships) that might not otherwise be obvious. This can lead to more empathetic interactions, and deeper connections – with ourselves and others.

CULTIVATE STILLNESS AND WISDOM

The aim here is to build your intuition, much like you would the muscles in your body. Do this practice regularly, especially during times of inner or outer conflict.

1 Choose a quiet place where you won't be disturbed and settle into a comfortable position.
2 Close your eyes and take a few deep breaths. As you inhale, feel your chest and belly expand. As you exhale, imagine releasing any tension or stress. Gradually let your breathing fall into a natural rhythm.
3 Allow yourself to settle into the stillness that emerges from being fully present in your body. If thoughts come, acknowledge them, but then gently bring your focus back to your breath. Stay in this state of calm awareness

for a few moments. If you find yourself drifting, it may be useful to say to yourself: "I welcome stillness."

4 Imagine your loved one standing in front of you and then visualize the relational field between you. Is energy flowing through it? Or is it stagnant? Can you see any colours? Is there anything different this field is requiring? Allow your intuition to guide you.

We live in a world built on separation and division: "This is mine and that is yours." And while this can be helpful when it comes to establishing boundaries, it's not the whole truth. *The truth is that we are all One, made up of the same fundamental energy. When we start to accept this and see that separation is merely an illusion, the way we view our relationships can change.* Quantum physics suggests that all elements of the universe – or even multiple universes – are interconnected through dimensions beyond our sensory perception. Therefore, if we can shift our own attitudes and behaviours, the relationship dynamic can also transform.

What's more, I like to think there is a "collective cloud", a kind of iCloud of universal ideas accessible to everyone. It's where spontaneous inspirations emerge, and from where we all unconsciously draw information. Can you try to access wisdom, insights and innovation from this collective bank? You don't have to be spiritual to do this, as a lot of people can tap into it through connecting to nature or an art form. The point is that whenever we feel particularly lost or uninspired, we can tune in to a universal pool of intelligence. It's okay if this all sounds a bit hocus pocus to you; just be open to the possibility of what I'm saying and then see if anything shifts.

Creating the Biosphere

We spoke earlier about how we all orbit each other, much like celestial stars do, but I also want to briefly touch on the idea that relationships are akin to mini biospheres. For those of you who flunked geography like I did, a biosphere is an ecological system where living organisms and non-living things grow and exist. Within a biosphere, all elements are interconnected. For example, if one species overgrows or disappears, it can disrupt the entire ecosystem. Just as a healthy biosphere relies on symbiosis, a healthy relationship depends on the mutual wellbeing of those involved.

This means that if something isn't working for one person, then it won't be working for the other one either, or for the environment that's being created. It's not conducive for evolution and growth. When we accept this, we start to hold our own experiences in higher regard.

Now, obviously I don't know where on the spectrum your loved one's mental health is, and if someone is hospitalized, severely schizophrenic or has no mental capacity, reciprocity may feel like a distant dream. But even gently expressing who you are to someone who is very unwell is still important – for everyone's sake, but above all for the sake of the relationship. *Authenticity builds intimacy.* If your loved one is very unwell, checking in with them about your relationship may be difficult at times, so consider ways for them to reciprocate in other ways. Andrea, 49, explains:

> My brother is schizophrenic and hospitalized. While he can't "give to me" in usual ways, I can share my love of music with him, and sometimes I sing to him. Recently, I've started writing songs about our relationship and childhood. His reaction is a bit hit and miss (on more than one occasion he's told me to "shut up!"), but there have also been plenty of times when he's applauded me and the songs have evidently made him very happy.

What's more, he's started to draw album covers for me based on them. It's like we are relating in this whole new way now.

Andrea and her brother are one example of connecting in a different way. Grant yourself permission to exist and engage on a nonverbal level, too. You may begin to notice the synchronicity, mystery and even telepathy that exists in the relational field. Remember, this goes both ways!

Relationships Are Reflections

Our relationships hold up a mirror reflecting back elements of ourselves, good and bad. Consider what your loved one represents to you. In intimate relationships, our partner often reflects our unfinished business, unresolved emotional wounds or unfulfilled desires, usually from childhood. In sibling relationships, our brother or sister might represent alternative routes our lives could have taken.

Being able to zoom out and see your relationship from a distance allows you to recognize such representations. This higher perspective prompts us to ask: "What is this relationship showing me about myself? Which characteristics do I need to develop to become more balanced?" For some, this might mean cultivating compassion; for others, developing acceptance or boundaries. In turn, this can help us navigate the relational terrain with greater awareness.

Society can place unrealistic demands on relationships, leading us to expect one person to fulfil all our needs. It's possible that you're on the receiving end of this, and that your loved one has unfair expectations of you. Or perhaps you're constantly attempting to change your loved one, rather than accepting them for who they are. It's also possible that you're both caught in a place of disappointment and unmet needs. This is where negative visualization can come in. Through visualizing potential challenges or losses ahead of time, you can both be better prepared when things don't go to plan, and experience greater contentment when they do.

As a therapist, I often have to resist the urge to "save" a client when things have gone wrong for them, recognizing that this would do them a major disservice, as I would prevent them from discovering answers for themselves. What's more, when I step out of my saviour complex and tolerate their discomfort, they can also learn to sit with it. If we can all learn to sit with the things that make us feel uncomfortable, we can expand our own edges and model tolerance for others.

Stepping back not only helps the other person, it helps us to confront the things we find difficult to endure. Namely, our own hopelessness, helplessness or despair. Our own shadow.

That's why we ultimately discover more about ourselves through being *in* relationship with others. Sure, solo practices that increase mindfulness, presence and stillness can majorly improve the quality of how we relate, but the real practice is to try to hold on to these things while in relationship. Sorry, monks, but it's a lot easier to stay Zen when no one disturbs you!

Internal Family Systems and Navigating Relational Dynamics

Internal Family Systems (IFS)[1] is a model of therapy created by Dr Richard Schwartz in the 1980s that recognizes that we all have different parts – or subpersonalities – inside of us who are just doing their best to try to protect us. The IFS model categorizes our internal parts into:

1 **Exiles:** These are often the wounded parts of ourselves that carry the pain and trauma from our past. They're protected by other parts to prevent those feelings from overwhelming us.
2 **Managers:** These parts work tirelessly to keep us functional and safe. They manage our daily lives by controlling any

behaviours that could lead to the Exiles' pain becoming apparent.

3 **Firefighters:** When Exiles' feelings threaten to break through, Firefighters attempt to extinguish the emotional intensity. This can involve impulsive or self-destructive behaviours, like substance abuse or disordered eating, which serve as distractions from the pain.

You might recognize these parts more easily in others, but they're within us all. In a relationship where one person struggles with their mental health, these parts interact in even more complex ways. For illustrative purposes, let's say the Manager part of you tries to maintain a sense of order and normalcy in the face of your loved one experiencing emotional distress. To do this, you might avoid certain topics or attempt to control a situation. This might prompt their Firefighter to leap into action and engage in behaviours that express their underlying turmoil – or they might numb it out altogether.

Conversely, if your loved one is depressed, their own Manager might be working overtime, trying to keep their pain under control. You might notice they become obsessive about work or their weight, or even phobic about something. If you attempt to break through this protective layer too forcefully, you might trigger their Firefighter, leading to an argument or withdrawal.

My point is that these internal dynamics, which are of course completely unconscious, give rise to losing strategies that hinder communication. Here are the five most common losing strategies that play out between people:

1 **Controlling the other person:** The Manager part might attempt to control the other person's actions to maintain stability, leading to resentment, secrecy or pushback.
2 **Withdrawing:** The Firefighter part might cause a person to suddenly withdraw from the relationship as a protective

measure. This withdrawal can trigger a response in the other person's Manager, who may attempt to re-engage or control the situation.

3 **Retaliating:** When Firefighters respond to perceived slights or emotional turmoil, they might retaliate, thereby escalating tensions and damaging the relationship.

4 **Not expressing yourself:** Managers might overly manage their image, creating a build-up of unspoken words and inauthentic interactions.

5 **Always needing to be right:** Managers or Firefighters can cause individuals to rigidly defend their perspectives, leading to diminished mutual understanding.

Take a moment to identify how you and your loved one might trigger specific parts of each other based on this model. For example, does their withdrawal trigger your Manager to micromanage their behaviour? Do your Firefighters clash or complement each other? Does your Manager's behaviour amplify or soothe their Exile's feelings?

Win–Win Solutions for Healthier Dynamics

By understanding the IFS model, we can create more conscious interactions, and begin to shift from losing strategies to win–win solutions.

It starts with getting to know your own parts. Identify when your Manager is controlling, or when your Firefighter is reacting. Notice what triggers these parts and what emotions they're trying to protect. If, say, you were the responsible one in your family from a young age, always telling people what to do to avoid danger and they didn't listen to you, it's likely your Manager will now do anything in your power to stop what you deem to be destructive behaviour in others.

Except perhaps now your Manager is more experienced and can recruit your loved one's more mature Manager to create a plan for when the Firefighters show up! When we gain a deeper understanding of our own protective mechanisms, it becomes easier to recognize the protective mechanisms in others (which can manifest in ways such as eating disorders, OCD, depression, addiction, etc.). Just as you learn to negotiate between different parts of yourself, you can use this approach in your relationships to create more compassionate and harmonious interactions.

IMPORTANT NOTE

The Internal Family Systems (IFS) model may not be appropriate for everyone, particularly those experiencing psychosis, paranoia or schizophrenia. The concept of having "parts" can be unproductive or harmful in these cases.

The Context of Romantic Relationships

Romantic relationships deserve a section of their own, because they can bring with them a whole different set of challenges and considerations, including issues connected to sex, commitment and break-ups.

The reasons we fall in love and choose the partner/s we do are multifaceted, but fundamentally remain a mystery. A blend of chemical, genetic, sociological, nurture, ancestral and free will all factor in. (For example, we know we're more likely to fall for people who have a different immune system to us, all in the name of evolution.)[2]

Freud talked about "repetition compulsion", which is when a person repeats a traumatic event over and over.[3] They do this because we all seek comfort in what is familiar and predictable. (The word "familiar" has the same origins as the word "family", and when someone is familiar to us, it's often because they remind us of our primary caregivers.) What's funny is that while writing this section in a café, I overheard a man in his fifties telling his two friends: "When I ultimately forgave my dead mother, I stopped going after relationships with women who were abusive toward me." I thought overhearing this was beautifully fortuitous, because it's similar to what I witness with so many clients. Seeking to heal an old wound with a person who reminds us of the original perpetrator rarely heals us, but instead re-traumatizes us! Incidentally, we know that someone is more likely to choose a partner with mental health issues if they come from a parent who had them.

If you're in a romantic relationship with someone who reminds you of your dysfunctional parent, the relationship is not necessarily doomed. Far from it. However, it's important to be aware of how it impacts on your commitment and the relational dynamics. Are you trying to fix them because you couldn't do that to your parent? Are you angry they can't meet all your needs, because your parent couldn't? Do you view them as the placid victim, because that's how you saw your ineffective mother? It's important to recognize that they are not them.

Sex and Intimacy Challenges

You might find yourself on the receiving end of your partner's decreased libido. This could be because they're too depressed to be intimate. Or maybe medication is impacting their performance. We know that most antidepressants and antipsychotics can lead to reduced sex drive, difficulty achieving arousal or orgasm and, in some cases, erectile dysfunction. These physical effects are the result of how these drugs interact with neurotransmitters in the brain, which are crucial not just for mood regulation but also for sexual function. It's useful to research such side effects in more depth, so that both you and your partner can have greater empathy and awareness about what's going on. For some men, taking sildenafil (Viagra) or tadalafil (Cialis) can alleviate SSRI-induced erectile dysfunction.[4] However, there are also nonmedical interventions to explore, such as timing sex before medication is taken, exercising together, using CBD and other stimulants on genitals, or addressing diet and lifestyle factors.

If your partner has experienced a history of abuse, gaining their trust may be challenging. Trauma can leave us feeling perpetually unsafe, leading to anxiety when engaging in intimacy. This may result in a heightened state of alertness even in non-threatening scenarios, making it difficult to relax and engage fully. For some, physical closeness can trigger memories of past abuse, leading to avoidant behaviours. This can be misinterpreted as disinterest or rejection, but is a protective response against potential harm.

Or perhaps you have noticed your partner disassociating during intimate moments or relying on substances to do the deed. These are coping mechanisms used to handle overwhelming emotions, insecurities or memories tied to past abuse.

Approaching these challenges requires sensitivity, patience and a willingness to understand the profound impact trauma can have. Educate yourself about trauma responses, including triggers and symptoms, to better understand your partner's behaviours and needs. Opening up emotionally requires vulnerability. But the fear of being hurt again can prevent someone from fully engaging in a relationship and sharing their true feelings. So, let them lead the conversation at their own pace; avoid pressuring them to share more than they're comfortable with.

This doesn't mean that it's easy to be on the receiving end of, of course. However, it's important to be aware of the very real challenges your loved one faces around sexual intimacy – and not to take it personally. Because it's not.

Intimacy is hard when we're disconnected from ourselves. Therefore, all you can do is support your loved one to reawaken to themselves and establish a healthier relationship with their own body through things like meditation, yoga, self-massage, enjoying baths and somatic therapy. In the case of previous sexual abuse, expressing your empathy and compassion for their past experiences is fundamental, as is letting them know that you expect nothing from them. They might sometimes confuse love for abuse, so remaining consistent and modelling healthy boundaries is key.

Or you might find yourself at the other end of the spectrum, whereby your partner's mental health challenges cause promiscuity. We see this a lot with bipolar disorder when someone is experiencing a manic episode. Promiscuity is also attributed to personality disorders, as those with a fragile sense of self might seek out the sexual attention of others. Those with a history of childhood sexual abuse can also unconsciously or even consciously select partners that re-enact their early experiences, and leave them feeling used. This ties in with repetition compulsion.

Everyone's personal boundary lines are very different, and you can't ever know how you'll react to a situation until you find yourself in it. The relationships I've seen survive such challenges involve the partner taking responsibility for their actions, and finding ways to deal proactively with their impulses or tendencies.

It's completely reasonable that you would need to understand how your partner has learned to deal with their compulsions, and vice versa. Behavioural theory proposes that all behaviours, including sexual ones, are learned responses to certain stimuli, which can be unlearned or modified through behavioural interventions – but a person has to be willing to do the work.

Too Scared to Leave a Relationship

Over the years I've worked with many clients, both male and female, who have found themselves in dysfunctional relationships that they find hard to leave. In some cases, their partner behaved in an abusive manner in the name of mental health. For example, high levels of anxiety can manifest in ways such as physically lashing out when stressed, name-calling, shaming and insisting that the partner stays by their side, night and day. While mental health issues can exacerbate negative behaviours, they do not excuse them. Abuse, whether physical, emotional or psychological, is not directly caused by mental health issues but can be influenced by them.

What do I mean when I say "abuse"? Well, abuse can be characterized by four main components:

1 It causes harm, damage or control over the other person.
2 The perpetrator is typically full of shame and regret afterwards, thereby pulling their partner back into the cycle.
3 It's kept a secret from others by both parties and there is an unspoken agreement that it must never be discussed.
4 The victim ends up feeling sad, bad or guilty, and doubts they're the one who is the victim.

Not long ago, I worked with a successful fashion designer, who was in a relationship with a much younger man, who was besotted with her. Very quickly, they moved in together and enjoyed some happy times nesting. However, before long he started drinking excessively and becoming passive-aggressive toward her, especially if she got back late from work. It was clear to me that her acclaim threatened him. Yet, rather than admit to this part of himself, he would put her industry down and tarnish her accomplishments.

His behaviour became more vicious and aggressive over time. But still, she wouldn't end the relationship. You see, a part of her believed what he was saying was true – and so she would make excuses for his cruelty. She would justify his behaviour and tell me: "He sees so much more for me than fashion." The idea of her throwing him out of her penthouse apartment brought up all the guilt she had toward her former best friend, who'd been an addict who couldn't get her life together. Eventually, my client did end the relationship, after he brought a young girl back to her apartment and subsequently trashed it, but it took a lot of therapy and soul-searching.

If you're wanting to end a relationship or take a break from someone who you view as unstable, I know this is a very difficult predicament to find yourself in – especially if you're married, or have a family together. Perhaps you also feel scared about what the other person would do if you left. Here's Sid, 51, talking about his experience:

> My wife's anxiety is really bad and most of her life has fallen to the wayside over the last five years – her career, social circle, independence. I've tried to support her as best as I can, but nothing has made any difference. The hardest part is she expects me to follow suit and let go of the things that make me happy. If I tell her I've made plans, or have to attend a work event, she's overcome with jealousy, starts to punch me and begs me to stay with her. I know the relationship isn't healthy anymore, but I fear what she'd do if I leave. She's already said a few times that she doesn't want to be alive and if she went, she'd stop being a burden to me.

Sid's case is complicated, because on the one hand his wife is clearly suffering, but on the other, her behaviour could be categorized as coercive control. Coercive control is a form of psychological abuse designed to control someone else's life systematically. The jealousy, physical altercations and emotional manipulation (such as using threats about ending her life to keep Sid from leaving) are all indicators of this form of abuse.

Coercive control is insidious, creating an ongoing environment of fear and dependency without necessarily leaving physical marks. It usually involves the gradual isolation of the victim from their support network, which undermines their social foundations and increases dependence. The abuser may even try to control resources such as finances, access to healthcare and transportation in a bid to restrict the other person's autonomy.

In my clinical experience, men find it a lot harder to recognize than women do, possibly because it undermines the notion that men have additional power or strength. Coercive control is more likely to occur if there is mental illness at play, which makes the loved one feel bad about leaving, and so the cycle of abuse perpetuates...

Typically, coercive control reflects underlying psychological distress and emotional problems, including personality disorders and past trauma. More surprisingly, it is also associated with anxiety and depression: the controlling behaviour becomes a misguided way to alleviate insecurity and perceived threats to the relationship. And the victim also ends up riddled with anxiety.

My personal belief is that most individuals who assert coercive control know what they're doing and, much like bullies, find ways to restrict the other person deliberately because of their own deep-seated inadequacies. Of course, there are always those who lack any form of self-awareness; having learned such patterns from their own families, they think these are normal aspects of behaviour. Regardless, people often justify their own controlling behaviour as being motivated by love and concern. While understanding this context can be helpful, it doesn't excuse the behaviour.

Circling back to Sid, his need for safety and respect within the relationship is paramount. So, what are his options?

1   Sid could be encouraged to express how he feels to his wife, using "I" statements which focus on his feelings and experiences. Clearly communicating his boundaries during these reflections is crucial, stating what is

acceptable and what isn't in their interactions. This might include which types of behaviours he can tolerate and what actions will compel him to take further steps to protect his wellbeing.

2 Sid could encourage his wife to seek help from a mental health professional, if she isn't already doing so, to manage her anxiety and any other underlying issues. However, he should be cautious about naming "coercive control" himself, as this could escalate matters.

3 Sid could consider seeking therapeutic support for himself to navigate his feelings and decide on his future steps in an informed and supportive environment.

4 Providing there is desire and buy-in from both parties, they could consider attending couples therapy, where Sid may be able to discuss his feelings more openly in the presence of a therapist.

5 If Sid decides to end the marriage, he should plan a safe exit strategy, based on support from his therapist and legal advisor. Prior to doing this, he might encourage his wife to connect with supportive networks, whether friends, family or mental health professionals, who can provide emotional support during this transition. He could even facilitate these connections himself to ensure she has a support system in place.

6 If there are serious concerns about either of their safety, he should contact professionals or emergency services immediately.

Extending kindness doesn't make you responsible for managing anyone's mental health. While ending a relationship doesn't negate the love or care you have shown, ensuring someone has support in place may be the best you can do as you step back. Remember, no one is responsible for anyone else's actions.

You might be thinking, "But my partner isn't of sound judgement – how can I absolve myself of responsibility?" The answer lies in personal choice. So, if you choose to continue to stay in a harmful or abusive scenario, then that is you exerting your own free will.

A fulfilling union is one where two people support one another's individuality and have each other's back, regardless of mental health difficulties. *Unconditional romantic love doesn't exist – nor should it.* If you're with a person who repeatedly disrespects your life choices, your boundaries and your trust, then it's almost always time to walk away. Coercive control is criminalized in the UK. In the US, some states like California and Connecticut are taking concrete steps to include it under domestic violence laws.

Change in relationships is possible but it requires not only individual determination but cooperation and understanding from both parties. Mental health issues don't preclude the ability to work on ourselves or the relationship, unless someone is severely incapacitated.

It's equally important to reflect on your own behaviour in relationships. Perhaps there are ways in which you might be unknowingly exerting control over your loved one who is struggling. Consider the possibility that what you perceive as help could sometimes feel like control to them, and embrace this awareness not as a fault, but as an opportunity to grow.

> **PROMPT:** Have your actions, however well intentioned, placed undue pressure on your loved one in a bid to control them? If so, what steps can you take today to ensure that your support is liberating for both you and your loved one?

Therapeutic Interventions

This chapter wouldn't be complete without emphasizing the lifeline that couples therapy and family therapy can offer. Not only do they provide external support, but they provide a safe space for relational dynamics. This can help each person to understand and empathize with the other's struggles, facilitating communication and conflict-resolution skills.

Family therapy extends these benefits to broader family dynamics. Research has shown that family environments characterized by communication deviance (unclear or vague communication) or high levels of expressed emotion can exacerbate mental health issues.[5] Family therapy aims to address these issues by improving communication patterns and reducing emotional over-involvement or levelled criticism, which is unhealthy for everyone.

When all is said and done, abuse affects everyone within the system, not just the direct victim. Systemic therapy approaches recognize these ripple effects and works toward healing not just the individual, but the relational network they're part of. This healing process acknowledges that our relationships often reflect our individual shadows, those parts of ourselves we may have trouble accepting. The transpersonal approach is that conflict, however painful it is, can catalyse growth and healing. Through finding peace with a loved one – which is not always the same as *making peace* – we can pave the way to find peace within ourselves.

CLOSING THE LOOP

"I think all comedians are born from unwell parents."
James, 60

What you don't yet know is that this book literally wouldn't exist if it weren't for my sister. Not only did she introduce me to the publishing house that ended up publishing *You Are Not Alone In This*, but she also worked tirelessly to support me along the way. Everything we went through together all those years back would eventually lead me to find my purpose and help others through writing about my experiences. I just had no idea this was the case at the time.

I think the same is true for most of the challenging things I've been through in my life; I've wilfully crafted them into shaping my narrative *for the better.* But if anyone has done that to an even greater extent, it's my sister. I appreciate we're two of the fortunate ones; I have a very capable and courageous sister, who has triumphed. However, I'm aware that not everyone shares this fortune, and it is with deep empathy that I address those of you who continue to navigate uncertainty. The principles I advocate are universal, grounded in the belief that "doing the work" is essential, not just for the wellbeing of our loved ones, but for ourselves.

My personal and clinical experiences, supported by research, have highlighted five key factors that most profoundly impact someone's ability *to support their loved ones without losing themselves.* These are:

1 that a loved one has a robust and personalized treatment plan in place
2 that you process all your feelings and find effective ways to manage stress
3 that you discover and maintain clear personal boundaries
4 that you actively seek support for yourself
5 that you find a purpose that is uniquely your own

Throughout this book, we've explored these in depth. You might have noticed that the majority of these factors (from 2 to 5) require you, the caregiver, to engage actively in self-work. Not because you should, but because you want to invest in your wellbeing and development not solely for the sake of your loved one but, crucially, for yourself.

Reclaiming Your Story

I wrote this book because a lot of people come into therapy when they're close to someone who is struggling with their mental health. Too often, the person in the supporting role ends up with mental health problem themselves. The toll can be huge – the incessant worrying about someone you love, the fear of saying or putting a foot wrong. Not to mention the fact that when people are hurting, they can hurt others, often through no fault of their own. I'm here to encourage you to be deliberate about stopping that cycle. Even when mental health is in the picture, there is a significant difference between being a victim of illness, or circumstance, and making victimhood your identity, or the identity of the person you love. Encourage them – and remind yourself – to maintain autonomy over your personal narratives.

Wherever you are on your own path, I urge you to find ways to reclaim not just your time but your story. Today, longer life expectancy isn't just a medical marvel, it's a sociological one. With longer lives come more chapters, more evolutions and, inevitably, more opportunities to begin again. Remember, it's important to grieve for what's lost, it's okay to feel uncertain, it's normal to fear. Yet take solace in the knowledge that this struggle signifies you're alive and capable of growth.

Throughout the enduring journey of supporting others, it's crucial to ask, "Who am I beyond this role?" Too often, we're ensnared by familial or societal demands that have outlived their usefulness. Sometimes, we get caught up conforming to external expectations rather than heeding our inner calling. Or we cut off parts of our personalities and emotions that we deem unacceptable. Is it time to honour your true essence, and reclaim the forgotten parts of yourself? This need not mean withdrawing your support, but fostering a more balanced approach that creates a win–win situation for you both.

Drawing inspiration from role models can be a useful tool to help us do this. They could be from literature, film, history or your personal sphere. What's important is they embody traits you aspire to develop. Then, when you are faced with a challenge, envision them within you. How would they navigate this obstacle? How would they practise resilience, empathy, or self-care? In transpersonal therapy, imagination is not just fantasy; it's your gateway to change.

An Alchemical Process

Alongside considering the qualities you're being summoned to cultivate, you might also find yourself asking questions such as: "What is this situation revealing to me? How can I use this situation as a force for good in my own life and the lives of others?"

This is the true meaning of alchemy: the idea of turning lead into gold. While it's not always possible to change our literal physical reality (spoiler alert: lead doesn't turn to gold no matter how hard I try), we can transform our perspectives. It is possible, at least figuratively, to turn something dark, heavy and dense into something of value. But it's not easy.

Victor Frankl, who wrote *Man's Search for Meaning* after surviving a concentration camp, said: "When we are no longer able to change a situation, we are challenged to change ourselves." And it's in this change – this adaptation of perspective – where we might discover an expanded, deeper sense of meaning.

Sometimes this means cultivating more acceptance that not everything is fixable. Sometimes there is no answer – and that's the answer. We're a society that loves to solve problems; to fix people and things. To make everything sanitized and perfect. But that isn't reality. And the more that we can accept and integrate shadow material, the more harmonious our society will actually be. Because then we stop trying to make others more like us, and accept that everyone is wholly unique and on their own path. We can't control everything – remember there is "Your Work, Their Work and God's Work". Focus on what is in your wheelhouse.

Speaking of which, a recent study found that caregivers who practiced acceptance experienced better mental health outcomes.[1] Accepting the reality of a situation, rather than continually fighting against it, allows caregivers to set healthy boundaries and focus on self-care. This acceptance does not mean giving up hope but rather finding a sustainable way to cope with a situation.

At the heart of this acceptance is recognition of every individual's autonomy – acknowledging their right to make choices about their life. This acceptance needn't mean passive resignation, but demands respect for their legal and ethical rights. While we might not always agree with the decisions of those we love, our role is not to control but to accompany and, where necessary, advocate on their behalf.

In embracing this complex reality, we learn not only about the limits of our influence but also about the depth of our compassion and love. When we recognize that no one is defined by their thoughts or emotions – including ourselves – we can more easily remain grounded.

Getting Untangled

Sometimes, as we've seen, you're simply not the right person to help your loved one. It's not your fault, but for whatever reason, it can't be you. The ultimate goal is still to ensure that your loved one receives the support they need to thrive, so if that means stepping back from aspects of their care and encouraging them to find the right key person to help them, then you are doing the right thing. Embrace the role that allows you to maintain a positive and supportive relationship, one that contributes to their overall happiness and mental health without being defined by it.

In the end, it's not about being right – or about being everything to someone – it's about offering them the right thing at the right moment. By recognizing your limits and respecting their needs, you create a more balanced dynamic that fosters genuine connection.

The more authentic you can be, the more authentic your relationship will be. So, notice when you say "yes" to those things you want to say "no" to, and vice versa. That doesn't mean you always have to say your truth, or do so with a lack of empathy. Consider whether there might be a way of behaving in a way that is true to you in spite of the complex situation.

The more we can model authenticity and be a whole person, the more we can influence others to be authentic and look at their own life and health as a whole, too. After all, an effective treatment plan requires the patient to be an active participant. You might also reframe a treatment plan as an integrative wellness plan, which doesn't just look at illness, but taps in to potential. And consider creating one for yourself too (see pages 269–70 for a template).

While we may not all have mental illness, we all have mental health, which requires intentional care and humility. So let's keep challenging how we perceive mental health. Digest and share articles, books, films and podcasts that explore the topic with nuance, sensitivity and hope.

Questions to Come Back To

As we approach the end of this book, I'd like to leave you with some final questions to reflect on that summarize the key points. Please revisit them whenever you need to:

- **Core needs:** What do I need in this relationship to feel respected and valued?
- **Comfort levels:** What behaviours or requests make me feel uncomfortable or anxious?
- **Apportioning time:** How much time and space would I like to dedicate to my loved one's mental health in order to feel balanced and at ease in myself?
- **Deal-breakers:** Which of my loved one's actions or behaviours are absolutely unacceptable to me?
- **Emotional capacity:** What am I willing and unwilling to take on emotionally in this relationship?
- **Personal boundaries:** What new boundary do I need to implement, or which old boundary do I need to change?
- **Food for the body and soul**: What else do I desire for myself?

Take Centre Stage

Just as you want your loved one to take responsibility for their wellbeing, you deserve to do the same. Take steps to foster:

- self-awareness
- a sense of purpose (outside of your supporting role)
- your own support network

While you might be in a supporting role when it comes to your loved one, you're not a support act in your own life. You're the star of the show – so embrace that role and the rest will fall into place.

HOLISTIC CARE PLAN TEMPLATE

Personal Information
Name:
Date of birth:
Today's date:
Medical practitioner/care worker (if applicable):
Emergency contact information:

Assessment of Wellbeing
Describe current status as well as things that help the areas of concern. You can use information from column "Things that support my health" on page 127.

Physical Pillar:
Emotional Pillar:
Intellectual Pillar:
Social Pillar:
Spiritual Pillar:
Financial Pillar:
Environmental Pillar:

Main objective:

SMART Goals Integration
Specific goal: What is the specific area of wellbeing you want to focus on?

Measurable: What measurable action can be taken?
Achievable: Is the goal realistic with the time and resources available?
Relevant: How does the goal relate to my core values?
Time-bound: What is the timeline for achieving this change?

Support Systems
Fill in four concentric circles of support that are varied and robust.

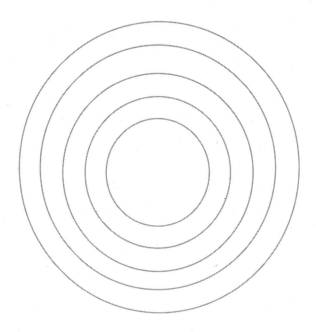

Evaluation and Feedback
Scheduled Review Dates: When will the plan be reviewed to assess progress and make necessary adjustments?

Feedback from care workers/medical practitioners (if applicable): Include feedback to ensure the plan remains aligned with medical advice and care needs.

REFERENCES

Introduction

1   Carers UK's annual survey of over 5,000 carers across
    the UK, 2015, www.carersuk.org/policy-and-research/
    state-of-caring-survey/
2   Navaie-Waliser, M, et al, "When the caregiver needs
    care: the plight of vulnerable caregivers", *Am J Public
    Health*, 92(3), 2002, pp. 409–13
3   National Alliance on Caregiving, "Young Caregivers in
    the US: Report on Findings", United Hospital Fund,
    2005, www.yumpu.com/en/document/view/43585724/
    young-caregivers-in-the-us-2005-national-alliance-for-
    caregiving
4   Cham, CQ, et al, "Caregiver Burden among Caregivers of
    Patients with Mental Illness: A Systematic Review and
    Meta-Analysis", *Healthcare (Basel)*, 10(12), 2022, p. 2423
5   Zhiya, Hua, and Dandan, Ma, "Purpose in life moderates
    the relationship between loneliness and caregiving
    stress among family caregivers of people with mental
    health problems", *Archives of Psychiatric Nursing*, 49,
    2024, pp. 99–105

1. Navigating the Path to Help

1   Tsang, YT, et al, "Caregivers as gatekeepers:
    Professional mental health service use among urban

minority adolescents", *Am J Orthopsychiatry*, 90(3), 2020, pp. 328–39

2   Giles, J, "Exposing the links between doctors and Big Pharma", *NewScientist*, 18 February 2009

3   "Adolescent and Young Adult Health Factsheet", World Health Organization website, 2023, www.who.int/newsroom/fact-sheets/detail/adolescents-health-risks-and-solutions

4   "Realising the Potential of Early Intervention", Early Intervention Foundation, 2018, www.eif.org.uk/report/realising-the-potential-of-early-intervention

5   See also: DSM-5, American Psychiatric Association, 2013, p. 645.

6   NHS statistics from 2020–2021

7   Chopra, Deepak, "UK Longevity Retreat", June 2024

8   "Circle of Care: A Guidebook for Mental Health Caregivers", National Alliance for Caregivers, 2023, www.caregiving. org/wp-content/ uploads/2016/02/ NAC_Mental_Illness_ Study_2016_FINAL_WEB. pdf

9   Zimmerman, E, "Mayo Clinic researchers demonstrate value of second opinions", Mayo Clinic website, 2017, newsnetwork.mayoclinic.org/discussion/mayo-clinic-researchers-demonstrate-value-of-second-opinions/

2. Communication and Building Dialogue

1   Thomas, M V, et al, "The Effect of Music on the Human Stress Response", PLOS ONE website, 2013, journals. plos.org/plosone/article?id=10.1371/journal.pone.0070156

2   American Physiological Society, "Stress hormones spike as
the temperature rises", ScienceDaily website, 25 April 2018,
 www.sciencedaily.com/releases/2018/04/180425131906. htm

3   Rogers, C, *Client-Centered Therapy*, Houghton-Mifflin, Boston, 1951

4   Cozolino, L, *The Neuroscience of Human Relationships: Attachment and the Developing Social Brain*, W.W. Norton
& Company, New York, 2014

5   Vecchi, G, et al, "Crisis Hostage Negotiation: Current strategies and issues in high-risk conflict resolution", *Aggression and Violent Behavior*, 10(5), 2005, pp. 533–51

3. Understanding Mental Health Conditions

1   Roberge, P, et al, "Generalized anxiety disorder in primary care: mental health services use and treatment adequacy", *BMC Fam Pract*, 16, 2015, p. 146

2   Gaudiano, BA, "Cognitive-behavioural therapies: achievements and challenges", *Evid Based Ment Health*, 2008, 11(1), 2008, pp. 5–7

3   National Autistic Society website, www.autism.org.uk/advice-and-guidance/topics/mental-health/ocd

4   Zangrilli, A, et al, "How do psychiatrists address delusions in first meetings in acute care? A qualitative study", *BMC Psychiatry*, 14, 2014, p. 178, www.ncbi.nlm.nih.gov/pmc/articles/PMC4067065/

5   Mestdagh, A, and Hansen, B, "Stigma in patients with schizophrenia receiving community mental health care: a review of qualitative studies", *Soc Psychiatry Psychiatr Epidemiol*, 49, 2014, pp. 79–87, link.springer.com/article/10.1007/s00127-013-0729-4

6   Díaz-Marsá, M, Carrasco, JL, and Sáiz, J, "A study of temperament and personality in anorexia and bulimia nervosa",
J Pers Disord, 14(4), 2000, pp. 352–9

7   Rorty, M, Yager, J, and Rossotto, E, "Childhood sexual, physical, and psychological abuse in bulimia nervosa",

Am J Psychiatry, 151(8), 1994, pp. 1122–6, pubmed.ncbi.
nlm.nih.gov/8037244/

8 Kreismann, J, *Talking to a Loved One with Borderline
    Personality Disorder*, New Harbinger Publications,
    Oakland, 2018

9 NHS, "Antisocial personality disorder", NHS website,
    2021,
    www.nhs.uk/mental-health/conditions/antisocial-personality-
    disorder/

10 School of Medicine and Public Health, "Psychopaths'
    Brains Show Differences in Structure and Function",
    University of Wisconsin website, 2017, www.med.wisc.
    edu/news/psychopaths-brains-differences-structure-
    function/

4. Taking a Holistic Approach

1 Leamy, M, et al, "Conceptual framework for personal
    recovery in mental health: systematic review and
    narrative synthesis", *British Journal of Psychiatry*, 199(6),
    2011, pp. 445–52

2 Krist, AH, et al, "Engaging Patients in Decision-Making
    and Behavior Change to Promote Prevention", *Stud
    Health Technol Inform*, 240, 2017, pp. 284–302, www.
    ncbi.nlm.nih.gov/pmc/articles/PMC6996004/

3 Mammen, G, and Faulkner, G, "Physical Activity and
    the Prevention of Depression", *American Journal of
    Preventative Medicine*, 2013, www.ajpmonline.org/
    article/S0749-3797(13)00451-0/

4 "How Swimming Improves Mental Health", swimming.
    org

5 NYU Langone Health / NYU School of Medicine, "Yoga
    shown to improve anxiety, study shows", ScienceDaily
    website, 12 August 2020, www.sciencedaily.com/
    releases/2020/08/200812144124.htm.

6   Butler, M I, and Mörkl, S, "The Mediterranean Diet and
     Mental Health", in Dinan, T, ed., *Nutritional Psychiatry: A
     Primer for Clinicians*, Cambridge University Press, 2023,
     pp. 39–54

7   Jacka, FN, et al, "A randomised controlled trial of dietary
     improvement for adults with major depression (the
     'SMILES' trial)", *BMC Med*, 15, 2017, p. 23

8   Appleton, J, "The Gut-Brain Axis: Influence of Microbiota
     on Mood and Mental Health", *Integr Med (Encinitas)*,
     17(4), 2018,
     pp. 28–32

9   Bilodeau, K, "Fermented foods for better gut health",
     Harvard Health Blog, Harvard Health Publishing website,
     2023,
     www.health.harvard.edu/blog/fermented-foods-for-
     better-
     gut-health-2018051613841

10   Dziedzic, A, et al, "The Power of Psychobiotics in
     Depression:
     A Modern Approach through the Microbiota–Gut–Brain
     Axis:
     A Literature Review", *Nutrients*, 16(7), 2024, p. 1054

11   Scholten, W, Batelaan, N, and Van Balkom, A, "Barriers
     to discontinuing antidepressants in patients with
     depressive and anxiety disorders: a review of the
     literature and clinical recommendations", *Ther Adv
     Psychopharmacol*, 10(10), 2020, ww.ncbi.nlm.nih.gov/
     pmc/articles/PMC7290254/

12   Schimelpfening, N, "Tips for Antidepressant
     Withdrawal Relief", VeryWellMind website, 2023, www.
     verywellmind.com/tips-to-reduce-antidepressant-
     withdrawal-symptoms-1066835

13   "How Does Vitamin B12 Help With Antidepressant
     Withdrawals?", MethylLife website, methyl-life.com/
     blogs/mental-health/how-does-vitamin-b12-help-with-
     antidepressant-withdrawals

14 Greer, M, "Strengthen your brain by resting it", APA website, 2004, www.apa.org/monitor/julaug04/strengthen

15 Besedovsky, L, Lange, T, and Born, J, "Sleep and immune function", *Pflugers Arch*, 463(1), 2012, pp. 121–37, www.ncbi.nlm.nih.gov/pmc/articles/PMC3256323/

16 "What are Sleep Disorders?", American Psychiatric Association website, www.psychiatry.org/patients-families/sleep-disorders/what-are-sleep-disorders

17 Newsom, R, and Dimitriu, A, "Cognitive Behavioral Therapy for Insomnia (CBT-1)", Sleep Foundation website, 2024, www.sleepfoundation.org/insomnia/treatment/cognitive-behavioral-therapy-insomnia

18 Tan, C, et al, "Recognizing the role of the vagus nerve in depression from microbiota-gut brain axis", Frontiers in Neurology, 13, 2022, p.1015–175

19 Gukasyan, N, et al, "Efficacy and safety of psilocybin-assisted treatment for major depressive disorder: Prospective 12-month follow-up", 2022, journals.sagepub.com/doi/10.1177/02698811211073759

20 Knatz Peck, S, et al, "Psilocybin therapy for females with anorexia nervosa: a phase 1, open-label feasibility study", 2023, www.nature.com/articles/s41591-023-02455-9#Sec2

21 Tugade, M M, and Fredrickson, BL, "Resilient individuals use positive emotions to bounce back from negative emotional experiences", *J Pers Soc Psychol*, 86(2), 2004, pp. 320–33, www.ncbi.nlm.nih.gov/pmc/articles/PMC3132556/

22 Lazarus, R S, "From psychological stress to the emotions: a history of changing outlooks", *Annu Rev Psychol*, 44, 1993, pp. 1–21, pubmed.ncbi.nlm.nih.gov/8434890/

23 Kendler, K S, et al, "Dimensions of religiosity and their relationship to lifetime psychiatric and substance use

disorders", *Am J Psychiatry*, 160(3), 2003, pp. 496–503, pubmed.ncbi.nlm.nih.gov/12611831/

24 Han, A, and Kim, T H, "Effects of Self-Compassion Interventions on Reducing Depressive Symptoms, Anxiety, and Stress: A Meta-Analysis", *Mindfulness* (NY), 5, 2023, pp. 1–29, www.ncbi.nlm.nih.gov/pmc/articles/ PMC10239723/

25 "Memory and Aging Project", Rush University Website, www.rushu.rush.edu/research/departmental-research/ rush-alzheimers-disease-center/rush-alzheimers-disease- center-research/epidemiologic-research/memory-and- aging-project

26 Budson, AE, "Why is Music Good for the Brain", Harvard Health Blog, Harvard Health Publishing website, 2020, www.health.harvard.edu/blog/why-is-music-good-for- the-brain-2020100721062

27 Oppong, T, "Psychological Secrets to Hack Your Way to Better Life Habits", Observer website, 2017, observer. com/2017/03/psychological-secrets-hack-better-life- habits-psychology-productivity/

28 "Mental Health at Work", World Health Organization website, 2022, www.who.int/news-room/fact-sheets/ detail/mental-health-at-work

29 Crowther, R, et al, "Vocational rehabilitation for people with severe mental illness", *Cochrane Database Syst Rev*, 2001; 2001(2), p.CD00308, www.ncbi.nlm.nih.gov/pmc/ articles/PMC4170889/

30 Ibid

31 Holt-Lunstad, J, Smith, TB, and Layton, JB, "Social relationships and mortality risk: a meta-analytic review", *PLoS Med*, 7(7), 2010, p. e1000316, pubmed.ncbi.nlm.nih. gov/20668659/

32 Arnold, R, et al, "Patient attitudes concerning the inclusion of spirituality into addition treatment", PubMed, pubmed.ncbi.nlm.nih.gov/12495793/

33 "The Facts", Money and Mental Health Policy Institute website, www.moneyandmentalhealth.org/money-and-mental-health-facts/

34 "Circle of Care Report", National Alliance for Caregiving, 2023, www.nami.org/wp-content/uploads/2023/08/CircleOfCareReport.pdf

35 Braverman, R, Holkar, M, and Evans, K, "Informal Borrowing and Mental Health Problems", The Money and Mental Health Policy Institute, 2018, www.moneyandmentalhealth.org/wp-content/uploads/2018/05/Money-and-Mental-Health-Informal-borrowing-report.pdf

36 IQAir Staffwriters, "How does outdoor air pollution affect my indoor air quality?", IQAir website, 2018, iqair.com/gb/newsroom/how-does-outdoor-air-pollution-affect-my-indoor-air-quality

37 Cui, X, et al, "Vitamin D and schizophrenia: 20 years on", *Mol Psychiatry*, 26, 2012, pp. 2708–20, www.nature.com/articles/s41380-021-01025-0

5. Creating an Emergency Plan

1 Borum, R, and Franz, S, "Crisis Intervention Teams may prevent arrests of people with mental illnesses", Mental Health Law & Policy Faculty Publications, 2010, Paper 537, http://www.gocit.org/uploads/3/0/5/5/30557023/crisis_intervention_teams_may_prevent_arrests_of_people_with_ment.pdf

2 Wilkinson, H, "The Importance of Early Mental Health Intervention", TalkWorks website, 2024, talk-works.org.uk/the-importance-of-early-mental-health-intervention/

3 Manwarren Generes, M, "Can You Die From Drug or Alcohol Withdrawals?", American Addiction Centers website, 2024, americanaddictioncenters.org/withdrawal-timelines-treatments/risk-of-death

4   "Suicide Prevention", World Health Organization, www. who.int/health-topics/suicide
5   "Samaritans Believes Reducing Self-harm is Key to Suicide Prevention", Samaritans, 2019, www.samaritans. org/news/samaritans-believes-reducing-self-harm-key-suicide-prevention/
6   Joiner, T, "Why People Die by Suicide", 2006
7   Engel, R, et al, "The Effect of Family Interventions on Relapse and Rehospitalization in Schizophrenia— A Meta-analysis", *Schizophrenia Bulletin*, 2001

6. Messy Feelings of Ambivalence

1   University of California at Davis, study by Katherine Conger.
2   Cowen, AS, "Self-report Captures 27 Distinct Categories of Emotion Bridged by Continuous Gradients", PNAS website, 2017, www.pnas.org/doi/abs/10.1073/ pnas.1702247114

7. Managing Burnout and Stress

1   "Caring in a Complex World: perspectives from unpaid carers and the organisations that support them", The King's Fund, 2023.
2   Pakenham, K, et al, "Relations between social support, appraisal and coping and both positive and negative outcomes in young carers", *Journal of Health Psychology*, 2007.

8. Setting and Holding Boundaries

1   "Unpaid care and domestic work", Action Aid website, 2024, www.actionaid.org.uk/our-work/womens-economic-rights/unpaid-care-and-domestic-work

2   "KPMG Study Finds 75% Of Female Executives Across
     Industries Have Experienced Imposter Syndrome In
     Their Careers", KPMG website, 2020, www.prnewswire.
     com/news-releases/kpmg-study-finds-75-of-female-
     executives-across-industries-have-experienced-
     imposter-syndrome-in-their-careers-301148023.html
3   Winicott, D, *Playing and Reality*, Routledge Classics,
     London, 1971.
4   Karpman, S, "Fairy Tales and Script Drama Analysis",
     karpmandramatriangle.com/pdf/DramaTriangle.pdf

9. Reclaiming You

1   Mayo Clinic Staff, "Caregiver stress: Tips for taking care
     of yourself", Mayo Clinic website, www.mayoclinic.org/
     healthy-lifestyle/stress-management/in-depth/caregiver-
     stress/art-20044784
2   The American Society of Training and Development
     (ASTD), 2015.
3   Bernabéu-Álvarez, C, et al, "Effect of support groups on
     caregiver's quality of life", *Family Process*, 61(2), 2022,
     pp. 643–58, onlinelibrary.wiley.com/doi/full/10.1111/
     famp.12684
4   Greenfield, C, "Fantastic Hobbies for Caregivers
     that Make Life Better", KAPOK website, 2023,
     multiculturalcaregiving.com/hobbies-for-caregivers/
5   Renehan, AG, Booth, C, and Potten, CS, "What is
     Apoptosis, and Why Is It Important?", *BMJ*, 2001,
     322(7301), www.ncbi.nlm.nih.gov/pmc/articles/
     PMC1120576/

10. Caring for Your Relationship

1   Schwartz, R C, *Internal Family Systems Therapy*, Guilford Press,
     1995.

REFERENCES

2   Sample, I, "Gene research finds opposites do attract", *Guardian*, 24 May 2009, www.theguardian.com/science/2009/may/24/genes-human-attraction.

3   Sigmund Freud, *Remembering, Repeating and Working Through*, London, 1914.

4   LeWine, H, "Sexual side effects of SSRIs: Why it happens and what to do", Harvard Health Publishing website, 2023, www.health.harvard.edu/womens-health/when-an-ssri-medication-impacts-your-sex-life.

5   Rund, B R, et al, "Expressed emotion, communication deviance and schizophrenia. An exploratory study of the relationship between two family variables and the course and outcome of a psychoeducational treatment programme", *Psychopathology*, 28(4), 1995, pp. 220–8, pubmed.ncbi.nlm.nih.gov/7480578/

Closing the Loop

1   Ye, F, et al, "Acceptance and Commitment Therapy Among Informal Caregivers of People With Chronic Health Conditions: A Systematic Review and Meta-Analysis", *JAMA Netw Open*, 6(12), 2023, p. e2346216, www.ncbi.nlm.nih.gov/pmc/articles/PMC10698615/

FURTHER RESOURCES

For a full list of resources and links, go to www.sophiescott.co, where you can also access my online programs.

Books

- *The Body Keeps the Score* by Bessel van Der Kolk – Groundbreaking exploration into how trauma is stored in the body and brain.
- *Man's Search for Meaning* by Viktor Frankl - Powerful narrative on finding purpose amidst suffering.
- *This Book Will Change Your Mind About Mental Health* by Nathan Filer – Fresh insights into mental illness and psychiatric treatments.
- *Wishful Drinking* by Carrie Fisher – Candid memoir of living with bipolar disorder by a Hollywood icon.
- *An Unquiet Mind* by Kay Redfield Jamison – Memoir written by one of the foremost authorities on bipolar disorder, who has experienced it first-hand.
- *The Color of Hope* by Vanessa Hazzard - Anthology amplifying the voices of people of color in their mental health journeys.
- *The Memory Palace* by Mira Bartók – Tales of growing up with a schizophrenic mother, and the lasting impact on a child's development.
- *It's Not You* by Dr Ramani Durvasula – Healing yourself from narcissistic abuse.
- *It Didn't Start With You* by Mark Wolynn – How to break free from inherited family patterns.

- *Cured* by Dr Jeff Redige – World-leading Harvard psychiatrist unlocks the secrets of good mental and physical health.
- *This Is Your Brain on Food* by M.D. Naidoo, Uma and Deepti Gupta – Cutting-edge research that explains how different foods affect mental health.

Online

- NAMI's Family-Family Education Program (US): Free 8-week course for caregivers.
- Turning Point (UK) www.turning-point.co.uk/services/drug-and-alcohol-support/friends-and-family/5-step-registration: Self-refer to get support if your loved one is struggling with addiction.
- Action for Happiness www.actionforhappiness.org: Resources and tips to lead a happier life.
- Calm App: Guided meditations and sleep tools for those looking to manage stress.
- The Optimum Health Clinic: Global award-winning clinic focused on treating chronic fatigue.
- The Embody Lab: Online hub to find somatic/bodywork therapists.

Support Groups

UK
- Carers UK: Supportive community and resources for unpaid caregivers across the UK.
- The Respite Association www.respiteassociation.org: Grants to caregivers to fund short breaks or holistic therapies like massage and yoga.

US
- Family Caregiver Alliance (FCA): Support services and information tailored to the needs of family caregivers.

- Embracing Carers: Global community and resources for unpaid carers.
- Huddol: A Canadian-based social network for caregivers to connect and exchange advice, experiences, and support.

Accredited therapists
- Psychology Today's Therapist Directory - Extensive directory of licensed and accredited therapists, counselors, psychiatrists, and psychologists across the US.
- BetterHelp – World's largest online therapy service providing affordable care.
- In the US, any person in crisis – or a person supporting someone in crisis – can call or text 988 or chat at 988lifeline. org/chat, any time to reach a trained counselor.
- UKCP Find a Therapist: www.psychotherapy.org.uk/Find accredited therapists across the UK (including integrative and art therapists).
- IAPT (NHS Talking Therapies): Free counselling across UK. Referrals can be made through GPs or self-referral.
- Relate (Relationship and Family Therapy) www.relate.org. uk: Relationship and family counseling. Some subsidized services available.

ABOUT THE AUTHOR

"With stress and mental health predicted to be the 'next global epidemic' Sophie's message is more critical than ever."

Forbes

Sophie Scott (UKCP, MABCP) is a leading integrative psychotherapist with a thriving private practice in central London. She has a particular interest in working with anxiety, burnout and existential crises in a holistic way, integrating mind-body practices. A steadfast advocate for psychoeducation, she has taught for many colleges and business schools, covering everything from human developmental theory to imposter syndrome.

Sophie likes to think she isn't your average psychotherapist – for one, she's fully aware of the trappings of modern living. As an entrepreneur, she founded BALANCE Magazine, the UK's award-winning wellness media brand, bringing mental and physical wellbeing to the masses. As the Editor-in-Chief for 6+ years, she championed innovation and accessibility across the industry, and was fortunate to work with A-list talent and spearhead partnerships with global brands.

Sophie regularly appears in the media speaking and writing about emotional health, the wellness industry and psychotherapy.

To find out more, visit her website – www.sophiescott.co – and sign up to her newsletter, The 2-min therapist.

ACKNOWLEDGEMENTS

This book is a deeply personal project, and I'm fortunate to have benefitted from the support of many brilliant people along the way.

First, to my family, who are my bedrock and constant cheerleaders. When I doubt myself to the point of paralysis, you take my hand and shepherd me to the next destination. You always believe in me, even if that sometimes means giving me the nudge to "just get on with it."

Daniel, my wonderful husband, you have spent countless late nights and early mornings helping me hone my ideas, craft chapter structures and patiently listen as I explained complex theories – despite having no formal training in them yourself. Your decency, wisdom and incredible ability to get to the heart of a matter are just a few of your gifts (your talents are endless). Thank you for supporting me through some hairy moments and for allowing me to show you how best to help when despair or anxiety take me hostage. Getting to do life with you makes everything right. I love you.

To my superstar sister, you have opened so many doors for me in life simply through your existence. And look how far we've come! Your go-getting attitude and fearlessness have been pivotal in shaping me – and this book. As one of the best literary publicists in the business, you've gotten this book into more hands than I could have imagined and have (shamelessly) promoted it whenever you could. Thank you for being my lucky star.

To our daughter, Billie Rose, who is almost two years old, the fact that I've managed to write this book while being your mother during "the toddler years" is a testament to your incredible and vast spirit. I see you, I love you and I will always be here for you.

To my parents, who made me who I am. I feel proud of our one-of-a-kind, eccentric family. I would choose you again and again. Thank you for the music.

To our other "parents", Aunty Stephanie and Uncle Michael, who have always offered Vikki and I a true sense of family. We love you and appreciate you more than you will ever know.

To the Osoffs, Scotts, my inspirational grandparents and my ancestors, I feel deeply connected to you all, and I miss you desperately.

A special thanks to my best friend of 29 years and second sister, Florence, who has remained as loyal and wise as the first day we met. You showed me that it was safe to trust someone outside of family – and in doing so, you became just that.

To all my other friends, girlfriends and Foundrs community – thank you for boosting my life.

Now, to the professional support: from our first conversation, I knew that working with Brittany Willis, my commissioning editor, was right. This may be our debut, but this book holds a deep personal significance for both of us. Thanks for trusting me and for being a steady hand throughout the entire process. You have been a constant source of support, common sense, and calm. I cannot wait to see your career soar.

Thank you to everyone at Watkins Media for your hard work and kindness. Special thanks to Fiona Robertson, Laura Whitaker-Jones, Christiana Spens, Hayley Moss, Melody Travers and the talented Rights team, Karen Smith and Uzma Taj. My gratitude also extends to Penguin Random House Publishing Services and Tantor Media.

To Sue Lascelles, my copyeditor, thank you for your meticulous work and kind encouragement.

I owe a great debt to Stacey Millichamp, one of the great psychotherapists of our time. When I walked into your practice aged 14, I had no idea how profoundly my life would change. You helped shape me into the person I am today and inspired me to become a therapist. Thank you for showing me that I could do it my own way.

Thank you to all the amazing lecturers, mentors and teachers at CCPE. My 6+ years of training there gave me a rock-solid foundation in psychotherapy. Special thanks to Nigel Hamilton, Susie Sanders (who challenged me when I said, "I want to help people" as my reason for becoming a therapist), Sandra Blais and Tamara Alferoff, who have been excellent supervisors and important parts of my concentric circles of support.

Thank you to Dr Ed Burns (I really enjoyed the DSM-5 lectures) and Dr Stefania Bonaccorso for sharing your compassionate and progressive views on psychiatry, and to Tom Pennybacker, who also helped me when I was seriously burnt out. I'm also grateful to Kevin Hamilton, Lois Elliott and Highgate Counselling Centre for believing in me when I was still a trainee. And to all the other mental health professionals who agreed to confidentially speak with me for this book.

To Alcoholics Anonymous, CODA, Pete Ward, Hannah Gentry, Hannah Dakin, Evgeny Shadchnev, Sally Assor and Dr. Deepak Chopra for your powerful insights. And a big thanks to everyone who has so kindly endorsed and supported this book – it really does take a village.

To the team at Carver PR – it's been a delight working with you again after all these years. Special thanks to Harriet Dunlea for tirelessly supporting me and this book, and to Olivia Mangroo for chasing down all the emails!

Dearest Emma Willis, thank you so much for lending your support to this book and for writing the Foreword. I am eternally grateful. And to Nader Dehdashti, thank you for championing me, being an advocate for mental health and for helping Emma to believe in this project.

Lastly, this book would not exist without the many clients I've had the privilege to work with over the years. Accompanying you on your journeys has been one of the greatest honors of my life. My deepest gratitude also extends to everyone who agreed to be interviewed anonymously for this book and who courageously and generously shared their stories with me.

I also want to acknowledge the amazing researchers, teachers, and experts whose work and insights in the fields of psychology, psychotherapy and beyond have shaped my thinking and influenced many aspects of this book.

To anyone else I may have unintentionally left out – any absent-mindedness is mine alone and speaks to the shared nature of so many of our stories.

INDEX